Inferiority Complex among the Urban Employed Dalits, Men & Women

Christian Heritage Rediscovered

The Series, as the name suggests, is meant to focus on Christian Faith & Living vis-à-vis topics like Literature & Poetry, Indigenous Philosophizing, Ethical Response towards Agriculture, Health & Healing, Science & Technology, Eco-Feminist Theology, Sociological Approach towards Human Rights, Law & Politics, Arts, History of Ideas, Ancient Civilizations, Cultural Contiguity, Religious Cosmologies & Mysticism, Footsteps of Famous Theologians, World Peace & Harmony, Global Capitalism, Network Marketing, Cybertheology, Population & Demographics, Epigraphic Studies, Contextualized Education, and many others. We welcome a Mss. on any topic/s mentioned, whether they are original works, scholarly monographs, collections of conference papers, revised dissertations, or translations of historical documents. Through the Series we, the Publishers, are striving to put forward published works that may help Institutions, Academic Bodies, Researchers, Scholars and the World at large in furthering their respective knowledge and understanding on the concerned subject. We welcome your comments on our efforts and further suggestions on how we can foster the upcoming thought provoking theologically grounded books.

Christian Heritage Rediscovered - 63

Inferiority Complex among the Urban Employed Dalits, Men & Women

Implications for Pastoral Care & Counselling

Epratha Sarathy

CWI

Christian World Imprints

First Published in 2019 by

Christian World Imprints
Christian Publishing & Books from India
H-12 Bali Nagar, **New Delhi-110015**
info@christianworldimprints.com
www.ChristianWorldImprints.com
Phone: +91 11 25465925

ISBN: 978-93-5148-266-6 (HB) ISBN: 978-93-5148-342-7 (PB)

Cataloging in Publication Data--DK
Courtesy: D.K. Agencies (P) Ltd. <docinfo@dkagencies.com>

Sarathy, Epratha, 1966- **author.**
Inferiority complex among the urban employed dalits, men & women : implications for pastoral care & counselling / Epratha Sarathy.
pages cm. -- (Christian heritage rediscovered ; 63)
Includes bibliographical references.
ISBN 9789351482666 (HB)
ISBN 9789351483427 (PB)

1. Inferiority complex--India. 2. Dalits--India--Psychology. 3. City dwellers--India--Psychology. 4. Working class--India--Psychology. 5. Pastoral care--India. 6. Dalits--Pastoral counseling of--India. I. Title. II. Series: Christian heritage rediscovered ; 63.

LCC BV4470.S27 2019 | DDC 259.086940954 23

Printed in India

DEDICATION

This book is dedicated to my
Adopted Mother Ms. Jane O'Hara, USA,
to my wife Dr. Rathna Sarathy
and to my children G. Daivashish Sarathy
and G. Daivanvesh Sarathy.

Contents

Foreword

I am delighted to write a foreword for the book "*Inferiority Complex among the Urban Employed Dalits, Men & Women: Implications for Pastoral Care & Counselling*" by Rev. Dr. Epratha Sarathy whom I have known for the last 26 years as a student at the United Theological College since I joined the Faculty in 1992. I had the privilege of guiding his doctoral dissertation during which I observed Dr. Sarathy's interests and passions with regard to the church and the society. His concern for the wellbeing of the downtrodden and the marginalized is always reflected in his ministerial commitment. Since July 2016 Dr. Sarathy is my colleague in the Christian Ministry department at the United Theological College, Bangalore. Hence, I have known the author as a student, friend, and colleague with high level motivation and passion for ministry. It is the pastoral counselling theory and practice with reference to the challenging Indian contextual realities that I find the content of this book intriguing.

Dr. Sarathy brings to discussion in this book the traditional caste-linked dominance and subordination which had seriously impacted the psychological and social makeup of men and women in the subaltern communities. Though there is marked transformation during the colonial and post-colonial independent India though various social, legal and political enactments that helped to improve the plights of the downtrodden communities, the author strongly contents that discrimination, subordination, victimization of still continues between the high and low caste communities. At the surface level of the social and political process one may not view the divisions and disparities but at the deeper social level one can find the discriminating dynamics. The author contends that it is not only among the rural communities but the educated and employed also experience such social isolation and psychological discrimination.

Dr. Sarathy's personal and family experiences, academic interest in knowing systematically the experiences of the Dalit communities, and his passion for ministering to the downtrodden led him to make an empirical study of the Employed Dalits in Bangalore in comparison with the non-Dalits in the same context. His primary hypothesis that the educated and Employed Dalits encounter experiences at work place that contributes to an Inferiority Complex is found validated. He employed psychological theories that help him to formulate a theological and theoretical framework that is relevant to understand the Indian Dalits who are educated and employed along with members of other communities.

Based on this framework he developed his methods that would allow him to measure various variables that allowed him to compare the Dalits with the Non-Dalits in the same context. The Dalits and the non-Dalits included in the study come with similar educational achievement, employment status, and income. Though there is no visible difference between the two groups at the surface level, it was found that on many counts that the Dalits were sidelined and discriminated with regard to the following: everyday social interactions; not sharing lunch time at work; not spending time during breaks; no invitation to the homes of the high caste groups; refusal to visit the Dalit homes by the non-Dalit colleagues; and lack of mentoring at work. Based on the findings of the study the author argues that the shadows of caste discriminatory mentality still continue at all levels of the Indian society.

Dr. Sarathy's exploration to understand the mental and emotional makeup of Women and Men is a significant contribution in the light of the contemporary social and political discourses on caste dynamics in the Indian society today. Though political and legal sanctions have provided measures to protect the dignity and wellbeing of the Dalit communities, the experiences at the grassroots level tell us a different story that reveals exploitation, discrimination, and isolation which is indication of the shadow of the caste mentality. The lower strata of the society still encounter visible and invisible struggles in their everyday life.

Not only the dirty vote bank politics but also the honor killings across India are compelling evidences for the shadows of caste mentality in contemporary India. It is in this context the author calls the church to be an agency for Holistic Pastoral Care and Counselling. Hence, I strongly recommend Dr. Sarathy's *Inferiority Complex among the Urban Employed Dalits, Men & Women: Implications for Pastoral Care & Counselling.*

Dr. Joseph George, Professor
Dean of Doctoral Division and Non-Research Studies
The United Theological College, Bangalore
August 5, 2018

Acknowledgments

This research has been a very enlightening and rewarding experience for me in an area that is of great personal interest. I thank our God Almighty for His enabling grace, help and guidance, for the good health and for all His providence through out my research work. I would like to acknowledge and express my gratitude to a group of people who provided generous amounts of support and cooperation during my research.

First of all, I would like to express my deepest gratitude to my Mentor Dr. Joseph George for his patience, guidance, encouragement, support, thought provoking insights which has been very valuable for me in every stage of this research. It would be appropriate to say that without his help it would not have been possible to complete this research. I also would like to thank his family members for their hospitality and politeness in receiving me in their home.

I am also very thankful to Dr. Nalini Arles for helping me during my assessment period and Dr. S. C. Paulraj, for helping me in formulating and conceptualizing the present research title. My special thanks to Dr. John Johnson (NIMHANS) for giving his precious time and helping me to structure my questionnaire scientifically. My sincere thanks to Rev. Dr. Sham P. Thomas for his concern shown towards me as a Tutor. My thanks also to all the former Deans of Doctoral Division, Rev. Dr. Joseph G. Muthuraj, Dr. I. John Mohan Razu, Rev. Dr. J.R. John Samuel Raj (present Principal) and the present Dean Rev. Dr. Evangeline Anderson-Rajkumar for their concern and encouragement towards my progress in research. My sincere thanks also to the Dean's office staff. I thank all the people who gave their valuable time and willingly participated in the data collection. This research was made possible because of their cooperation.

I am greatful to Rev. Dr. Samson Prabhakar, former director of SATRI and all the office staff for their encouragement and support. I am also thankful to Rev. Dr. O.V. Jathanna, former Principal of United Theological College, Bangalore for his motivation and encouragement in my research. I thank my brother Rev. Richard Kishore for his technical assistance and editorial work and Mr. John Sunder Boopalan for helping me in grammatical corrections.

Last, but not least, I would like to thank my family: My Adopted Mother Ms. Jane O'Hara, USA, for generously providing family scholarship to do my studies. I am greatly indebted to her for the love, care, encouragement, support and prayers through out my research. This research would not have been possible without her financial help and motivation. My wife Dr. Rathna and children, Daivashish and Daivanvesh for their unconditional love and support, for their encouragement and prayers for this research. My brothers and sister for their inspiration and my parents for giving me life and for sending me to school.

Epratha Sarathy

Preface

The study "Inferiority Complex among Employed Dalits in Bangalore: Implications for Pastoral Care", is the original title of the research and the title has been changed with the permission from the Senate of Serampore College (University) for the purpose of publication as "Inferiority Complex among the Urban Employed Dalits, Men & Women: Implications for Pastoral Care & Counselling". This research was undertaken in the context of the persistent deprivation and oppression of Dalits due to continued existence of a solid core of the phenomenon of caste. The old caste hierarchies sway in spite of a solid core of abolition of untouchability and the discrimination policy in post-independent India. In spite of the positive change for Dalits, in terms of their educational achievement, occupational improvement, political assertion and influence, they are still unable to get rid of the stigma of untouchability and thus suffer from psychological problems. Education is seen as the key to fundamental change in social structures and social attitudes. Indeed, education has been the only avenue available to Dalit masses in rising up from positions of degradation, gaining self-respect and employment. As a result the Employed Dalits have considerably improved their standards of lifestyle and there has been a shift from ascribed status to achieved status. However it is not very clear, whether this has helped them to improve their self-image. Hence this study was undertaken with a purpose to find whether there are any psychological problems, particularly, "Inferiority Complex among the Employed Dalits, Men & Women in Bangalore", and to draw implications for Pastoral Care.

In order to understand the research problem, the theoretical framework was built around the subject, 'Caste and Identity', and 'Personality Theories and Contextual issues in relation to Inferiority Complex'. The second chapter provide insights into the research problem by dealing with the meaning, definition and characteristics of caste and untouchability. It also traces the origin of caste and untouchability from different viewpoints with special reference to Ambedkar and Gandhi. The later part elaborates on how the Dalits asserted and claimed their identity demanding their Constitutional Rights with the help of Dalit Movement before and after Ambedkar. The third chapter provide insights in the concepts of

Inferiority Complex and it was well understood in the light of different personality theories, focusing mainly on the interpersonal relationship, which were essential and necessary to do the Empirical research on Inferiority Complex among the Urban Employed Dalits, Men & Women.

This is an Empirical Study with a quantitative approach. The locale of the study was Bangalore and the sample consisted of 240 subjects, 120 Employed Dalits as experimental group of which 60 subjects were male and 60 subjects female and 120 Non-Employed Dalits as control group of which 60 subjects were male and 60 subjects were female. Purposive Sampling Method was used to draw subjects from Hindustan Aeronautical Limited (HAL), Graphite India Private Limited (GIPL), and Karnataka State Government Services (KSGS) in Bangalore City with the help of the records of the Employees Associations. The background information was gathered using demographical sheet, and questionnaire developed by the researcher. Rosenberg Self-Esteem Scale (RSE), Self Esteem Inventory, Social Distance Scale was used to find out the Inferiority Complex among Employed Dalits. Statistical tests employed in this study were unpaired t-test, 'T' test, Analysis of Variance, and the results were tested for significance using the Fisher's test at the 5% and 1% level of confidence.

As part of the summary of Finding and Testing of Hypothesis, the investigation reveals that there is significant effect of Inferiority Complex among Employed Dalit subjects and significantly higher among Employed Dalit female subjects. The investigation also revealed that there is significantly higher level of Inferiority Complex among group D Male Employed Dalits, and group C Female Employed Dalits. The Employed Dalit subjects belonging to group D were the most affected by Inferiority Complex on the whole. Thus hypothesis 4.1, that Employed Dalits in Urban settings seemingly develop a higher level of Inferiority Complex compared to the Non-Dalits in the same context is accepted.

The hypothesis 4.2, In spite of their educational and economic development the Employed Dalits experience Inferiority Complex that is seemingly caused by the stigma of untouchability is accepted. The investigation revealed that there is significant effect of Inferiority Complex among Employed Dalits in spite of being well placed in the society by having good education, own housing facility, and economic conditions. The investigation also revealed the major ways of how Employed Dalits are affected by Inferiority Complex. They are affected by Inferiority Complex when sharing food with others at work place, topping the list followed by restriction, caste identity, criticism, and relationship with superiors, relationship between families, relationship in the canteen, celebrating festivals, inter-personal relationships, and lastly relationship with subordinates.

The hypothesis 4.3, There seems to be a link between the level of Inferiority Complex and the level of socio-economic achievements is accepted. The investigation revealed that there is significant effect of Inferiority Complex among group D Male Employed Dalits, and group C Female Employed Dalit subjects.

The investigation also revealed that 69(57.47%) of Employed Dalits whose length of service is between 1-20 years were significantly affected by Inferiority Complex. The Study found that 75(62.47%) of Dalit subjects lived in their own houses, in comparison to 68(56.64%) of Non-Dalits subjects and the highest 40(33.32%) of subjects among Employed Dalits were graduates in comparison to 15(12.49%) among Non-Dalits. It is also found that 41(34.15%) among Employed Dalit subjects were drawing salary between Rs.15001.00 to 20000.00 in comparison to 23(19.15%) among Non-Dalit subjects.

The outcome of the research significantly indicates that Employed Dalits are suffering from Inferiority Complex as compared to the Employed Non-Dalits. The hypothesis has been tested and was found to be true. The Employed Dalits in Urban setting seemingly develop a higher level of Inferiority Complex when compared to Non-Dalits in the same context. In spite of their educational and economic development the Employed Dalits experience Inferiority Complex that is seemingly caused by the stigma of untouchability. There seems to be a link between the level of Inferiority Complex and the level of socio-economic achievements. The implications for Pastoral Care were made based on the finding of the research to technically address the issue of Inferiority Complex. The methods suggested are derived from a variety of schools in Pastoral Care and Counselling for the treatment of Inferiority Complex among Urban Employed Dalits, Men and Women.

List of Abbreviations

AD	After Death
ANOVA	Analysis of Variance
BC	Before Christ
BCs	Backward Castes
BSP	Bahujan Samaj Party
D	Dalit
Df	Difference in Frequency
DS4	Dalit Shoshit Samaj Sangharsh Samiti
EAP	Employee Assistance Programmes
F	Female
GIPL	Graphite India Private Limited
HAL	Hindustan Aeronautical Limited
KSGS	Karnataka State Government Services
LSTC	Liberator, Shepherd, Therapon, and Counsellor
M	Male
MMPI	Minnesota Multiphasic Personality Inventory
ND	Non-Dalit
NIMHANS	National Institute for Mental Health and Neurological Sciences
OBCs	Other Backward Castes
PG	Post Graduate
PUC	Pre-University College
REBC	Rational Emotive Behavioural Counselling
RET	Rational Emotive Therapy
RSE	Rosenberg Self-Esteem
SANS	Scale for Assessment of Negative Symptoms
SCs	Scheduled Castes

SD	Standard Deviation
SEI	Self Esteem Inventory
SFC	Solution-Focused Counselling
Si	Social Introversion
Sig	Significance
STs	Scheduled Tribes
U.P	Uttar Pradesh

List of Tables

Chapter 1

Introduction and Methology

1.1. Statement of the Problem

The traditional patterns of dominance-subordination have undergone marked transformations in colonial and post-colonial periods. The post-independent India has witnessed two major landmarks towards the establishment of an egalitarian society, which is the legal abolition of untouchability and the discrimination policy.[1] Even though untouchability is legally abolished, it is not extinct.[2] Old caste hierarchies stand disrupted and new hierarchical social formations have emerged which are not strictly tied to caste and ritual purity. Yet, the continued existence of a solid core of the phenomenon of caste is most clearly evident in the persistent deprivation and oppression of Dalits. Dr. Manmohan Singh, then Prime Minister of India, speaking after inaugurating Dalit-Minority International Conference in New Delhi, said "I recognize, even after 60 years of constitutional and legal protection and state support, there is still social discrimination against Dalits in many parts of our country. The political, social, cultural and intellectual battle against such discrimination must continue."[3] He further states: "Dalits have faced a unique discrimination in our society that is fundamentally different from the problems of minority groups in general. The only parallel to the practice of "untouchability" was Apartheid in South Africa. Untouchability is not just social discrimination. It is a blot on humanity."[4] The positive change for Dalits, in terms

1 Ravindra Patil, "Search for Identity among Dalit Middle Class in Maharastra," *Social Action* 50/1 (Jan-Mar, 2000): 70-79.

2 Padma Velaskar and G.G. Wankhede, "From Old Stigma to New... Exploring the Changing Identity to Urban Educated Dalits," *The Indian Journal of Social Work* LVII/1 (Jan 1996): 121.

3 Dr. Manmohan Singh, *Unbroken People* 2, 8 (Jan 2007): 14.

4 Ibid.

of educational achievement and occupational improvement, political assertion and influence has come slowly as a result of reservation policy.[5]

The reservation policy has helped some dalits to get better education and this education holds a central place in Ambedkar's ideology of liberation. Education is seen as the key to fundamental change in social structures and social attitudes. Indeed, education has been the only avenue available to Dalit masses in rising up from positions of degradation, and also for gaining self-respect and employment.[6] As a result, the Employed Dalits have considerably improved their standards of lifestyle and there has been a shift from ascribed status to achieved status.[7] However it is not very clear, whether this has helped them to improve their self-image. It is found that in spite of their development, the Dalits are unable to get rid of the stigma of untouchability and thus suffer from inferiority complex.[8] Mendelsohn and Marika in their research found that the Dalits are facing inferiority problems and are not feeling comfortable in the institutions in which they work.[9]

Several scholars have done research in this particular area; Dahiwale conducted a study about the Self-Employed Dalits of Kolhapur. His study focus was on the occupational mobility of Dalits and brought out the difference between the Dalits who were engaged in the traditional and modern occupation.[10] Showeb on the other hand chose three categories of Chamars, who were traditionally employed, government employed and students. He observed the fact that the traditionally employed Chamars were unable to bring about change in their occupational life because of their poverty and ignorance. He noted that the educated with the help of reservation and other State benefits have raised their socio-economic status but are alienated and cut-off from the large section of their community.[11] Nandu Ram also focused on the Central and State government Employed Dalits in Kanpur. He mainly focused on occupation and social mobility, and found that employment has a positive impact on their achievements leading to an impressive change among the present generation compared to their forefathers.[12]

5 Padma Velaskar and G.G. Wankhede, "From Old Stigma to New… Exploring the Changing Identity to Urban Educated Dalits," 115-116.

6 Ibid., 121.

7 Ravindra Patil, "Search for Identity among Dalit Middle Class in Maharastra," 70-79.

8 C. Parvathamma, "The Weaker Sections of Society-The Scheduled Castes in India," *Sociological Bulletin* 30/1 (March 1981): 54.

9 Oliver Mendelsohn & Marika Vicziany, *The Untouchables: Subordination, Poverty, and the State in Modern India* (New Delhi: Foundation Books, 2000), 266-267.

10 S.M. Dahiwale, *Emerging Entrepreneurship among Scheduled Castes of Contemporary India: A Study of Kolhapur City* (New Delhi: Hindustan Publishing House, 1989), 47-62.

11 M. Showeb, *Educated and Mobility among Harijans* (Delhi: Vohra Publishers, 1986), 1-8.

12 Nandu Ram, *The Mobile Scheduled Caste: The Rise of New Middle Class* (Delhi: Hindustan Publishing House, 1998), 8-9, 42.

All these scholars are from the school of social work and successfully attempted in highlighting the achievements and problems of Employed Dalits from their own perspective. These studies have pointed inferiority as one of the problems and no one appears to have investigated whether the Employed Dalits have improved their self-esteem as a result of their educational and career achievement. Also it does not appear to be very clear, what are the factors related to their low self-esteem. It is from here the Counsellors and Psychologists need to continue the work started by the Social Scientists. It is with this challenge and motivation I am attempting to find the level of Inferiority Complex among the Employed Dalits in comparison with non-Dalits, within the framework of socio-demographic variables.

1.2. Elaboration of the Problem

Neither the traditional Hindu society nor the Muslim rule in India could provide adequate opportunities to untouchables or Dalits to improve their status in social, economic, religious and educational milieu. It is an historical fact that the Dalits in India are the original inhabitants and one of the earliest indigenous communities who had been denigrated as dasa (slave), avarna (without caste) or achhuta (untouchable).[13] Mohan describes the untouchables as a people without a name and without a place in the social organization of the time due to various forms of Brahmanical exploitation.[14] Girijamma, Woman President of Dalit Jagruti Samiti, has cried out that "for more than 3500 years the Hindu religion has treated the Dalit people as low and untouchable and has perpetrated atrocities on them."[15] As a result they remained in great oppression without opportunities for growth and development. But the British rule in India brought certain changes in the socio-economic conditions of dalits. Nandu Ram pointed out that British enacted several laws to remove social and religious disabilities of dalits; "at the provincial level, steps were taken, as 'welfare measures', to provide the scheduled castes with various facilities, such as opening of schools and hostels, fee remissions, scholarships, boarding grants, and book allowances, to promote their studies and pursue industrial and technical training. Some reservation was also made in appointment of candidates belonging to these castes to government jobs."[16] A number of laws were passed against the inhuman practice of untouchability and all state controlled public places were thrown open to Dalits. Besides these, they had also new opportunities created in the British army, industries and the media. Similarly, the Christian Missionaries with the help of some Dalit leaders worked hard to create a better-off section or new class among Dalits.

13 D.K. Sahu, "Ministry from the Margin", *Indian Journal of Theology* 45/1 & 2 (2003): 2.

14 A. Mohan, "The Growth of Contemporary Buddhism and its significance for Church's Mission," *Indian Journal of Theology* 47/1 & 2 (2005): 107.

15 M.C. Raj, *Dalitology* (Tumkur: Ambedkar Resource Centre, 2001), 25.

16 Nandu Ram, *The Mobile Scheduled Caste: The Rise of New Middle Class,* 8.

Along with this after the Independence, the Government of India continued the efforts by adopting more comprehensive measures for the welfare and development of the scheduled castes or Dalits. But ritual pollution, caste exploitation and other legacies of Indian civilization such as Varna system still continue. Whereas the reservation policy has helped some Dalits in their education and employment which has led to a shift from 'ascriptive' to 'achieved' status. The employed dalits are well aware of their traditional, hierarchical and occupational status, which is socially, ritually and occupationally inferior. That is why they want to develop their status with the help of modern education and government employment, which is secular and prestigious. It means they break ties with old traditions and traditionally practiced occupation.[17]

The positive gain for the Dalits is that they have realised the importance of education and its benefits for the improvement of socio-economic status. This is the reason they are engaged in educating their children and enrolling them for higher education and professional courses in well-known educational institutions and prestigious universities. These children of better-off Dalit parents are the second-generation learners after independence, who with the help of reservation policy are able to get admission in prestigious educational institutions and later acquire well-paid white collar jobs in government and private sectors. But inspite of their improvement, it seems they are facing severe negative consequences and have become the worst target of victimisation by the upper castes due to their class elevation. The conversations with Dalits in various institutional settings reveal a forbidding world of deprecation and exclusion from the otherwise common culture of the institution. The oppression of Dalits is taking a different shape in the form of compartmentalisation, hypocrisy and avoidance strategies. Despite their progress of achieving employment, it is highly doubtful that there has been any inward change between Dalits and non-Dalits at the work place.[18] In the perception of higher castes, the success of Dalits is frequently considered as state favoritism and that is the reason the upper castes term the Employed Dalits as 'Government Brahmins', and 'sons-in-law' of government. Calling them by such derogatory terms means devaluing or undermining their success and the status of the job held by them. In this way, the taunting and wrong perceptions of higher castes lead to a self-depreciation process among the Dalits.[19]

The danger of one having inferiority complex is that one does not attain the needed development in personality. The overcoming of inferiority complex is necessary for the maximum development of an individual.[20] People with the attitude of inferiority learn to avoid competitions and criticisms and make no

17 Ravindra Patil, "Search for Identity among Dalit Middle Class in Maharastra," 70-79.

18 Oliver Mendelson & Marika Vicziany, *The Untouchables: Subordination, Poverty, and the State in Modern India,* 66-267.

19 B.S. Waghmare, "Dilemma of Dalit Middle Class and Ambedkarism," (October 1991): 4.

20 S.P. Chaube, *Developmental Psychology* (New Delhi: Neelkamal Publications, 2003), 65.

attempts to attack problems directly and substitute activities as satisfaction for their drives. They show a marked sensitivity to criticism and apply all criticism to themselves. They frequently cross streets to avoid meeting people and shun social groups. The attitude of inferiority is a generalised habit of reacting with a strong fear to all social situations, particularly to those involving competition or criticism. This attitude is acquired by a long sequence of experiences from the childhood. When inferiority is in the process of formation, the individual is learning to react with fear to criticism and to competition with others, thus leading to persistent and intense defensive behaviour.[21]

1.3. Operational Definitions

- **Inferiority Complex:** Inferiority refers to the feeling of low self-esteem about oneself in relation to others. Inferiority complex is a condition in which a person continues to feel depleted self-esteem.
- **Employed Dalit:** Dalits are those who were considered untouchables are presently termed as Scheduled Castes, irrespective of their religious affiliation. Dalits who have attained employment in government and private sectors on merit or with the help of reservation will be considered as Employed Dalits.
- **Pastoral Care:** The oppression of Dalits has affected them not only physically, but also socially, culturally, and religiously. This multi-sided suffering has given them an inferior social status, so pastoral care is the ministry that strives to bring out the Dalits from the historical captivity that led them to physical, social, cultural and religious multi-sided suffering. These factors gave them a multi-faceted identity that they are outcaste, untouchables and slaves. Pastoral care is a human relationship of caring with concern for what others are thinking, feeling and doing. Pastoral care is an expression of hope for the recovery of their past identity and transformation into full and liberated human being.
- **Pastoral Caregiver:** Pastoral caregiver is a person irrespective of religion, caste and culture. Pastoral caregiver is a person who is interested in helping the Employed Dalits overcome their inferiority complex. It can be a Counsellor, Pastor, Priest, Poojari, Social Worker, Psychiatrist, or any other person.

---

21 L.F. Shaffer, *The Psychology of Adjustment* (New York: Hougton Mifflin Co., 1936), 150-151. "She Taunted me over my Caste," *Times of India* (Bangalore), 11 June 2009, 6. Mr. Puttanna, Office Manager, allegedly slit the throat of Prof. Chandralekha of Sarada Vilas College of Pharmacy in Mysore, and hacked her to death. "I killed Chandralekha, who ill-treated me on the basis of my caste and played a big role in sacking me... As I belonged to a lower caste the staff kept a distance while communicating with me... Since my childhood I have been experiencing such treatment at my work places. Earlier, I worked as an officer in a bank and took voluntary retirement in 2001. Owing to financial crisis I applied for a job here five months back," Puttanna told Times of India.

1.4. Hypothesis

- The Employed Dalits in urban settings seemingly develop a higher level of inferiority complex when compared to the non-dalits in the same context.
- Inspite of their educational and economic development the Employed Dalits experience inferiority complex that is seemingly caused by the stigma of untouchability.
- There seems to be a link between the level of inferiority complex and the level of socio-economic and educational achievements.

1.5. Method of Data Collection

1.5.1. Locale of the Study

The researcher worked as a pastor and chaplain for the past fifteen years in Bangalore and has a fairly good acquaintance of the geographical area of Bangalore. The locale of the study chosen to collect the data is Hindustan Aeronautical Limited, Bangalore, Graphite India Private Limited, Bangalore, and Karnataka State Government Services in Bangalore city.

1.5.2. Sample

The Dalit and non-Dalit subjects were selected through Purposive Sampling Method from the records of the Employees Associations. In Purposive Sampling, the choice of the researcher is very important and the units will be selected according to the objectives of the research. According to Adolph Jenson, "A purposive selection denotes the method of selecting a number of groups or units in such a way that selected groups together yield as nearly as possible the same averages or proportion as the totality with respect to those characteristics which are already a matter of statistical knowledge."[22] The experimental group consists of 120 Employed Dalits and the control group consists of 120 Employed non-Dalits, a total of 240 subjects.[23] The Employed Non-Dalit subjects were controlled against the gender, education, employment, marital status and professional status of the Employed Dalit subjects. Inclusion Criteria of the Experimental and Control group consists of Group A, B, C, D Employees in the locale of the study.

22 S. Kapila, *Methods of Social Research* (Jalandhar: New Academic Publishing Co, 2001), 78.

23 The Classification of the Sample will be as follows:
Group A Dalit Employees, (Male= 15 + Female =15) n= 30
Group B Dalit Employees, (Male= 15 + Female =15) n= 30
Group C Dalit Employees, (Male= 15 + Female =15) n= 30
Group D Dalit Employees, (Male= 15 + Female =15) n= 30
Total N= 120.

1.5.3. Research Tools

This is an empirical study with a quantitative approach. The word 'Empirical' means relying on experiment or observation, and empirical study is guided by practical experience rather than theory.[24] The primary data were collected through a structured questionnaire. Apart from the primary data, a secondary source of information was collected from journals, research papers, and other types of published materials. The following instruments were used to collect the data for the purpose of the research work.

1.5.3.1. Socio-Demographical Details

The socio-demographical details include variables such as gender, age, marital status, people group, type of residence, employment, income, education background, professional background, and length of service.

1.5.3.2. Questionnaire

There is a lack of standardised scales to measure the inferiority complex among the Employed Dalits. The author developed the questionnaire relevant to the Indian context by adopting the appropriate items from the following standardised scales, such as MMPI Si1 Inferiority- Personal Discomfort Scale,[25] MMPI Si2 Discomfort with others Scales,[26] MMPI-2 Si Social Introversion Scale,[27] Emotional Stability Test,[28] Self-Esteem Inventory,[29] Social Behaviour

---

24 Gardner Lindzey, et.al., *Psychology* (2nd edition). (New York: Worth Publishers, 1978), 641.

25 http://www1.umn.edu, Minnesota Multiphasic Personality Inventory 27 items Si1 Inferiority - Personal Discomfort Scale- developed by Serkownek.

26 http://www1.umn.edu, Minnesota Multiphasic Personality Inventory 14 items Si2 Discomfort with others Scale developed by Serkownek.

27 http://www1.umn.edu, Three subscales namely Shyness/Self-Consciousness, Social Avoidance, and Self/Other Alienation will be employed or used. James N. Butcher, et.al, New Subscales for the MMPI-2 Social Introversion (Si) Scale. *A Journal of Consulting and Clinical Psychology.* September 1989 Vol. 1, No. 3, 169-174.

28 A. Sen. Gupta and A.K. Singh, "Test of Emotional Stability", *Psychological Studies* 30/1 (1985): 121-123. ***Emotional Stability Test***: was originally developed by Singh, in terms of eight dimensions. 1. To have control over one's emotions, 2. To reply boldly to a question in a group, 3. To consider elements in their proper perspectives, 4. To talk confidently with others, 5. Freedom from common phobic reactions, 6. To face personal comments and criticisms realistically, 7. Freedom from doubts over other's actions and reactions, 8. To have correct account of one's merits and demerits. Three items relating to each of the first seven dimensions and four relating to eighth dimension were written by Gupta and Singh, making it a set of 25 items.

29 H. Sam Sananda Raj and Immanuel Thomas, "Certain Correlates of Self-Esteem: A Factor Study", *Psychological Studies* 31/2 (1986): 119-124. Self-esteem Inventory is a 25-item inventory developed for measuring the self-esteem of secondary school students of Kerala State. The inventory makes use of direct self-reports for the purpose. The items are intended to

Questionaaire,[30] Scale for Assessment of Negative Symptoms (SANS).[31] **The Inclusive Criteria:** for selecting the items from the just mentioned standardized scales were based on the following, that is identity, due respect, restriction, celebrating festivals, segregation, relationship with superiors, appreciation, criticism, competitions, social avoidance, relationship with subordinates, initiating discussion, freedom of self-expression, interpersonal relationship, suspicious attitude, relationship between families, relationship in the canteen, and sharing food. The items which were not relevant to the study were considered to be **Exclusive Criteria.**

1.5.3.3. Rosenberg Self-Esteem Scale (RSE)

The Rosenberg self-esteem scale was developed by Morris Rosenberg, and the scale can be used to assess global self-esteem and it is one of the most widely used self-esteem tests among psychologists and sociologists.[32]

1.5.3.4. Self-Esteem Inventory

Was developed by James Messina, and Constance Messina, and is widely used to assess self-esteem.[33]

---

tap self-evaluation from a variety of behavioural domains, including social, academic, physical, and emotional aspects.

30 Pramod Kumar, "Supervisor's Authoritarianism and Ingratiation among Workers", *Psychological Studies* 31/2 (1986): 165-168. Social Behaviour Questionnaire a 21-item 5-point rating scale entitled to measure different forms of ingratiation, *viz.*, opinion conformity, self-enhancement, name-dropping, changing with the situation, and instrumental dependency and self-degradation.

31 P. John Mathai, et.al., "Evaluation of the reliability of the Scale for Assessment of Negative Symptoms," *Psychological Studies* 28/3 (1984). The Scale for Assessment of Negative Symptoms (SANS) was developed by N.C. Andreasen (1981) from two other instruments, thought, language and communication (Andreasen 1979) and the Affect Rating Scale (Andreasen, 1979). The SANS includes five negative symptoms complexes, viz., Affective Flattening, Alogia, Abolition-Apathy, Anhedonia-Associality and Attentional impairment. These negative symptoms have been renamed and redefined by a group of scholars from NIMHANS in more specific terms to ensure reliability by P. John Mathai.

32 www.selfesteem2go.com, The Rosenberg Self-esteem Scale was developed by Morris Rosenberg, Ph.D., (deceased) in 1965. (Reference: Society and the Adolescent Self-Image. Princeton, N.J.: Princeton University Press).

33 www.Coping.org - James J. Messina, Ph.D. & Constance M. Messina, Ph.D., Coping.org is a Public Service of James J. Messina, Ph.D. & Contance M. Messina, Ph.D., Email: jjmess@tampabay.rr.com – 1999-2007. Note: Original materials on this site may be reproduced for any personal, educational, or noncommercial use as along as one credits the authors and website.

1.5.3.5. Social Distance Scale

A modified form of Bogardus Social Distance Scale of six items by Kuppaswamy further modified by the researcher to suit the population of the present work.[34]

1.5.4. Procedure of Data Collection

The author sought permission and co-operation from the concerned Officers in the Personnel Departments and the Employees Associations in the locale of the study. The Employed Dalit subjects were gathered from the records of the Scheduled Caste Employees Associations and the Employed non-Dalit subjects were gathered from the records of the Personnel Departments in the locale of the study. An initial rapport building session was arranged to discuss the need and purpose of the research. A contract was made between the researchers and the subjects with regard to participation and confidentiality. Different tools were given to assess the necessary data from the subjects.

1.5.5. Analysis

Statistical data are presented in the 2 × 2 contingency tables[35] in the form of frequency and percentage. The Measures of Central Tendency and Measures of Variability are used to organize and interpret the data. The Correlation Methods were used to measure if there is any significant relationship between the variables. The t-test, the analysis of variance (ANOVA) will be used and the results will be tested for significance using the Fisher's test at the 5% and 1% level of confidence.

1.6. Scope and Limitations of the Study

The research focuses its attention on Employed Dalits and their inferiority complex. In order to achieve this, the Employed Dalits are compared against the control group. It also focuses on the Socio-demographic variables, such as gender, education, employment and marital status of Employed Dalits as against the control group of Employed Non-Dalits. The magnitude of the inferiority complex among different categories as found in the classification of the sample will be brought out. The findings will be summarised to bring out the implications for Pastoral Care. There is lot of scope for this study in future, the inferiority complex among different categories of Employed Dalits can be studied separately and the findings can be very useful for the betterment of Employed Dalits.

However, there are certain limitations in the research. It is not a longitudinal study and is only limited to the urban Dalits working in the following sectors: Hindustan Aeronautical Limited in Bangalore, Graphite India Private Limited,

34 A modified form of Bogardus Social Distance Scale of six items by Kuppaswamy is further modified by the Researcher to suit the populatin of the present work.

35 G.R. Basotia, & K.K. Sharma, *Research Methodology Made Simple* (Jaipur: Mangal Deep Publications, 2002), 239. Contingency tables are also called bivariate tables or cross-tabulations. In contingency tables all combinations of categories of all variables are presented.

Bangalore and the State Government Service in Bangalore. It does not include other categories of Dalits, such as the self-employed, rural, and unemployed Dalits, so the finding cannot be generalised.

1.7. Purpose of the Study

- To find out whether there is any inferiority complex among the employed dalits and if so to what extent.
- To study the relationship between inferiority and status inconsistency, alienation, discrimination, deprivation, oppression, victimization, submissiveness, subordination, and domination.
- To suggest guidelines to pastoral care based on the findings of the study.

1.8. Significance of the Problem

There has been considerable research done in the area of Dalit studies with reference to their socio-economic, occupational, and educational problems. Most of these studies have been done in the North Indian Context. Wankhede identified and critically analysed the social and educational problems of the Scheduled Castes with reference to the educated Scheduled Castes in their social context, comments that these issues have not been identified and empirically studied at regional levels or at an all-India level.[36] In particular, as far as my knowledge is concerned there is not much research carried out in the South Indian context. Moreover, less attention has been given to psychological problems, more specifically inferiority complex.

So this work becomes significant because there is not much research done particularly on inferiority complex among the Employed Dalits. It is also significant because the study is going to help the Employed Dalits by providing ways and means to come out of the inferiority complex so that they will develop their personalities to some extent. It will also will help the church and society by providing appropriate ways to work with the Employed Dalits.

1.9. Review of Literature

Adler in his book "Understanding Human Nature" refers inferiority as the basis of abnormal behaviour and it determines the goal of an individual's existence. According to Adler, the principle force of life is striving for superiority or self-assertion. In normal individuals this is adjusted to reality and integrated with social drives, thus leading to reasonable satisfaction through achievement. In childhood the urge for superiority is dissatisfied in many directions because of the child's weakness and helplessness and the supremacy of his parents. This situation may be forced by the presence of actual physical defects, by imagined defects, by excessive parental strictness or by other factors. In such circumstances, the

---

36 G.G. Wankhede, "Social and Educational Problems of Scheduled Castes: Some Critical Insights," *The Indian Journal of Social Work* 60/3 (July 1999): 397-418.

individual acquires a hidden inferiority complex. According to Adler, Inferiority arises from the frustration of the individual's desire for superiority, which is subject to continual frustration and makes it difficult for him to adopt the give-and-take of a socialized human being.[37] Adler's work in finding the inferiority complex should be appreciated, but he is talking about inferiority in the western context and his viewpoints are not empirical in nature. He is mostly talking about the physical inferiority in the childhood and of different nature. He says that inferiority arises out of the desire for superiority, but in the case of Dalits in India, it may not be the same. It is a problem of survival for the Dalits in India.

Heinrich was involved in the work of the North India Church for fifteen years and has shed light on many psychological factors of the suppressed people. He was assigned to work in the city of Rawalpindi, a city in the Mohammedan territory North of Jhelum River. He observed that inferiority feeling among Dalits is part of the pattern of untouchability, which is a force of religious sanction. He says, "His apparent submissiveness and acquiescence in his miserable condition is part of the pattern of untouchability."[38] And thus suffers real or imagined disadvantage.

The oppressive conditions of Dalits have shaped their emotional development and have led them to inferiority. Inferiority feeling leads a person to an unsocial behaviour. He found striking parallels between the people of Israel while living in Egypt and the Negroes in America and the Dalits in India. He felt that the "conditions that are constantly forcing upon the Negro a feeling of inferiority are quite similar to those under which the Depressed Classes of India labour."[39] Further he remarks: "It has been more than a coincidence that both among the Negroes in the South and the Christian sweepers of North India there has been recognition of their likeness to Israel in bondage and on the way out."[40] Heinrich was a missionary in North India and was mainly working among a few congregations. His findings were mainly through observation and not empirical in nature. His actual findings were that there is inferiority complex among Dalit Christians; however he never used the concept of Dalit Christian. But he gives a generalised statement that Dalits are suffering from the problem of inferiority complex as part of the pattern of untouchability. He was a missionary and it is surprising that he failed to link pastoral care to the problems that the Dalits are facing.

Harold Isaacs shared insights gained from stories told by 50 highly articulate Dalit informants. He described the urban Dalits as in a kind of 'semi-limbo,'

---

37 Alfred Adler, *Understanding Human Nature* (London: Allen & Unwin Ltd, 1927), 69.

38 J.C. Heinrich, *The Psychology of a Suppressed People* (London: The Aberdeen University Press, 1937), 3.

39 J.C. Heinrich, *The Psychology of a Suppressed People* (London: The Aberdeen University Press, 1937), 10.

40 Ibid., 41.

not integrated with other middle class Indians or the mass of their own people. "As the educated ex-untouchables pull up and away from the sodden bleakness of their past estate, they do not quite get *nowhere*, not neither do they reach *somewhere*. They are people who want above all to become different from what they were and what their fathers were. They want to leave all that behind, to forget it, to blot it out, but they come into a situation where too little is changing too slowly; a society still governed by caste does not allow them to abandon their past, to forget it, to blot it all out. What they move into becomes a kind of semi-limbo."[41] Isaacs experienced that many young people hiding their caste to get food and lodging, to win acceptance or at least to avoid rejection. At work place the background of a Dalit was kept as a secret because friendship with colleagues were broken if they were known to be outcaste. Consequently, some Dalits went to great lengths to hide their outcaste background. Others tried to lead a non-Dalit life in public while living a Dalit private and family life. Yet others have chosen neither to hide nor to publicize their outcaste, "At almost any point of contact with the caste Hindu world, the satisfaction of a man's simplest needs often depended on his readiness to conceal his caste identity and, if need be, to falsify it."[42] Most of the parents faced the problem of how and when to tell their children about their outcaste, because most of them believed "that awareness of the past status was enough to instill feelings of inferiority."[43] This was the main reason most of the parents delayed saying anything about it so that their children would not develop inferiority complex during their early years. This research was carried out by Isaacs while he was in America mainly concentrating on the highly intellectuals among the Dalit community. He is moreover talking about the Dalit middle class and the tension that they have with their own people.

Mendelsohn and Marika found that the Dalits face inferiority problems and are not feeling comfortable in the institutions they work. They found that "conversations with Dalits in various institutional settings reveal a forbidding world of deprecation and exclusion from the otherwise common culture of the institution."[44] The oppression of Dalits is taking a different shape, "compartmentalisation, hypocrisy and avoidance strategies are the external face of a major waning of oppression of untouchables, but in the absence of more rigorous internalization they are of limited utility in more intimate situations."[45] Despite their progress of achieving employment, they felt "it is highly doubtful

41 H.R. Issacs, *India's Ex-Untouchables* (New York: John Day Company, 1965), 128.

42 Ibid., 143.

43 Ibid., 151.

44 Oliver Mendelsohn & Marika Vicziany, *The Untouchables: Subordination, Poverty, and the State in Modern India,* 267.

45 Ibid., 267.

that there has been any general change of heart on the issue of caste hierarchy and untouchable inferiority in particular."[46]

Hasnain is emphasizing that the process of development is same for everybody and Dalits have to make use of the available resources. He challenges the Dalits by saying that "the weaker sections have to accept the hard core realities as to put double efforts and surpass those who had been their master. There is a need to make them aware that there is no place for the feeling of inferiority, shame, and repentance in the development process of a people as in the psychological sense the weaker sections are not inferior to anybody as far as their abilities, cognitive and psychological resources are concerned."[47] Therefore, he feels the weaker sections of the society should work out strategies to overcome age-old stigmas. He asserts that the Dalits in the midst of the culture of poverty finds it difficult to adapt to the harsh realities of life and thus protect themselves with a philosophy of life, which is characterized by inferiority. By this an individual is deprived of "opportunities and consequently brings restrictions on them for the optimal development of cognitive, emotional and behavioural spheres of their personality."[48] Hasnain is mixing the Dalits and Dalit Muslims in the weaker sections of the society. He feels that the problems of the Dalit Muslims are completely neglected and are not addressed. But I feel that Dalits irrespective of their religion are the downtrodden and weakest among the weak.

Nandu Ram mainly focused on the scheduled caste middle class family and he asserts that caste consciousness in the country has become certainly more pervasive and powerful in public life. He observed "after Independence, several more comprehensive and systematic measures have been adopted, under the policy of protective discrimination, for the socio-economic betterment of scheduled castes and for protecting them from various social and economic disabilities."[49] He studied the implications of the 'reservation policy in modern India and gives credit to the reservation policy for this development of Scheduled Castes but speculates that there is a growing jealousy and resentment. Nandu Ram's sample of 240 Dalits drawn from the various cadres of central and state government employees in Kanpur, U.P. included not only sweepers, peons, clerical and technical staff, but also supervisors as well as class II and class I officers. He found that the degree of occupational mobility from their forefathers was impressive. Their achievements in terms of social mobility and a new identity have been analyzed and measured within a theoretico-methodological perspective devised

46 Ibid., 266.

47 N. Hasnain (ed)., *Weaker Sections: Psycho-Social Perspective* (New Delhi: Gyan Publishing House, 1998), 19. This book is a collection and presentation of the papers presented at a two day seminar conducted by the Department of Psychology at the Jamia Millia Islamia to commemorate the 98th birth anniversary of Dr. Zakir Husain.

48 N. Hasnain (ed), *Weaker Sections: Psycho-Social Perspective,* 18.

49 Nandu Ram, *The Mobile Scheduled Caste: The Rise of New Middle Class,* 11.

for the purpose. He observes that the mobile scheduled castes are looking for a positive impact of their achievements on their traditional social status.[50] Nandu Ram is mainly concerned with the social and occupational mobility and finds that there is an impressive change among the present generation from their forefathers.

Dahiwale made a study of 230 self-employed Dalits in Kolhapur, Maharashtra. He selected 30 subjects in their traditional occupations and the remaining 200 subjects engaged in modern occupations, such as doctors, lawyers, chartered accountants, radio or watch repairs, owners or workers in various kinds of engine manufacture and repair shops, transportation, selling eatables, cycle sales and repair, skilled construction work, painting and tailoring. He mainly focuses on the occupational mobility of Dalits.[51] Dahiwale is showing the difference between traditional occupation holders and modern occupation holders. But my question is, can we call watch repairs, radio repair, selling vegetables as modern occupation? What is clear is that they are ready to give up their traditional occupations.

Showeb concentrated on exploring a single outcaste group known as Chamar, numerically the most predominant and spatially the most widespread group among Scheduled Caste groups in Uttar Pradesh. The author has adopted a comparative framework. Three different segments of Chamars – the traditionally employed, 'the government employed, and the students' residing in Varanasi were chosen to measure the change in the attitudes, life styles and the socio-economic conditions of this outcaste group. He observed the fact that "it is clear that shoe making continues to be the main occupation not only in their fathers' generation but in that of the respondents' as well."[52] Thus, the traditionally employed Chamars were unable to bring about any change in their occupational life because of their poverty and ignorance. However, the educated with the help of reservation and other state benefits have raised their socio-economic status but they are alienated and cut-off from the large section of their community.[53] In a different direction Showeb while studying about education and mobility among Harijans, observed that the Dalit students on the other hand have high educational and economic aspirations. He points out that they are under achievers in their educational career and occupational career. He underscored the fact that mere state intervention is not enough, but feels adequate initiative and drive should come from within the community in a more organized way.[54]

Parvathamma gives some account of frustration prevalent among the Scheduled Castes in post-Independence India. She believes that the ban on untouchability remains more or less a legal fiction. She comments that, "During

50 Ibid., 8-9, 42.

51 S.M. Dahiwale, *Emerging Entrepreneurship among Scheduled Castes of Contemporary India: A Study of Kolhapur City*, 47-62.

52 M. Showeb, *Educated and Mobility among Harijans*, 47.

53 Ibid., 1-8.

54 Ibid., 5-8.

the post-independence period, in contemporary India, under the parliamentary democracy, these issues are of vital importance precisely because the problems continue unabated and are becoming sources of social unrest in spite of protectionist policy adopted by the Government."[55] She also discovered a big gulf between the scheduled caste politicians, the educated and the common people. She pointed out that the "Scheduled Caste politicians firstly do not wish to be identified as Scheduled Caste leaders. Secondly there is a growing tendency among the Scheduled Caste politicians to overlook and brush aside the problems of scheduled Castes precisely because 'general' votes in 'reserved' constituencies outnumber the Scheduled Caste votes."[56] In general, it is an up hill task for a Scheduled Caste politician to emerge as an effective and accepted leader.

Padma Velaskar and Wankhede explores the issue of the changing identity of educated neo-Buddhists of Maharashtra, located in urban, upper class/caste dominated context. The specific focus was on Buddhist Dalit male students in the elite educational institutions. The paper brings out some aspects of identity formation of this group of students and the manner in which it is shaped by inter-group relations and interactions. More specifically, it is concerned with exploring the basis, organization and assertion of the social identity, and its social and socio-psychological consequences. Their analysis has thrown light on factors that account for the persistent subordination of the Dalits. On the other hand, Velaskar and Wankhede have further explored some complex issues by asking some crucial questions like, have they actually achieved what they set out to achieve. What is the character of the new social identity that they collectively carry? How do they experience it in their daily lives? To what extent have they been able to wipe out their "original" negative, stigmatized identity and achieve esteem and prestige in society? What have been the escapes and the freedoms that the present allows or confers? What are the sources and channels of these freedoms? How does the past affect the present? How is the sum total of individual experiences manifest at the group level?[57]

Wankhede in particular identified and critically analyzed the social and educational problems of the Scheduled castes with reference to the educated Scheduled Castes in their social context. He analysed the problems of those among them who have achieved social status, which is contrary to their traditional stigmatized social status. Wankhede specifically tried to understand the educational problems in the context of the old and new social problems. He observed that "the stigma of caste and untouchability continues to exist"[58] and in

---

55 C. Parvathamma, "The Weaker Sections of Society-The Scheduled Castes in India," 51.

56 Ibid., 60.

57 Padma Velaskar and G.G. Wankhede, "From Old Stigma to New... Exploring the Changing Identity of Urban Educated Dalits," 115-135.

58 G.G. Wankhede, "Social and Educational Problems of Scheduled Castes: Some Critical Insights," 405.

his study shows how social problems obstruct the motivation level, quality and utility of education. He examined the processes in the educational system and Scheduled Caste homes to see how the social and educational problems manifest themselves at micro levels. However, he accepts that "these issues have not been identified and empirically studied at regional levels or at an all-India level."[59] He says though there are inherent handicaps, like past is linked with the present and that is directly affecting their educational progress, but however education has proved to be the best means for their over-all development. He accepts that their emotional achievements need to be analyzed within the parameters of their socio-cultural and economic conditions.[60]

In the above review of literature, there has been a considerable research done in the area of Dalits. In particular about the self-employed Dalits, traditionally employed Dalits, State and Central government employed Dalits and students. The main area of focus was to find the positive and negative factors that contributed towards their occupational mobility, social mobility, and educational mobility. It is agreed by most of the scholars that the employment has a positive impact on their achievements leading to an impressive change among Dalits of the present generation compared to their forefathers. Most of the scholars involved in the research are from the background of social work and hence they are limited to these variables. On the other extreme the Psychiatrists attend to the problems of mental illness. The area which is not covered in detail is the psychological aspect; that too Dalits in particular from a pastoral care and counselling perspective. Moreover, most of the research done is in the context of North India and so it cannot be generalised. So there is an urgent need to address Dalit issues in India from a pastoral care and counselling perspective. It is with this challenge and motivation I am attempting to find the level of Inferiority Complex among the Employed Dalits in comparison with non-Dalits, within the framework of socio-demographic variables.

---

59 Ibid., 399.

60 G.G. Wankhede, "Social and Educational Problems of Scheduled Castes: Some Critical Insights," 397-418.

Chapter 2

Caste and Identity
An Overview

2.1. Introduction

Vikas Jha and Imran Ali comment that, "the Hindu social order is based on two pillars, i.e., the caste system and untouchability. These social institutions which control the social, economical and political life of its people, is not founded on the principle of liberty (or freedom), equality and fraternity, but on the principle of inequality in every sphere of life... The unequal Hindu social order denies dignity and self-respect to Dalits in India which are dear to every human being and are expressed and communicated in interaction with other human being."[61] Caste system in India is the main feature of Hinduism and the world's longest surviving social hierarchy based on ritual purity. An individual becomes a member of a particular caste by birth and remains within the same caste until his or her death.[62] The traditional explanation given by the Hindu religions and legal texts, the Shastras and the Manu Smriti placed the Untouchables outside the four castes or varnas which fixed a person based on birth and heredity according to divine ordination.

The practice of discrimination or deprivation and subtle forms of ill treatment meted out to every Dalit enforces a sense of loss of identity of themselves. It is a sense of a denial of human worth, and against the affirmation of one's essence and existence, as a human person in relation to other humans. Identity and self-image are closely related and not the same. Self-image refer to how a person looks at him or herself, one's conception of one's own self, whereas

61 Vikas Jha and M. Imran Ali, "Atrocities on Dalits in Haryana and Rajasthan – A Comparitive Study: Religion as Oppressive," *Religion and Society* 51, 1 (March 2006): 44.

62 M.N. Srinivas (ed), *Caste: Its Twentieth Century Avatar* (New Delhi: Viking, 1996), ix.

identity means how other people look at someone. Thus, self-image is purely subjective and self-denied, although external influences can and do affect how one comes to define oneself. Identity, on the other hand, is socially a matter of constant negotiation between one's self and the other people in one's social world. The debate in the recent past over reservations in the private sector unfolds competing communities and social categories of our caste-structured hierarchical pyramidal structure of our society. Ambedkar perceived caste worldview as both self-alienating and other-alienating. Dalits have been excluded traditionally on the basis of caste system and thus suffering from inferiority complex, which is the result of the stigma of untouchability.[63] This chapter aims to provide insights into the above problem by dealing with the meaning, definition and characteristics of caste and untouchability. It also traces the origin of caste and untouchability from different viewpoints with special references to Ambedkar and Gandhi. The later part elaborates on how the Dalits asserted and claimed their identity demanding their Constitutional Rights with the help of Dalit Movement before and after Ambedkar.

2.2. The Origin of Caste and Untouchability

Caste is a term derived from a Portuguese word, *'casta,'* meaning breed, lineage, or race.[64] Caste is generally used as an equivalent for the more famous and also the more appropriate Indian word Jati. The word 'Jati' etymologically means 'something into which one is born'. Jati is a term used to identify the different social segments within the caste-based Hindu society. Later on the word 'Jati' is specialized to denote caste, which is acquired by birth. It is occasionally used by good ancient authorities as equivalent to 'varna'. Ghurye views[65] caste from the etymological understanding and arrives at a point that caste in India is a Brahmanic child of the Indo-Aryan culture, framed in the land of the Ganges and Jamuna and thence transferred to other parts of the country. This racial origin of the principal feature of the caste system is further supported by the early term 'varna' meaning colour used to specify the orders in society.[66] Though there are conflicting views about the origin of caste, there is absolute agreement among scholars about its nature and functions. People belonging to one caste will not interdine or intermarry with other castes. Each caste has its own customs, rituals, family deities and food habits. According to Ambedkar, it is mainly the custom

63 *India Today* (Bangalore), 5 June 2006, 25. The soft-spoken Minister for Social Justice and Empowerment, Meira Kumar speaking to the Managing Editor of India Today, Shankkar Aiyar and Special correspondent Neeraj Mishra on the subject reservations in the private sector, said that "Merit is used to practice mental untouchability."

64 Sarajit Kumar Chatterjee, *The Scheduled Castes in India* (New Delhi: Gyan Publishing House, 2008), 15.

65 G.S. Ghurye, *Caste and Race in India*, 5th Edition, (Bombay: Popular Prakashan, 1969), 162.

66 Ibid., 176.

of endogamy that has preserved the castes and prevented one caste from fusing into another.[67]

The above view is accepted by many scholars such as Kroeber, who defined caste as "endogamous and hereditary subdivision of an ethnic unit occupying a position of superior or inferior rank or social esteem in comparison with other subdivisions"[68] It is further elaborated by the renowned scholar, Srinivas who says "caste is a hereditary, endogamous, usually localized group, having a traditional association with an occupation and particular position in the social hierarchy of caste. Relations between castes are governed, among other things, by concepts of pollution and purity and generally maximum commensability occurs within the caste."[69] It is much more focused by Risley, "as a collection of families or groups of families bearing a common name; claiming common descent from a mythical ancestor, human or divine; professing to follow the same hereditary calling; and regarded by those who are competent to give opinion as forming a single homogeneous community."[70]

An eminent anthropologist, Hutton concluded his major work, Caste in India, by locating the origins of caste in the taboos and divisions of labor in the pre-Aryan tribes of India as well as in their efforts at self-preservation in the face of invasion. According to him, the dominant view traces the origins both of caste and untouchability to the Aryans themselves and to their ways of relating to the peoples of India with whom they came into contact. The Aryans, a series of related and highly self-conscious tribes sharing a common language and religion, began their invasions of India from the northwest around 1500 BC. For centuries they remained in seemingly constant conflict with the indigenous peoples, whom the Aryans looked down upon as culturally inferior and excluded as ritually unclean. Once conquered by superior military technology, some of these peoples withdrew into regions as yet unoccupied by the Aryans, while others were incorporated as separate and inferior castes within Aryan-dominated society.[71] Vivekananda Jha and Prabhati Mukherjee have examined references to social stigma, to untouchability, and to the precursors of castes later considered untouchable in the early Sanskrit, Pali and Prakrit literature. These literatures were produced by the dominant Aryans and are basically representing their views that Candala are of particular importance. Although, the Candala were severely stigmatized in the

67 V.T. Rajshekar, *Caste: A Nation with the Nation* (Bangalore: Books for Change, 2002), 4.

68 A.L. Kroeber, *Caste, Encyclopedia of the Social Sciences* (New York: McMillan, 1980), 254.

69 M.N. Srinivas, *Caste in Modern India and Other Essays* (Bombay: Asia Publishing House, 1962), 106-108.

70 Sir. H.H. Risley, *The People of India,* 2nd Edition, (London: W Thacker Co., 1915), 67.

71 J.H. Hutton, *Caste in India: Its Nature, Function and Origins,* 4th Edition, (London: 1963), 207.

later Vedic age, it was only in the period between 600 BC and 200 AD that untouchability appears as such.[72]

On the other hand, it is generally observed that untouchability is not an independent institution in itself but is a consequesence of the caste system. According to Ambedkar, the "idea of pollution" is by no means a peculiarity of caste as such. It usually originates in priestly ceremonialism and in particular case of the general belief in purity. Consequently, its necessary connection with caste may be completely denied without damaging the working of caste. Whereas untouchability, which originated initially in the contempt and hatred of Buddhism by the Brahmanical forces, became an integral and essential part of Hindu Social habit observed by the caste Hindus all over the country. Even though it is not an essential part of other religions, it has no doubt intruded because other religions imitated Hinduism. In this sense untouchability is a unique feature of Hinduism. It is also treated as a permanent stain acquired by reason of birth in an untouchable community, and it could not be obliterated by any way. The National Commission reports a similar view for Scheduled Castes and Scheduled Tribes, that "untouchability" as – the imposition of social disabilities on persons by reason of their birth in certain castes.[73] The notion of untouchability was so deeply rooted in the minds of the caste Hindus that they considered it was but a religious act. It is their misconceived belief in the pollution or defilement by the touch of untouchables that does not permit them to discard the 'custom' of untouchability. The above understanding of the caste Hindus means, in the words of Ambedkar, that untouchability is the notion of defilement, pollution, contamination and there is no ways and means of getting rid of that defilement. It is a case of permanent hereditary stain, which nothing can cleanse,[74] neither religious rite nor act. Manmohan Singh, the Prime Minister of India has rightly said that, "untouchability is not just social discrimination. It is a blot on Humanity."[75]

---

72 Vivekananda Jha and Prabhati Mukherjee, "Stages in History of Untouchables," *The Indian Historical Review* II, (July 1975): 14-31.

73 National Commission for Scheduled Castes and Scheduled Tribes, Highlights for the Report for the year 1994-95 & 1995-96 (New Delhi: Government of India, 1997), 2. The National Commission for Scheduled Castes and Scheduled Tribes is a constitutional body set up pursuant to Article 338 of the India Constitution. It has been entrusted with the responsibility of ensuring that the safeguards and protections which have been given to Scheduled Cates and tribes are implemented by the various implementing agencies.

74 B.R. Ambedkar, *The Untouchables*, Vol. 7, (Bombay: Govt. of Maharastra, 1990), 26.

75 Dr. Manmohan Singh, *Unbroken People,* 2, 8, (Jan 2007): 14-16.

Shinde[76] defines Untouchability as "A nation-wide institution indicating three features of often observing pollution, asking to live outside of village and not giving equal legal protection of law."[77] The committee on Untouchability headed by Elayaperumal, defines that "Untouchability is a basic and unique feature of the Hindu social system and order. It is generally held these days that it is an economic backwardness of the people concerned. But the simple fact is forgotten that while economic issues are present in all other countries untouchability is a unique problem confronted in this country only. It does not require much research to realise that the phenomenon of untouchability in this country is fundamentally of religious and political origin. Untouchability is not a separate institution by itself; it is an outcome of the institutions of the Caste system of Hindu society. It is an attitude on the part of a whole group of people. It is spirit of social aggression that underlies this attitude."[78]

As usual, the attention and exposure that the indigenous people gained and the opportunities they experienced gave some of the several groups from among those lumped together as the 'depressed classes' a new sense of identity. It forced them, as well as the other Hindus who had been party to their subjugation to question their situation. It was in this process that in 1909 the problem of the lowest castes was first conceptualized under the rubric of 'untouchability'. Shridhar Ketkar used the term in a study of the caste system published in September 1909,[79] soon afterwards, in October 1909, the Maharaja of Baroda used the term 'untouchable' in the course of an address that he delivered to the 'depressed classes' mission in Bombay.[80]

Every Caste Hindu who believes in the Vedas, also believe in the Varnashrama, caste system and the caste purity or taboo. It is stated in the Purusha Sukta, part of the Rigveda, that God created the Brahmin, Kshatriya, Vaisya and Sudra respectively from the mouth, arms, thighs and feet. The untouchables, however, were not Savarnas. They were known as Avarnas. Hence in the hierarchy of the caste system they were more degraded and treated as outcastes, untouchables, whose touch was considered to be blasphemous. The Bhagavad Gita while narrating the duties of each and every Varna states categorically "by worshipping

76 According to Shinde, there were five different causes for the origin of untouchability. The original sources is found in the Marathi version of the book of V. R. Shinde, *Bharatiya Asprushancha Prashna* (Marathi), 78-79. 1976. For the translation of the same can be referred to R.K. Kshirsagar, *Dalit Movement in India and its Leaders.*

77 R.K. Kshirsagar, *Dalit Movement in India and Its Leaders* (New Delhi: M.D. Publications, 1994), 14.

78 National Commission for Scheduled Castes and Scheduled Tribes, *Highlights for the Report for the year 1994-95 & 1995-96* (New Delhi: Government of India, 1997), 2.

79 Shridhar Ketkar, *The History of Caste in India* (Ithaca: Taylor and Carpenter, 1909), 86.

80 Sayaji Rao III, *Maharaja of Baroda. Speeches and Addresses* (London: Macmillan Co., 1912), 244.

through the performance of his own duty (Dharma) man attains perfection." Performing one's own duties or Dharma was, thus made essential for salvation. Therefore, none could afford to challenge the Dharma revealed in the religious books. Ultimately, the habit of untouchability formed Achar Dharma of all the caste Hindus. Therefore, this theory does not explain the origin of untouchability, but explains it in terms of fabricated belief in caste purity, taboo and inequality of castes.[81]

Stainly Rice explains the origin of Untouchability with the help of the theory of race and occupation. According to him, the untouchables were non-Aryan and non-Dravidian aboriginals. They were conquered and subjugated by the Dravidians first and thereafter by the Aryans. Accordingly, there were two invasions of India, first by the Dravidians and second by the Aryans. The Aryans defeated the non-Aryans, reduced them to mere 'serfs' and assigned to them only menial or filthy occupations.[82] The concept of caste owes its origin to the Vedic ideals of Varnashrama Dharma. The Hindu religion divided the society into four classes, which included an occupational hierarchy as each caste was allotted a particular kind of work.

The origins of caste and of untouchability lie deep in India's ancient past and the evidence of those origins provided by the archeological and literary sources now available is, at best, circumstantial. Consequently, scholars have been forced to engage in considerable speculation in their efforts to reconstruct the past history of untouchability. Whatever is available now are not hard and clear facts but a variety of competiting theories, all of which have proven difficult to substantiate in a convincing manner. Asha Krishnan comments that as the society became more complex, the caste system became more rigid and orthodox. It changed to a system where a person's caste was fixed for his lifetime dependant on his birth. The rigidity of the caste system fell heavily on the lowest caste, namely, the Shudras and amongst them a further division was made into touchables and untouchables. The Untouchables, in the main, represented the class of people who were engaged in performing unclean work. These classes of people were condemned for life to the curse of Untouchability, once they were born in a family of Untouchables. Untouchables were only to do impure or unclean tasks. In the course of time, this caste system developed an inhuman rigidity, under which certain communities were treated as defiled or impure whose members, the untouchables, supposedly caused pollution to ordinary Hindus by touch or proximity. Hence, they were excluded from the ordinary social and religious privileges of Hinduism.[83]

The Untouchable was subjected to indignities, which would be disgusting to any modern mind. The Untouchable was born impure and treated as the lowest of the low while he or she lived. There was absolutely no way by which they

81 Bhagavad Gita, Ch. IV.

82 Stainly Rice, *Hindu Customs and their Origin* (London: George Allen Unwin, 1937), 13-15.

83 Asha Krishnan, *Ambedkar and Gandhi* (Mumbai: Himalaya Publishing House, 1997), 9-10.

could come out of the pale. Their children were condemned to Untouchability from their very birth; they were born as Untouchables, lived as Untouchables and died as Untouchables. Religious knowledge was denied to them and could not enter Hindu temples. The priest would not officiate in the event of life in which, in the case of other castes, his attendance was essential. The Untouchable was compelled to live in his separate quarters with others of his or her class, generally in the unsanitary outskirts of the village. They could not use the village well. By reason of their birth, they had to suffer indignity treating them as one whose touch and shadow defiled the caste Hindu and their environment. The Untouchable thus was socially segregated, economically exploited and politically excluded from educational and growth opportunies.[84] According to Aiyappan, the term untouchability denotes "the socio religious practice of which Hindus keep a large number of lower castes from touching or coming near their persons, houses, temples, tanks and sometimes even public road."[85]

Caste system is based on Veda, Manusmriti and other religious scriptures, whereas untouchability is based on traditional contempt of Buddhism, and continuation of beef eating by the so-called untouchables. Caste system prescribes certain rules of "Internal" behaviour as a distinct unit as such for other castes, whereas untouchability is a rule of "external" behaviour with the so-called lower castes, and later on into thousands of castes and sub-castes; whereas 'untouchability' divides the Hindu society into 'Touchables' and 'Untouchables'. Caste system is comparatively more ancient than the institution of Untouchability.[86] Yet, caste system has consolidated the institution of Untouchability by enforcement of several disabilities and restrictions under the fabricated belief in 'purity' of the so-called high castes and 'Impurity' of the so-called lower castes. As such caste and Untouchability are so interwined and cannot be separated. In spite of this, the minute observations reveal that both are separate institutions, at least, at their inception.[87]

2.3. Hindu Religious Scriptures on Caste and Untouchability

It is generally observed that Untouchability is a unique feature of Hinduism. The Karma theory, expounded in the Gita states that man attains salvation by worshipping God through performance of one's own duties as decided by the religious scriptures consequently all the Hindus, including touchables and untouchables, strongly believe that there was no salvation except by complying with the rules of caste system as expounded and interpreted by Brahmins who had the right to that effect. Most of the religious gurus and pujaris believed

84 Asha Krishnan, *Ambedkar and Gandhi*, 9-10.

85 A. Aiyappan, *Social Revolution in a Kerala Village: A Study in Cultural Change* (Bombay: Asia Publishing House, 1965), 37.

86 B.R. Ambedkar, *Castes in India; their Mechanism, Genesis and Development*, 7.

87 R.K. Kshirsagar, *Untouchability in India, Law and Abolition*, 23-26.

in the sanctity of untouchability and they had practiced and enforced several disabilities based on untouchability. Whereas Manu States those four varnas were divinely ordained from the very beginning. From the Mouth of Purusha, the Self-Existent one, came the Brahman, from his arms came the Kshatriyas, from his thighs came the Vaishyas, and from his feet came Shudras. Other castes were the result of alliances between members of these four original varnas. The Candala, whom Manu considered the offspring of a Brahman woman and a Shudra man, the worst possible combination, was to be excluded from all considerations of dharma. According to Manu, the ancient Indian Lawgiver, untouchability is the punishment for miscegenation between a member of a high caste and that of a low caste or an outcaste. The children of such an unequal pair become untouchables and the greater and social gap between the two parents, the lower the status of their children. The consequences are also more severe if the mother is of superior caste. Thus, the offspring of a Brahmin father and a Sudra mother is called Nishada; the child becomes a fisherman. The offspring of Sudra father and a Brahmin mother is called Chandala; he is the most degraded of all mortals. To Manu, a degraded occupation is not the cause of untouchability; rather untouchability condemns a person to a low and impure occupation. In later times, racial mixture was added as a factor of impurity. In the period after Manu, increasing numbers of the members of the lower castes belonged to different races and cultures. Practice of untouchability was intensified and applied to more groups in the years following AD 200, while Chandala became a label not simply for a tribe but for all whom the Aryans considered to be at the very bottom of society.[88]

Most of the religious authorities, Shastras and Puranas have advocated the divine origin of the caste system. So the general feeling among the Hindus is that it has been established by the order of God and so it should be religiously followed. High castes among the Hindus are considered pure while the lower castes are considered as polluted. Certain scheduled castes were supposed to be so polluted that even their touch would invite elaborate purificatory ritual for members of the higher caste.

2.4. Gandhi on Caste and Untouchability

Gandhi's movement for Harijan uplift began in 1932 and in spite of the efforts to bring some legislation to lay down the law prohibiting the practice of untouchability; it was only during the period when congress ministries came into power in the provinces that some legislation got under way.[89] According to Gandhi, untouchability was not part and parcel of the caste system, but was a logical and inevitable outcome of the caste idea. He preached eradication of

88 V.S. Nargolkar, "Removal of Untouchability, Goals and Attainments," *Indian Journal of Social Work* XXX, 3, (July 1969): 189.

89 G.S. Sharma, *Legislation and Cases on Untouchability and Scheduled Castes in India* (New Delhi: Allied Publishers, 1975), 2.

untouchability while cherishing the caste system in which it has its very root. He 'jealously' guarded Caste, the root and source of the evil.[90] Gandhi said, "Injustice is being done all the world over, but we have given it the sanction of religion. These distinctions have not been created by God. The Harijans are on the lowest rung of the ladder not because of any inherent defects but only because they have been kept down by the so called higher castes. God has bestowed on them the same talents that he has given to us, but we deny them opportunities for using them. They should surely have the same rights and privileges and the same opportunities of growth that we enjoy."[91]

Gandhi's views on Untouchability are made clear in his early speeches and writing. Gandhi while addressing the students in Bombay in February 1916, stated Untouchability as, "It has been handed to us from immemorial times. I think that these miserable, wretched, enslaving spirits of Untouchability must have come to us when we were in a cycle of our lives at our lowest ebb and that evil has stuck to us and it remains with us… It is to my mind a curse that has come to us and as long as it remains with us, we are bound to consider that every affliction that we labour under in this sacred land is a fit and proper punishment for the great crime that we are seized with fear, and we have got our superstitious veneration for our family traditions and for the members of our families."[92]

When the orthodox Hindus tried to justify untouchability, Gandhi lashed out, "That religion and that nation will be blotted out of the face of the earth which pins its faith to injustice, untruth or violence. God is light, not darkness, God is love, not hate, God is truth, not untruth. God alone is great. We His creatures are but dust. Let us be humble and recognise the place of the lowliest of His creatures. Krishna honoured Sudama in his rags… Love is the root of religion"[93]

In order to convince Gandhi that the practice of untouchability had religious sanction and was integral part of Hinduism, the orthodox Hindus always quoted Hindu scriptures such as vedas, upanishad, smritis and puranas. Gandhi initially did not believe what the Shastras said about the Untouchability. He firmly believed that the basic tenets of Hinduism were based on love and universal tolerance. In the long run, Gandhi instead of attacking the Hindu religion, he modified his strategy to use religion. He diverted the attention of the Hindus from Shastras to the other equally respected and popular treatises on Hindu religious philosophy such as Bhagvad Gita. He proclaimed himself as a sanatanist (orthodox Hindu). By this he meant that he believed in Vedas, the Upanishads, the Puranas, the

90 Sanjana J.E., *Caste and Outcaste,* (1946), XIV.

91 M.K. Gandhi, *Caste Must go, the Sin of Untouchability* (Ahmedabad: Navjivan Publishing House, 1964), 32.

92 M.K. Gandhi, *Caste Must go, the Sin of Untouchability*, 32.

93 Ibid. The original source was published in *Young India*, 12 June, 1924.

Avtars and rebirth, and the Varnashrama dharma (caste system).[94] He agreed with the orthodox Hindus that the Varnashrama dharma was an inseparable part of Hinduism and was based on the natural law of heredity. Gandhi stated, "Varna means predetermination of the choice of man's profession. The law of Varna is that a man shall follow the profession of his ancestors for earning his livelihood. Every child naturally follows the 'colour' of his father, or chooses his father's profession. Varna, therefore, is in a way the law of heredity... It is not a human invention but an immutable law of nature."[95] Gandhi believed in the theory of 'Action' and 'Incarnation' as endorsed in the Gita and explained that by his good karma (deeds) in his present life a Shudra could be born a Brahmin in his next birth. In other words, the Untouchable in his present life was only atoning for his bad karma in his previous birth. They need to perform their duties to the best in order to rise to a higher caste in the next generation.

2.5. Ambedkar on Caste and Untouchability

One of the theories on Caste and Untouchability put forward by Ambedkar is that they are the Broken Men. The theory is based on the use of words 'Antya, Antyaja and Antyavasin'. They are derived from the root 'Antya'. The names Antya, Antyaja and Antyavasin are given to certain communities by the Hindu Shastras. According to some Hindu Pundits Antya means an Untouchable. Ambedkar does not agree with them. He writes, "The argument is absured and does not accord with the Hindu theory of the order of creation. According to it, it is the Shudra who is born last. The Untouchable is outside the scheme of creation. The Shudra is Savarna. As against him the Untouchable is Avarna, i.e., outside the Varna system. The Hindu theory of priority in creation does not and cannot apply to the Untouchable."[96]

According to Ambedkar, Antya means end of the village and not end of creation. The name 'Antya' was given to the people who lived on the outskirts of the village. The people who lived on the 'Antya' of the village were called 'Antyaja'. The people who lived on the outskirts of the village were alien tribes. They were different from the tribes who live inside the village. He says there was a stage in the history of India when broken men or women belonging to other tribes-the aliens, who were different from the settled tribe inside the village, were allowed to settle on the outskirts of the village. But they were required to do certain duties for the villagers and in return were given certain rights. But undoubtedly they were not Untouchables. According to Ambedkar, only at a later stage, these Broken Men or rather their descendants must have turned into Untouchables. The present-day Mahars of Maharastra, he holds, are the descendants of the Broken Men. Mahars

94 M.K. Gandhi, *Caste Must go, the Sin of Untouchability*, 32. The original source was published in Young India, 27 April, 1927.

95 Ibid. The original source was published in Young India, 24 November, 1927.

96 B.R. Ambedkar, *The Untouchables who were they and why they became Untouchables?* 32-33.

live on the outskirts of villages and are Untouchables. One of the rights claimed by Mahars is to appropriate the dead animals belonging to villagers.

At one time all people in India were eating beef. Especially Brahmins ate it abundantly. They were priests. Thousands of cows were offered to them for their yajna every day. In the name of their several imaginary gods, thousands of innocent cows were slaughtered every day. The killing of cows was carried on in the name of their religion. The ritualists hardly had a day on which there was no cow sacrificed and they were not invited to eat beef-steak. What were their Yajnas? If it is to be quoted in the exact words of Ambedkar, "The Yajna of the Brahmins was nothing but the killing of innocent animals carried on in the name of religion with pomp and ceremony with an attempt to enshroud it in mystery with a view to conceal their appetite for beef."[97]

Manu, the lawgiver had permitted them to kill cows and eat beef. For generations the Brahmins were eating not merely meat but beef also. But at a later period Brahmins were compelled to give up beef eating. They had to take to vegetarianism. To find out the reason why the beef-eating Brahmins took to vegetarianism, we have to read carefully the history of the Buddhistic period in India. At one time Buddhists were the majority people in India. Buddhism continued to be the religion of the masses for hundreds of years. And then naturally Brahmanism was attacked on all sides and was on the decline. So there was strife between Buddhists and Brahmins. Brahmins had lost their power and prestige. So as this was the condition of the Brahmins, they had to make all efforts to regain their power and prestige. They had to fight Buddhism, which had a great hold on the masses. Animal sacrifice was the essence of Brahmanism and Buddhism was deadly opposed to it. Buddhism had been opposing animal sacrifice, and the agricultural population who depended on their bullocks and cows for irrigation and livelihood, naturally respected Buddhism and reacted against Brahmanism. So the Brahmins had to find out a way to defeat the Buddhists. So what did they do? The Brahmins themselves became the extreme followers of Buddhism but were still called Hindus. The extreme followers of Buddhism gave up meat-eating altogether and became pure vegetarians. Their object was to snatch away the supremacy the Buddhists had over them. Not only did they give up meat eating but they also began to worship the cow.

Buddhism is opposed to animal sacrifice but at the same time, it has no particular affection for the cow. Ambedkar summed up saying, "They wanted to oust the Buddhists from the place of honour and respect which they had acquired in the mind of the masses by their opposition to the killing of the cow for sacrificial purpose. To achieve their purpose the Brahmins had to adopt the usual tactics of a reckless adventurer. It is to beat extremism by extremism. It is the strategy which all rightists use to overcome the leftists. The only way to beat the Buddhists was to

97 B.R. Ambedkar, *The Untouchables who were they and why they became Untouchables?* 100.

go a step further and be vegetarians."[98] Ambedkar writes that, "The worship of the cow is the result of the struggle between Buddhism and Brahmanism."[99] The cow was made a sacred animal and the beef eating received religious sanctions. But the broken men continued to eat beef and were thus kept away on the outskirts of the village as separate class and were made untouchables by the sacred men who lived inside the village. Ambedkar summed up saying, "Once the cow became sacred and the broken men continued to eat beef, there was no other fate left for the broken men except to be treated unfit for association, i.e., as untouchables."

It was sometime in the 4th Century A.D., during the period of the Gupta Kings who were the champions of Hinduism, the Brahmins succeeded in making cow-killing a capital offence. "Taking the ban on beef-eating as a point to reconnoiter from, it follows that the date of birth of untouchability must be intimately connected with the ban on cow-killing and on eating beef," and thus Ambedkar concludes his theory on Origin of Untouchability and Untouchables in India. Since religion has divided the society, into four different classes, Ambedkar said, "I want religion, but I do not want hypocrisy in the name of religion. I like that religion which teaches his followers to have relation with others on the basis of liberty and fraternity."[100] Religion has played an important role in spreading the Caste system in Indian society. That is why Ambedkar said, "religion must be matter of principle only. It cannot be matter of rules. The moment it degenerates into rules, it ceases religion as it kills responsibilities which is the essence of a truely religious act."[101] He added, "caste does not result in economic efficiency, caste cannot and it has not improved the race. Caste has, however, done one thing. It has completely disorganized and demoralized the Hindus."[102]

2.6. Dalits Consciousness for Separate Electorates

The above section helps us to understand the whole concept of caste and untouchability which is the core issue leading to the problem of inferiority complex among Dalits, whether employed or not. The following section is more of an initial Dalit consciousness towards the road of progress and prosperity. The Dalits under the leadership of Ambedkar demanded that their representation should be made by separate electorates. A separate electorate means an electorate composed exclusively of untouchable voters who are to elect an untouchable as their representative to the Legislature. The Hindus Agree that certain number of seats is to be reserved for untouchables to be filled only by untouchables. But they insist that the untouchable who is to be the representative of the untouchables in the Legislature should be elected by a mixed electorate consisting both of the

98 B.R. Ambedkar, *The Untouchables who were they and why they became Untouchables?* 119.

99 Ibid., 121.

100 B.R. Ambedkar, *Annihilation of Caste* (Jalandhar: Beem Patrika Publication, 1970), 42.

101 Ibid., 6.

102 Ibid.

Hindus as well as of the untouchables and not by an electorate exclusively of the untouchables. In other words there is still a controversy over the question of joint versus separate electorates. Here again Ambedkar wants to set out the pros and cons of this controversy.

The objection to separate electorate raised by the Hindus is that separate electorate means the fragmentation of the nation. The reply is obvious. First of all, there is no nation of Indians in the real sense of the word. The nation does not exist, it is to be created; and Ambedkar thought it would be admitted that the suppression of a distinct and a separate community is not the method of creating a nation. Secondly, if it is conceded – as the Hindus have done – that untouchables should be represented in that Legislature by untouchables then it cannot be denied that the untouchable must be a true representative of the untouchable voters. If this is a correct position then separate electorate is the only method by which real representation can be guaranteed to the untouchables. The Hindu argument against separate electorate is insubstantial and unsupportable. The Hindus admit the premises on which the political demands of the untouchables are based. Separate electorate is only a consequence, which logically follows from those grounds.[103]

Special electorates are devised as a means of protecting minorities like the untouchables to determine what kind of electorate is necessary for its protection. These are questions to which the Hindus cannot answer. The reason is that the real objection to separate electorates by the Hindus is different from this alleged objection raised in the name of a nation. The real objection is that separate electorate does not permit the Hindus to capture the seats reserved for the untouchables. On the other hand the joint electorate does.[104]

In the Government of India Act of 1919, there was a provision which has imposed an obligation on His Majesty's Government to appoint at the end of ten years a Royal Commission to investigate into the working of the Constitution and report upon such changes as may be found necessary. Therefore, in 1928 a Royal Commission was appointed under the Chairmanship of Sir Johan Simon. Indians expected that the Commission would be mixed in its personnel. But Lord Birkenhead who was then the Secretary of State for India was opposed to the inclusion of Indians and insisted on making it a purely Parliamentary Commission. At this, the Congress and the Liberals took great offence and treated it as an insult. They boycotted the Commission and carried on a great agitation against it. To diminish this feeling of opposition it was announced by His Majesty's Government that after the work of the Commission was completed representative Indian would be assembled for a discussion before the new Constitution for India was settled. In accordance with this announcement representative Indians

103 B. R. Ambedkar, *Mr. Gandhi and the Emancipation of the Untouchables* (Bombay: Thacker & Co., Ltd. 1943), 31-33.

104 Ibid.

were called to London at a Round table Conference with the representatives of Parliament and of His Majesty's Government.[105]

On the 12th November 1930, His late Majesty King George V formally inaugurated the Indian Round Table Conference. From the point of view of Indians the Round Table Conference was an event of great significance. Its significance lay in the recognition of His Majesty's Government of the right of Indians to be consulted in the matter of framing a constitution for India. For the untouchables it was a land mark in their history. For, the untouchables were for the first time allowed to be represented separately by two delegates who happened to be Ambedkar and Dewan Bahadur R. Srinivasan. This meant that the untouchables were regarded not merely as a separate element from the Hindus but also of such importance as to have the right to be consulted in the framing of a Constitution for India.[106]

Gandhi in response to the British Government's decision on the representation of minorities, writes, "I have read the British Government's decision on the representation of minorities and have slept over it. In pursuance of my letter to Sir Samuel Hoare and my declaration at the meeting of the Minorities Committee of the Round Table Conference on 13th November 1931, at St. James Palace, I have to resist your decision with my life. The only way I can do so is by declaring a perpetual fast unto death from food of any kind save water with or without salt and soda. This fast will cease if during its progress the British Government, of its own motion or under pressure of public opinion, revise their decision and withdraw their scheme of communal electorates for the Depressed Classes, whose representatives should be elected by the general electorate under the common franchise, no matter how wide it is."[107]

Therefore, on the 20th September 1932, Gandhi commenced his 'fast into death' as a protest against the grant of separate electorates to the untouchables. The fast however created a problem, and that problem was how to save Gandhi's life. The only way to save his life was to alter the Communal Award, which hurt the conscience of Gandhi very much. The Prime Minister had made it quite clear that the British Cabinet would not withdraw it or alter it of its own, but that they were ready to substitute for it a formula that may be agreed upon by the Caste Hindus and the Untouchables. As Ambedkar had the privilege of representing the Untouchables at the Round Table Conference, it was assumed that the Untouchables would not be valid unless Ambedkar was a party to it. The surprising fact is that Congressmen did not only question his position as the leader of the Untouchables of India but it was accepted as a fact. All eyes

105 B.R. Ambedkar, *Dr. Ambedkar on Poona Pact* (Jalandhar: Bheem Patrika Publication, 1973), 7-8.

106 Ibid.

107 B.R. Ambedkar, *Dr. Ambedkar on Poona Pact*, 7-8. Letter written by Gandhi in objection to the separate electorate from Yeravada Central Prison, on August 18th, 1932.

naturally turned towards him as the man of the moment or rather as the villain of the section.

As for Ambedkar, it is no exaggeration to say that no man was placed in a greater and graver dilemma than he was then. It was a mysterious situation. Ambedkar had to make a choice between two different alternatives. First, humiliation as a part of common humanity, to save Gandhi from sure death and secondly, the problem of saving for the Untouchables the political rights which the Prime Minister had given them. Ambedkar responded to the call of humanity and saved the life of Gandhi by agreeing to alter the Communal Award in a manner satisfactory to Mr. Gandhi.[108] His agreement is known as the Poona Pact.

Poona Pact is an important historic agreement, which was signed on 24th September 1932, between Ambedkar and the Hindu leaders in Yervada jail of Poona in Maharastra State. Although, the Scheduled Castes through this agreement got representation in legislature, facilities in education and reservation in Government services, many of them are still unaware of it, when and where it was signed, how it changed the political face of our country and what it obtained for the Scheduled Castes people. The history of Poona Pact reveals the attitude of Gandhi towards the demands of Scheduled Castes and the struggle waged by Ambedkar for getting rights for his people.[109]

The Indian National Congress, till framing the Constitution of India, never mustered a firm stand over the issue of the removal of untouchability. If the brief history of the Indian National Congress with its controversy over social reforms is closely studied, one will get an impression that it had taken favourable decision on the social uplift of the untouchables in its initial phase only. The main reason for not focusing on the social uplift of the untouchables is because they decided that it should not divert from its main objective of winning freedom. It feared that attention to social reforms would have a harmful effect on the national struggle. This trend continued further. However, in 1895, the Indian National Congress' tone turned to be sympathetic to social reforms. The Indian National Congress in its Annual Session at Calcutta in 1917 passed a resolution to the effect of bringing of social justice to the Depressed Classes and removing their disabilities forced by traditional customs. This was all done under the Presidentship of Annie Besant.[110]

The Indian National Congress was split up into two camps: one professing social reforms but at the same time not favouring the Congress to be an instrument to steer them, and the other advocating to exclusion of social reforms from its programme. The historical split of the Indian National Congress at Poona in 1895 ruined the fate of the pro-social reforms plank. These happenings unfolded the trend in the Indian National Congress and in 1917 the Congressmen evinced a

108 B.R. Ambedkar, *Dr. Ambedkar on Poona Pact*, 54-55.

109 The text of the Poona Pact is presented in the Appendix 2.

110 B.R. Ambedkar, *What Congress and Gandhi have done for the Untouchables?* (Bombay: Thacker and Co., n.y), 68ff.

sympathetic attitude towards social reforms. The Congress movement came under the leadership of Gandhi in 1922 and he gave it a new life. It became broad-based. The objective of raising the social and economic status of the depressed classes was included in the committee and appointed another committee was appointed to study the problems of the untouchables.[111]

The All-India Congress Committee was exposed concerning its sincerity about the issue, when it ridiculously handed over the task of removing untouchability to the Hindu Mahasabha in May 1923. The problems of the untouchables engaged significant attention from holding First Round Table Conference (1930). Two representatives of the untouchables were invited for the same and this recognised the fact that the interests of the untouchables were different from those of the Caste Hindus. For sharing the work of Round Table Conference various committees were formed. Ramsay MacDonald chaired the committee on Minorities, the then British Prime Minister.[112]

In fact it was not for the first time that the problems and difficulties of the Depressed Classes were put before the British Government. Earlier the Montague-Chelmsford Report made certain recommendations for safeguarding their special interests. But the recommendations were petty and did not touch the core of the problem. The First Round Table Conference was given a memorandum by Ambedkar which covered adequate representation of the Depressed Classes in legislatures, measures against boycott or threat of boycott, protection against discrimination, adequate reservations in services, right to redressal against prejudiced action, or neglecting their interests, formation of special department for taking care of untouchables and representation in cabinet.

The Minorities Committee agreed to award separate electorates to the Depressed Classes and this caused a big hue and cry among the Caste-Hindus. It was also made clear that the minorities should be taken upon the provincial and federal executives. If a small minority did not get representation in Cabinet, a minister specially charged with the duty to safeguarding their interests was to be appointed. The public service commissions were to reconcile the interests of various communities. The Committee pointed out that the Minorities and Depressed Classes were free to refuse their consent to any constitution that, they felt, could not safeguard their interest.

In the First Round Table Conference, the Congress was not a party. Mahatma Gandhi, after a comprise between the Congress and British Government, was chosen to represent the Congress. The situation, with his entry into the Round Table Conference, got complicated; because he was not ready to accept untouchables as a separate entity. Gandhi resisted special representation to the untouchables; to this Ambedkar's reaction was very bitter. He took Gandhi's opposition to separate representation to untouchables as a war against them. He

111 B.R. Ambedkar, *What Congress and Gandhi have done for the Untouchables?*, 68ff.

112 Ibid.

was also annoyed by the reference made by Gandhi that their communities did not elect the representatives of minority communities and that they were merely the nominees of the British Government.[113]

Ambedkar feared that the power was likely to be transferred to the high castes by the British Government. As such, he made it amply clear that the transfer of power should be designed in such a manner that it should not fall into the hands of the elite of Hindus or Muslims but to be distributed among the various communities in proportion of their population. The Muslim, Sikhs, Depressed Classes, Christians and Anglo-Indians concluded a pact. It was read out to the then British Prime Minister on November 13, 1931. Gandhi's reaction to this pact was very bitter and strong. The recognition, which the minorities gave to the Depressed Classes, angered Gandhi. He could understand the claims of other minorities except those of the untouchables. He was not prepared to sell the vital interests of the untouchables even for the sake of winning freedom.[114]

It is very interesting to see how prejudicially the Congress and its leaders approached the issue of the untouchables. Since it was agreed that the number of untouchables in legislatures and administrative services would be fixed in proportion to their population, very unkind under-estimation of their population was made. The census commissioner in 1931 estimated the population of the untouchables in the United Provinces at 12.6 millions, while the Provincial Government at 6.8 millions, but the provincial Franchise committee at 0.6 million only. All this exposed the tendency of the caste-Hindus. Earlier the Congressmen were not interested in the population of the untouchables but when they came to know that seats were offered to them on the basis of their population would slice from their bread, and then they went out and out to show the number of untouchables as low as possible.

Gandhi's reasoning to the opposition to the separate electorate was different. He feared that since the Untouchables had been spread in the caste-Hindu population all over the country, the caste Hindus could do great harm to the untouchables in the manner they would like due to the economic dependence of the untouchables on them. Ultimately Gandhi announced that if he would go unheeded and the decision regarding separate electorate was not changed he would go on fast unto death.

The Government declaration of 1932 regarding communal representation recognised separate constituencies for the Depressed Classes but gave them two votes, one for community candidate and another for general candidate. Gandhi stuck up to his stand. According to Ambedkar as Gandhi was a signatory to request the British Prime Minister to arbitrate; it was his moral duty to accept the decision of the arbitrator. However, he continued to communicate with the

113 B.R. Ambedkar, *What Congress and Gandhi have done for the Untouchables?* 68ff.

114 B.R. Ambedkar, *What Congress and Gandhi have done for the Untouchables?,* 68ff.

British Premier requesting him to revise the decision and not only that but to exercise his pressure for the same.

Ramsay MacDonald, in reply, said that the scheme announced was in no way to cause a separation of Depressed Classes from the Hindu fold and that he was quite unable to understand the reason behind Gandhi's decision which possibly he took under a misapprehension of the actual facts.[115] As MacDonald was not ready to waive his decision, Gandhi started his fast on the scheduled date 20th September 1932. Ambedkar turned furious at Mahatma's decision and declared that Gandhi did not want to die. Responding to the call of humanity he showed willingness to alter his plan to make it agreeable to Gandhi. After the negotiations between Gandhi and Ambedkar the Poona-Pact came out. But the dispute between Gandhi and Ambedkar did not end there.

Gandhi did not take a firm stand on the question of untouchability. He proclaimed that untouchability in any form and in any shape would be a crime, while he cautioned that taking an untouchable into ministry would be a dangerous principle and, that the protection of the neglected classes should not be carried to an extend which would harm them and harm the country.[116] The high caste-Hindus and particularly Brahmins were occupying important positions in the ministry and administrative services. The Brahmins were trying to maintain their dominance by employing less qualified non-Brahmins. The policy of the congress in practice was not helpful to the untouchables. It might be due to the leadership and due to their general mental make-up. Gandhi showed a dual policy as far the temple-entry to the untouchables was concerned. In Shikshan, Gandhi wrote that it was not possible that the Antyajas should have the right to enter all the existing temples. As long as the law of caste and ashram had the chief place in Hindu religion, to say that every Hindu could enter every temple was a thing that was not possible then.[117] However, afterwards Gandhi joined the Temple-entry movement, with a view to reduce the increasing importance of Ambedkar among the Depressed Classes.

The views of the Congress and its leaders were not liberal on Untouchables. It was the spontaneous effect of the public opinion. Certainly, the public opinion was sympathetic to the untouchables and it was not prepared to give their rightful claims to them. This was evidently clear in the dropping of the Temple-Entry Bill. Ranga Iyer drafted the temple entry bill. But when the Government of India took a decision to dissolve the Assembly and to order fresh elections, the congress members withdrew their support to this Bill. Moreover, they had to see their own political fate sinking. Thus, their political wisdom prevented them from supporting the Temple Entry Bill. It was the case with Gandhi, he began as an opponent to Temple Entry, when the untouchables put their demands for

115 B.R. Ambedkar, *What Congress and Gandhi have done for the Untouchables?* 86.

116 B.R. Ambedkar, *What Congress and Gandhi have done for the Untouchables?* 99.

117 Ibid., 107.

political rights then he changed his position and became a supporter of Temple Entry. When the Hindu members gave a threat to defect if the matter of temple entry was persuaded to a conclusion, Gandhi again abandoned Temple Entry. [118]

It became increasingly clear that the interests of the depressed classes were not safe in the hands of the Congress and its leaders. To avoid this danger, it was necessary to represent certain safeguards for them in the constitution itself. It was to be done through guarantee of minimum representation to them in legislatures, executives and administrative services. Ambedkar knew it all well and therefore, he constantly fought for constitutional safeguards. The greatest contribution of Ambedkar and the Congress, which represented the views of Gandhi, for the cause of the Scheduled Castes, was that in the Constitution of India, the Fundamental Rights including equality before the law were made applicable to all citizens of India, irrespective of Caste and creed. It should not be forgotten that Ambedkar was the only member of the Scheduled castes in the Constituent Assembly who was elected on a non-congress platform. The Congress dominated the constituent Assembly. Although Ambedkar had a major role as Law Minister in the drafting of the Constitution, all the provisions were much debated and examined by various important persons. It would not be wrong to say, therefore, that the provisions of the Constitution granting equal rights to the Scheduled Castes materialised the dreams of both Gandhi and Ambedkar, who without doubt were the greatest emancipators of the Untouchables in modern India. Both of them strove for the upliftment of the Scheduled Castes, but concentrated on different areas and their work was complementary and supplementary to each other. Ambedkar worked primarily amongst the Scheduled Castes and fought for their political rights to secure for them social and economic justice. Gandhi worked primarily among Caste Hindus to bring about a change of heart towards the Scheduled Castes and to ensure that the Scheduled Castes remained within the Hindu fold. In assessing their roles, it would not be wrong to say that Ambedkar was the saviour of Scheduled Castes while Gandhi was the saviour of Hinduism. In their rivalry, Gandhi emerged the winner as even after his death, his views were accepted by Ambedkar.[119]

Both Gandhi and Ambedkar were great men. While Gandhi was the Father of the Nation, Ambedkar was the Father of the Indian Constitution. While Gandhi was an apostle of peace and non-violence, Ambedkar became a convert to Buddhism which preached universal peace and non-violence. Both of them worked tirelessly for the emancipation of Scheduled Castes, though their means differed. For Gandhi, the change had to come primarily in the hearts of caste Hindus. He staked his life for retaining the Scheduled Castes within the Hindu fold. Gandhi wanted political freedom before the rights of various classes could be secured. Ambedkar agitated for separate electorates but showed generosity of

118 B.R. Ambedkar, *What Congress and Gandhi have done for the Untouchables?* 125.

119 B.R. Ambedkar, *What Congress and Gandhi have done for the Untouchables?* 125.

spirit and gave up this demand to save Gandhi's life. It is unfortunate that Gandhi died on 30 January 1948 and could not see for himself the progress made by the Scheduled Castes. Ambedkar was fortunate enough to see himself the initial progress made by the Scheduled Castes arising out of the safeguards provided in the Constitution. Ambedkar and Gandhi envisioned their social emancipation and worked with dedication for this goal.[120]

2.7. The Dalit Movement

The organizational or institutional efforts made by Dalit leaders for the liberation of the downtrodden masses could be termed as Dalit Movement. It is a movement of protest against untouchability, casteism and superstitions. It aims at the uplift of the Dalits. It is a movement to regain self-respect and equal human status in the society. The means by which it could operate were bringing awareness among Dalit masses about their own 'identity' as human beings equal to other human beings, inculcating in them the attitude of protest against all sorts of injustice and oppressions and raising organizational strength and pressure against all the forces of inequality in a peaceful manner.[121]

The objective of Dalit movement was, obviously to liberate the historically known untouchable classes from the most oppressive practice of untouchability observed ruthlessly by the caste Hindus, and to bring the former on a par with socio-cultural level of the privileged classes, so that they could be brought to the national mainstream. The basic idea involved in the Dalit movement is to reconstruct the society on the basis of new value. The objective of Dalit Movement is to emancipate the Dalits from the threshold of untouchability and caste system. However, the strategies, ideologies, approaches, ways and means varied from leader to leader, place to place, and from time to time. The 'Dalit consciousness' came to the fore in different forms and shapes.[122]

However, the process of Dalit Movement could be characterized as follows:

First in the form of 'Sanskritization', used by Srinivas while analyzing the process of change in the traditional social structure in India. He states that Sanskritization is "the process by which a 'low' Hindu caste, or tribal or other group, changes its customs, ritual, ideology and way of life in the direction of a high and frequently, 'twice born' caste. Generally such changes are followed by a claim to a higher position in the caste hierarchy than that traditionally conceded to the claimant caste by the local community."[123]

Babasaheb Ambedkar in fact explained the phenomenon of Sanskritization long ago by the term 'imitation', in the context of formation of the castes. He had very firmly stated that almost all the classes in the pre-caste society followed

---

120 Ibid.

121 R.K. Kshirsagar, *Dalit Movement in India and its Leaders*, 4-5.

122 Ibid.

123 M.N. Srinivas, *Social Change in Modern India* (Bombay: Orient Longman Ltd., 1972), 6.

the priestly Brahmin class in their attempt to upgrade their social status by way of 'imitation' of certain Brahmanic manners and customs and by 'differentiation' from other groups. This process led to the formation of the castes. It was but natural because the tendency to imitate is a deep-seated one in the human mind. He stated that the laws of imitation flow from the higher to the lower. The extent or intensity of imitation varies inversely in proportion to social distance from the superior caste, and the source of imitation must enjoy status in the group. The Brahmin priestly class was treated as 'semi-Gods', as such the other groups followed them. Thus, each group intentionally prohibited its members from mingling into another through the custom of endogamy and formed its own caste. They imitated certain manners, customs and rituals of Brahmins to raise their status.[124]

Although, the untouchables imitated the Brahmins and their locally dominant high caste groups, their social status remained unchanged. However, it should be noted that the imitation of the high caste manners by the Dalits, which was strictly prohibited, was but an assertion of their right to equality in the initial stages of the Liberation Movement. Some of the families could develop the habit of maintaining cleanliness and cultural standard. Though it was not a protest, it was a craving for a better life standard at least according to the established norms.[125]

The Dalits were treated as 'outcaste' or 'Panchamas' and they were asked to maintain spatial distance from the caste Hindus in the major village community. They were culturally different from the caste Hindus. Their food habits, recreation, language, rituals and ceremonies, deities, manners of worship, etc, were different from those of the caste Hindus. They developed a sense of separateness or isolation from each other. The situation became worse due to increasing incidents of atrocities, suppression and exploitation. All these situations, naturally gave rise to another new movement called Adi-Hindu Movement. This Movement gave the Dalits an 'identity' in terms of Adi-Hindus. The main reason behind this was that the Dalits were the original inhabitants of India and they were not Hindus and untouchability was forcibly imposed on them. Accordingly, the Dalits in different States, called themselves as Adi-Andhras in Andhra, Adi-Karnataka in Karnataka, Adi-Dravidas in Tamil Nadu, Adi-Hindus in Uttar Pradesh and Adi-Dharmis in Punjab.[126]

De-Hinduization was another form, which means complete distant and protest against Hinduism. Dalits were experiencing ruthless and widely practiced untouchability by the caste Hindus. So they realized that unless they desert that exploitative order, there was no liberation for them. De-Hinduization is rejecting Hinduism and embracing non-Hindu religions like Islam, Christianity,

124 B.R. Ambedkar, *What Congress and Gandhi have done for the Untouchables?* 125ff.

125 B.R. Ambedkar, *What Congress and Gandhi have done for the Untouchables?* 125ff.

126 Ibid.

Sikhism or Buddhism mainly to get rid of untouchability and to develop their moral and financial conditions. Dalits in order to speed up the Dalit Liberation Movement joined with another movement called the Communist Movement. But Communism could not create the necessary confidence in the minds of Dalits. The Communist Movement was invariably in the hands of the high caste people and they could not realize the crucial role of caste in the Indian social structure. The Communists believed that if the material condition is changed, then the super structure of caste and untouchability would be changed.[127]

Dalit Liberation Movement is, of course an inseparable part of the politico-cultural history of India. It is true that the Indian National Movement was determined to liberate the country from the bondage of foreign imperialism, but this process was not going to be complete and final unless all the sections of the society, including the so-called untouchables were to be free from the stigma of untouchability. The Dalit leaders fulfilled this uphill task of liberation of the Dalits. They were the real precursors of liberty, equality and social justice in India – they commanded attention of the national politicians by their voices and influenced and shaped the national politics in a befitting manner. Their role in setting up universal human values, narrowing the social distance between the touchables and untouchables and in setting up a democratic polity cannot be easily ignored or underestimated.[128] However, the pity is that the history of the Dalit Liberation Movement has not been properly interpreted and duly recorded in a consolidated and widespread manner as such.[129]

In order to fight against the socio-economic problems, Babasaheb Ambedkar formed the Independent Labour Party in 1936. He tried to abolish the exploitative *khoti* system prevailing in the *Konkan* part of Maharastra, and *Veti* or *Maharaki* system – a wage-free hereditary service to the caste Hindus in the local administration. He was of the view that all the key industries, including agriculture should be nationalized in the interest of the nation as a whole. Politicization was another movement, which means "The orientation of people to political perspectives and political actions."[130] This is very much necessary in every community; however Babasaheb Ambedkar said that, "the problem of the Depressed Classes will never be solved unless they get political power in their own hands. If this is true, and I do not think that the contrary can be maintained, then the problem of the depressed classes is, I submit eminently, a political problem and must be treated as such."[131] The Dalits were politically not conscious and thus they needed such an orientation and inspiration to enter the power structure of the state in order to solve their problems.

127 B.R. Ambedkar, *What Congress and Gandhi have done for the Untouchables?* 125ff.

128 R.K. Kshirsagar, *Dalit Movement in India and its Leaders*, 3.

129 R.T. Jangam, *Political Sociology* (New Delhi: Oxford & IBH Publishing Co., 1980), 167.

130 Ibid.

131 Bhagawandas (ed.), *Thus Spoke Ambedkar* I. 24.

The process of politicization had a greater impact on the then apolitical and ignorant Dalits. They could successfully evolve their identity as a separate group and performed their role in national politics. The British Government, Indian National Congress and Muslim League had to take cognizance of the separate identity of Dalits. Everybody tried to win over their confidence. Mahatma Gandhi, with his organization of Harijan Sevak Sangh tried to win the confidence of Dalits. He was successful to some extent but could not counter the overall impact of Ambedkarite movement on the masses. However, the contribution of Mahatma Gandhi to the Dalit liberation cannot be ignored. He tried to convince non-Dalits masses to give up untouchability and tried to bring the Dalits elites into politics.

Dalit Movement was, of course, based on a well-defined objective, which was to abolish untouchability and establish a new social order based on liberty, equality and fraternity. During the period of 100 years (1857-1956) several leaders and their ideologies and strategies became popular. The leadership of some of them was confined to certain regions and field. After 1920 onwards the mission of Ambedkar became more popular and effective; and it spread almost throughout India. After the death of Ambedkar, [132] the responsibility of leadership fell upon the shoulders of Dadasaheb Gaikwad. He had a good mass identity in the movement and was a natural choice for the top job. The problem of land was the biggest challenge and the most glorious event in the post-Ambedkar Dalit Movement.[133] Though the Dalit masses were interested in this issue, the leadership was not impressed with it. They disproved Gaikwad's struggle as being communist and declared that it had no place in Ambedkarian agenda. They accused Gaikwad of being intellectually incapable of comprehending the subtleties of Ambedkar's ideology and hence unsuitable to step into his shoes. Then came the era of disintegration. The Republican Party of India split and hence people lost confidence in it because it continued to split. The Dalit Panthers was born in early 1970's. Surprisingly, the Dalit Panthers spoke the language of rebelliousness and militancy, which created waves. These waves had shaken the foundations of the established order in the country and in essence demonstrated what the wrath of the inferior could be. It provided a valuable insight that was pathetically missing in the Dalit politics. Going by their policy, Dalit panthers had broken many new grounds in terms of radicalising the political space for the Dalit movement. They

---

132 www.postambedkar.htm, This paper was presented by Anand Teltumbde, in the Seminar on the Post-Ambedkar Dalit Movement organized by the department of Political Science, University of Pune. On 27-29, (March 1997).

133 Even during the days of Babasaheb Ambedkar, the mass struggle for land had never materialized in direct terms and at such a scale. At the most, it could be said to have materialized symbolically in the form of a struggle for abolition of 'Khoti'- a kind of landlordism that prevailed in the Konkan region of Maharashtra. At any rate, as a mass struggle for land at the national level, it did not have any parallel in Indian history.

imparted the proletarian - radical class identity to Dalits and linked their struggles to the struggles of all oppressed people over the globe.[134]

Kanshiram came up with a different approach of identifying all the SCs, STs, BCs, OBCs and religious minorities as 'Bahujan'. He started off with a non-political organisation of government employees belonging to Bahujana, identifying them to be the main resource of these communities. It later led to the formation of an agitating political group called as DS4 - the Dalit Shoshit Samaj Sangharsh Samiti, which eventually became a full-fledged political party - the Bahujan Samaj Party (BSP). Kanshiram's strategy has proved quite effective in only certain parts of the country. Apart from these broad political trends, there are many regional outfits like Dalit Mahasabha in Andhra Pradesh, Mass Movement in Maharashtra, Dalit Sena in Bihar, etc. Another trend in the Dalit movement emphasises the spread of Buddhism as its goal. As in politics, there are numerous organisations devoted to this task. According to them, Buddhism was the result of Ambedkar's mission and hence, the true Ambedkarite not only had to be a Buddhist but also had to work for the spread of Buddhism.[135]

Conclusion

This chapter provides the theoretical framework for this particular research on "Inferiority Complex among Employed Dalits in Bangalore: Implications for Pastoral Care." A deeper understanding of caste and untouchability is very much necessary for this research to be done. Whatever benefits the present day Dalits are enjoying is because of some great leaders like Ambedkar, Gandhi and others, who have toiled hard to represent the cause of the Scheduled Castes and saw that there is a provision in the Constitution of India granting equal rights to the Scheduled Castes. The later part of this chapter provides the process, struggles, debates and tension among the leaders in order to arrive at a point. The Chairman of the National Knowledge Commission, Sam Pitroda, in an interview to the India Today asks a question, "Should children carry caste labels in this age?"[136] It is a sad story that caste labels are very much seen as the main identity even in the present day context. Caste is a mind-set and will there be a change in future? Is there an escape for the Dalits from the stigma of untouchability, which leads to inferiority complex? This chapter as explored the background of how and where the inferiority complex originates and the next chapter will provide insights into the Inferiority Complex in particular.

---

134 www.postambedkar.htm.

135 www.postambedkar.htm.

136 *India Today* (Bangalore), 5 June 2006. 24.

Chapter 3

Personality Theories and Contextual Issues in Relation to Inferiority Complex

3.1. Introduction

Dalits in India belong to the culturally stigmatized social group that leads them to develop inferiority complex, which is in other words known as lower self-esteem, lower well-being, and higher psychological distress. Culturally stigmatized people select and interpret social events to protect themselves and so the cultural stigma and positive identity are related to self-esteem, well-being, and product of distress. In my review of literature the usage of the concept of inferiority complex is very much replaced by the usage of the concept of low self-esteem, which means that other people are better looking, better achievers, or more successful than oneself. So in this chapter, I will be using the concepts of inferiority complex and low self-esteem synonymously. The inferiority complex is well understood in the light of different personality theories and so this chapter will focus mainly on the interpersonal relationship and different theories of personality, which I believe are essential and necessary to do the present empirical research on Inferiority Complex among Employed Dalits in Bangalore.

3.2. The Importance of 'Self'

The self occupies a prominent role in psychology. Executive self and self-esteem are two important aspects of the self-system. People are motivated to protect and enhance their self-esteem.[137] *Executive Self* refers to the agentic aspect of the self-system. The part involved actively in monitoring itself, choosing how to

137 Michelle B. Neiss, et.al., "Executive Self, Self-Esteem, and Negative Affectivity: Relations at the Phenotypic and Genotypic Level," *Journal of Personality and Social Psychology* 89, 4 (2005): 593-606.

behave, and enacting chosen responses. The executive self encompasses several phenomena; including control beliefs refer to people's conviction that they can control many aspects of their lives and their confidence in effecting change. *Self-Esteem* refers to the extent to which one values him/herself and it constitutes one of the important parameter of well-being and or quality of life. Self-esteem is the overall evaluation of the self-reflecting how much individuals accept and like themselves.[138] Self-esteem is central to the individuation of the human person, it arouses the need to be loved and delighted. Humans feel insecure when they don't feel good about themselves which leads them to ground their identity around which the structure of explicit personhood is formed. In this case they can develop a deformed non-person, masked as a person. Maslow acknowledged the interdependence of self-esteem and esteem of others, and regarded self-esteem as more essential. He stressed the point that lasting and healthy self-esteem is based on the deserved respect of others. And, of course, for Maslow, real self-esteem was a precondition of entering the highest developmental phase of self-actualization in which one desires 'to become everything that one is capable of becoming'. So both Maslow and Rogers make a very close connection between self-esteem and self-actualization.[139]

Self-Esteem also refers to an individual's overall positive or negative evaluation of the totality of the self. It refers to the self's evaluation of the self, or an attitude an individual has toward him/herself. There are two dimensions of self-esteem; the competence dimension and the worth dimension. The competence dimension is the degree to which individuals view themselves as capable and effective, whereas the worth dimension is the degree to which people feel they are of value. There are both cognitive and affective dimensions of self-esteem. The attitudes a man/woman has toward him/herself are cognitive in that they represent thoughts and self-perceptions he/she has of him/herself. The internal thoughts about the self become affective when they tend to move in either a negative or positive direction. There are two important types of self-esteem; global and specific. Individuals have attitudes towards themselves as a whole and as well as specific attitudes toward certain aspects of themselves are referred as global self-esteem. Specific self-esteem is related to behaviour, and is closely related to competence and self-efficacy, and it tends to be good predictor of behavior or performance.[140]

Human experiences and perceptions of the self have clear affective implication. Lack of control and feeling of hopelessness put people at an increased

---

138 Radhey Shyam & Sudesh Yadav, "A Study of Depression, Self-Esteem and Social Support amongst Institutionalized and non-Institutionalized Aged," *Journal of Personality and Clinical Studies* 18 (2002): 81.

139 Abraham. H. Maslow, *Motivation and Personality* (New York: Harper & Row, 1970), 67.

140 M. Rosenberg, C. Schooler, C. Schoenbach, & F. Rosenberg, "Global Self-Esteem and Specific Self-Esteem: Different Concepts, different outcomes," *American Sociological Review* 60 (1995): 141-142.

risk of depressive symptoms. Whereas feelings of mastery are associated with greater life satisfaction and lower occurrence of depressive symptoms. People with higher levels of self-esteem have lower levels of negative affect and higher levels of positive affect, enjoy greater life satisfaction, and report lower levels of depressive symptoms. Theoretically, feelings of low self-esteem are seen as both a symptom and a cause of depression. Feelings of self-worth reflect a sense of connection to others and low self-esteem reflects a need for approval and interpersonal connections. People with low self-esteem are particularly needy of others' acceptance because they are operating at a chronic inclusion deficit. Unfulfilled needs for acceptance sensitize low-self-esteem people to the social cues in their environments, focusing their mental energies on interpreting the meaning of events that might prove to be informative of another's caring. People with low esteem generally anticipate rejection from others and believe that the acceptance and approval of others is conditional in nature.[141]

Information-processing models of self-regulation provide a framework for understanding the relation between the executive self, self-esteem, and negative affectivity. Individuals perceive the environment, evaluate the right between actual and desired states, and attempt to reduce discrepancies. This corresponds to the agentic and self-regulatory aspects of the executive self. Individuals then evaluate the effectiveness of their behaviour, assessing whether they have brought the self closer to the desired outcome. Success or failure in meeting individual goals has consequences for self-esteem and, ultimately, overall affective state.[142]

3.3. Theories of Personality

3.3.1. Adler's Theory of Personality

Adler[143] first began his theorizing in the field of abnormal psychology. He formulated a theory of neurosis before and than broadened his theoretical scope to include the normal personality.[144] His main argument was that every individual strives for superiority and when this is let down, a person feels inferior and an "inferiority complex" results. An individual then attempts to compensate for this inferiority by asserting him/herself in other ways. If this compensation activity gains recognition, the inferiority feeling may be overcome and if the compensation is ill-advised and anti-social, it constitutes neurosis. The thwarted self-assertion causes neurotic disorders.

141 M.R. Leary, E.S. Tambor, S.K. Terdal, & D.L. Downs, "Self-Esteem as an Interpersonal Monitor: The Sociometer Hypothesis," *Journal of Personality and Social Psychology* 68 (1995): 518-519.

142 Michelle B. Neiss, et.al., "Executive Self, Self-Esteem, and Negative Affectivity: Relations at the Phenotypic and Genotypic Level," 593-606.

143 Calvin S. Hall and Gardner Lindzey, *Theories of Personality* (New York: John Wiley & Sons, 1973), 119ff.

144 This occurred during 1920's.

To treat neurosis according to Adler, one must discover the 'style of life' which a person adopted in his/her early childhood in the family. This should be clearly explained that the individual understands his/her inferiority complex and the failure of his/her compensatory efforts. An individual then should be guided towards goals more socially acceptable and more within his/her capacity for achievement.[145] Adler's theory of personality is an extremely economical one in the sense that a few basic concepts, such as imaginary or fictional finalism, striving for superiority, inferiority feelings and compensation, social interest, style of life and, creative self, sustain the whole theoretical structure.

Adler's major contributions are that, he assumed that man/woman is motivated primarily by social urges. According to Adler, man/woman is inherently a social being. He/she relates himself/herself to other people, engages in co-operative social activities, places social welfare above selfish interest, and acquires a style of life which is predominantly social in orientation. Adler did not say that man/woman becomes socialized merely by being exposed to social processes; social interests inborn although the specific types of relationships with people and social institutions which develop, are determined by the nature of the society into which a person is born. Adler's second major contribution to personality theory is his concept of creative self. Adler's self is a highly personalized, subjective system, which interprets and makes meaningful the experiences of the organism. Likewise, it searches for experiences, which will aid in fulfilling the person's unique style of life; if these experiences are not to be found in the world the self tries to create them. A third feature of Adler's psychology, which sets it apart from classical psychoanalysis, is its emphasis upon the uniqueness of personality. Adler considers each person to be an unique configuration of motives, traits, interests, and values; every act performed by the person bears the endorsement of his own distinctive style of life. Adler made consciousness the centre of personality, which makes him a pioneer in the development of an ego-oriented psychology. Man/woman is a conscious being; is ordinarily aware of the reasons for his/her behaviour. He/she is conscious of his inferiorities and conscious of the goals for which he/she strives. More than that, he/she is a self-conscious individual who is capable of planning and guiding his/her actions with full awareness of their meaning for his/her own self-realization.[146]

Adler put forth the idea of organ inferiority and overcompensation very early in his career. At that time, he was interested in finding the answer to the long lasting question of why people become sick or suffer some affliction, become sick or afflicted in a particular region of the body. One person develops heart trouble, another lung trouble, and a third lumbago. Adler suggested that the reason for the site of a particular affliction was a basic inferiority in that region, an inferiority that existed either by virtue of heredity or because of some developmental abnormality.

---

145 S. Stansfeld Sargent, *Basic Teaching of the Great Psychologists*, 187.

146 Calvin S. Hall and Gardner Lindzey, *Theories of Personality*, 120-121.

He then observed that a person with a defective organ often tries to compensate for the weakness by strengthening it through intensive training.

Soon after he had published his monograph on organ inferiority, Adler broadened the concept to include any feeling of inferiority; those that arise from subjectively felt psychological or social disabilities as well as those that originate from actual bodily weakness or impairment. At this time, Adler equated inferiority with unmanliness or femininity, the compensation for which was called "the masculine protest." Later, on the other hand, he subordinated this view to the more general one that feelings of inferiority arise from a sense of incompletion or imperfection in any sphere of life. For instance, the child is motivated by his feelings of inferiority to strive for a higher level of development. When he/she reaches this level, he/she begins to feel inferior again and the upward movement is initiated once more. Adler contended that inferiority feelings are not a sign of abnormality; they are the cause of all improvement in man/woman's lot. Of course, inferiority feeling may be exaggerated by special conditions such as spoiling or rejecting the child, in which case certain abnormal manifestations may ensue, such as development of an inferiority complex or a compensatory superiority complex. But under normal circumstances, the feeling of inferiority or a sense of incompleteness is the great driving force of mankind. In other words, man/woman is pushed by the need to overcome his/her inferiority and pulled by the desire to be superior. Adler was not a proponent of hedonism. Although, he believed that inferiority feelings were painful he did not think that the relief of these feelings was necessarily pleasurable. For him the goal of life is perfection and not pleasure.[147]

3.3.2. Rogers' Theory of Personality

His theory was presented in his book, 'Client-Centered Therapy', and elaborated and more informally described in his book, 'On becoming a person'. Rogers characterizes his theory of personality in the following manner: "This theory is basically phenomenological in character and relies heavily upon the concept of self as an explanatory concept. It pictures the end-point of personality development as being a basic congruence between the phenomenal field of experience and the conceptual structure of the self-a situation which, if achieved, would represent freedom from internal strain and anxiety, and freedom from potential strain; which would represent the maximum in realistically oriented adaptation; which would mean the establishment of an individualized value system having considerable identity with the value system of any other equally well-adjusted member of the human race."[148]

147 Calvin S. Hall and Gardner Lindzey, *Theories of Personality*, 120-121.

148 Carl Rogers, *Client-Centered Therapy; Its Current Practice, Implications, and Theory* (Boston: Houghton Mifflin, 1951), 532.

Rogers focused his attention to change and development in personality, and preferred two constructs, which are of fundamental importance to his theory and may even be regarded as the basis upon which the whole theory rests. These are the organisms and the self. *The organism,* psychologically conceived, is the locus of all experience. Experience includes everything potentially available to awareness that is going on within the organism at any given moment. This totality of experience constitutes the phenomenal field. The phenomenal field is the individual's frame of reference, which can only be known to that particular person. "It can never be known to another except through empathic inference and then can never be perfectly known."[149] How the individual behaves depends upon the phenomenal field (subjective reality) and not upon the stimulating conditions (external reality). *The Self,* for Rogers was an important element in the experience of the client, and his/her goal was to become his/her real self. He feels that when clients are given opportunity to express their problems, they tend to talk in terms of their self. A self is a portion of the phenomenal field that gradually becomes differentiated. Rogers' theory becomes clear in his discussion of congruence and incongruence between the self as perceived and the actual experience of the organism.[150] Organism and self are subject to strongly influences from the environment and especially from social environment. Rogers' main focus was that the evaluations of an individual by others, particularly during childhood, tend to favour distancing between experiences of organism and experiences of the self. If these evaluations are positive, then there will be no distancing between organism and self. Rogers' says, "If an individual should experience only unconditional positive regard, then no conditions of worth would develop, self-regard would be unconditional, the needs for positive regard and self-regard would never be at variance with organismic evaluation, and the individual would continue to be psychologically adjusted, and would be fully functioning."[151]

3.3.3. Freud's Theory of Personality

According to Freud, the personality is made up of three major systems, the id, the ego, and the superego. Each of these provinces has its own functions, properties, components, operating principles, dynamisms, and mechanisms, but still interact so closely with one another that it is difficult to disentangle their effects and weigh their relative contribution to human behaviour. To Freud, behaviour is always the product of an interaction among these three systems, which do not mostly operate without the other. *The Id* is the original system of the personality;

---

149 Rogers, "A Theory of Therapy, Personality, and Interpersonal Relationships, as Developed in the Client-Centered Framework." *Psychology: A Study of a Science,* S. Koch (ed.), Vol. 3. (New York: McGraw-Hill, 1959), 210.

150 Ibid., 205-206.

151 Rogers, "A Theory of Therapy, Personality, and Interpersonal Relationships, as Developed in the Client-Centered Framework." 224.

it is the matrix within which the ego and the superego become differentiated. The id consists of everything psychological that is inherited and that is present at birth, including the instincts. It is the reservoir of psychic energy and supplies all the power for the operation of the other two systems. It derives its energy in close touch with the bodily processes. Freud calls the id as the 'true psychic reality' because it represents the inner world of subjective experience and has no knowledge of objective reality.[152]

The Ego comes into existence because the needs of the organism require appropriate transactions with the objective world of reality. The basic distinction between the id and ego is that the former knows only the subjective reality of the mind whereas the latter distinguishes between things in the mind and things in the external world. The ego is said to be the executive of the personality because it controls the gateways to actions, selects the features of the environment to which it will respond, and decides what instinct will be satisfied and in what manner. The ego performs these highly executive functions and integrates the conflicting demands of the id, the superego, and the external world. Though ego plays an important role, it has no existence apart from the id, and it is not completely independent of the id. Its principle role is to mediate between the instinctual requirements of the organism and the conditions of the surrounding environment; its subordinate objectives are to maintain the life of the individual and to see that there is productivity.

The superego is the internal representative of the traditional values and ideas of society as interpreted to the child by his/her parents, and reinforced by means of a system of rewards and punishments imposed upon the child. The superego is the moral arm of personality; it represents the ideal rather than the real and it serves for perfection rather than pleasure. Its main concern is to decide whether something is right or wrong so that it can act in accordance with the moral standards authorized by the agents of society. The main functions of the superego are to inhibit the impulses of the id, particularly those of a sexual or aggressive nature, which are highly condemned by the society, and to persuade the ego to substitute moralistic goals for realistic ones, and to strive for perfection. In a very general way, the id may be thought of as the biological component of personality, the ego as the psychological component, and the superego as the social component.[153]

3.3.4. Carl Jung's Theory of Personality

Jung's theory of personality is usually identified as a psychoanalytic theory because of the emphasis that it places upon unconscious processes. Perhaps the most prominent and distinctive feature of Jung's view of man/woman is that it

152 S. Freud, *New Introductory Lectures on Psychoanalysis,* Vol. 2 (Penguin Freud Library, 1933), 105-108.

153 S. Freud, *The Ego and the Id.* Vol. 11 (Penguin Freud Library, 1923), 374.

combines teleology with causality. Man/woman's behaviour is conditioned not only by his/her individual and racial history (causality) but also by his/her aims and aspirations (teleology). Both the past as causality and the future as potential guide of one's present behaviour. Jung's view of personality is prospective in the sense that it looks ahead to the person's future line of development and retrospective in the sense that it takes account of the past. For him, there is constant and often creative development, the search for wholeness and completion, and the yearning for rebirth.

Jung's theory places strong emphasis upon the racial and phylogenetic foundations of personality. He sees the individual personality as the product and container of its ancestral history. The foundations of personality are archaic, primitive, innate, unconscious, and probably universal. Jung emphasises the racial origins of personality. Man/woman is born with many predispositions that have been given to him/her by his/her ancestors; these predispositions guide his/her conduct and determine in part what he/she will become conscious of and respond to in his/her own world of experience. An individual's personality is a resultant of inner forces acting upon and being acted upon by the outer forces. The total personality or psyche, for Jung, consists of a number of differentiated but interacting systems. The principal ones are *the ego, the personal unconscious and its complexes, the collective unconscious and its archetypes, the persona, the anima and animus, and the shadow.* In addition to these interdependent systems there are the *attitudes of introversion and extraversion, and the functions of thinking, feeling, sensing, and intuiting.* Finally, there is the *self,* which is the center of the whole personality.

The Ego is the conscious mind. It is made up of conscious perceptions, memories, thoughts, and feeling. The ego is responsible for one's feeling of identity and continuity from an individual's own viewpoint and it is regarded as being at the center of consciousness. *The personal Unconscious* is a region adjacent to the ego. It consists of experiences that were once conscious but which have been repressed, suppressed, forgotten, or ignored and of experiences that were too weak in the first place to make a conscious impression upon the person. The contents of personal unconscious are accessible to consciousness, and there is a great deal of two-way traffic between the personal unconscious and the ego. *A complex* is an organised group or constellation of feeling, thoughts, perceptions, and memories, which exist, in the personal unconscious. It has a nucleus, which acts as a kind of magnet to it or 'constellating' various experiences. *The Collective Unconscious* is one of the most original and controversial feature of Jung's personality theory. It is the most powerful and influential system of the psyche and in pathological cases overshadows the ego and the personal unconscious.[154] Collective unconscious is the storehouse of hidden memory traces inherited from man/woman's ancestral

---

154 C.G. Jung, *The Archetypes and the Collective Unconscious*, 2nd edition, (New Jersey: The Princeton Press, 1968), 155.

past, a past that includes not only the racial history of man/woman as separate species but his/her pre-human or animal ancestry as well. Racial memories or representations are not inherited as such; rather we inherit the possibility of reviving experiences of past generations. They are predispositions, which set us to react to the world in a selective fashion. These predispositions are projected on the world. The *archetypes,* are the structural components of the collective unconscious and are called by various names such as dominants, primordial images, images, mythological images, and behaviour patterns. An archetype is a permanent deposit in the mind of an experience that has been constantly repeated for many generations. It is a universal thought form/idea, which contains a large element of emotion.[155]

The Persona is a mask, which is adopted by the person in response to the demands of social customs and traditions and to his/her own inner archetypal needs. Persona is a role, which is assigned by the society and expects him/her to play in life. It is a public personality, which displays certain aspects to the world. When the ego identifies with the persona, the individual becomes more conscious of the play, which is other than his/her genuine feeling.[156] He than becomes alienated from him/herself and his/her whole personality takes a flat or two-dimensional quality. Thus he/she instead of becoming an autonomous human being, becomes a mere reflection of the society. Jung ascribes the feminine side of man's personality and the masculine side of woman's personality as archetypes. The feminine archetype in man is called the *anima;* the masculine archetype in woman is called the *animus.*[157] The animal side of man/woman's nature typifies the shadow. *The shadow* archetype is responsible for the appearance in consciousness and behaviour of unpleasant and socially guilty thoughts, feeling, and actions.[158]

The concept of self is probably Jung's most important psychological discovery and represents the climax of his intensive studies of archetypes. For him, self is the mid-point of personality, around which all other systems are constellated. It holds all the above systems together and provides the personality with unity, equilibrium, and stability. Jung distinguishes two major attitudes or orientations of personality, the *attitudes of extraversion* and the *attitude of introversion.* The extraverted attitude familiarises the person toward the external, objective world; the introverted attitude familiarises the person toward the inner, subjective world.[159] These two opposing attitudes are both present in the personality but ordinarily one of them is dominant and conscious while the other is subordinate and unconscious. There are four fundamental *psychological functions: thinking, feeling, sensing, and intuiting. Thinking* is ideational and intellectual. By thinking

155 Ibid., 153.

156 Ibid., 20.

157 Ibid., 153.

158 Ira Progoff, *Jung's Psychology and its Social Meaning* (New York: The Julian Press, 1953), 181.

159 C.G. Jung, *Psychological Types* (New York: Harcourt, Brace & World, 1933), 27.

man/woman tries to understand the nature of the world and him/herself. *Feeling* is the evaluation function; it is the value of things, whether positive or negative, with reference to the subject. The feeling function gives man/woman his/her subjective experiences of pleasure and pain, of anger, fear, sorrow, joy, and love. *Sensing* is the perceptual or reality function. It yields concrete facts or representations of the world. *Intuition* is perception by way of unconscious processes and hidden contents. The intuitive man/woman goes beyond facts, feeling, and ideas in his/her search for the essence of reality. Thinking and feeling are called rational functions because they make use of reason, judgment, abstraction, and generalization. They enable man/woman to look for lawfulness in the universe. Sensation and intuition are considered to be irrational functions because they are based upon perception of the concrete, particular, and accidental.[160]

3.4. Inferiority Complex

Inferiority complex is a condition in which extreme feelings of inferiority, often derived from childhood frustration, manifest themselves either in the form of an aggression or withdrawal and silence.[161] The Oxford Thesaurus provides synonymous words for inferiority, such as unimportant, insignificance, lowliness, inadequacy, and deficiency, worthlessness, lesser, lower, subordinate, lowly, subservient, humble and servile.[162] Inferiority Complex is also known by different terms such as *Unhealthy Self-Esteem.* In every person there is a compulsive attempts to extract confirmation of one's superiority from others. If exaggerated self-esteem is threatened, then vital efforts are made to defend it, and if the attempt is shattered then there will be serious psychological difficulties such as mental health disaster. *Low Self-Esteem* is equally unhealthy, a major psychological core, an exaggerated self-devaluation, takes on a variety of referents such as inferiority complex, inadequacy, self-doubt, and unworthiness. *False Humility* is the counterpart of negative self-esteem, is a reverse form of pride in one's badness. Thinking more highly of ourselves than we ought to think is pride. Thinking less highly of ourselves than we ought to think is false humility.[163]

Adler introduced the term "inferiority complex", into psychology and defined it as a complex of ideas centered on real or imaginary handicaps and colored by feeling of discouragement. He contended that these feelings of inferiority complex restruct a person's conscious desire for power and self-assertion.[164] On the other

160 Ira Progoff, *Jung's Psychology and its Social Meaning*, 98-114.

161 *New Webster's Dictionary* (New York: Delair Publishing, 1971), 493.

162 Laurence Urdang, "Inferiority," *The Oxford Thesaurus* (Oxford: Clarendon Press, 1993), 220.

163 C.R. Ridley, "Self-Esteem," *Dictionary of Pastoral Care*, Rodney J. Hunter (ed.). 1131.

164 Roberta Roesch, "Depression", *The Encyclopedia of Psychic Disorders*, Vol. 1 (New Delhi: Viva Books, 2004), 3.

hand, Sargent identified Jungs[165] description of inferiority Complex as a feeling of very low self-esteem and that other people are better looking, better achievers, or more successful than oneself. Ideas that are linked together and related to feelings that affect an individual's behaviour and personality are called a complex. The formation of complexes begins in the same manner as is the case with sentiments. Drives and emotions are active in the background of formation of complexes. Complexes are the sum total of our frustrated attitudes. The complexes take root in the mind when one's mental set-up does not function in an orderly and organised way. They are like knots in a piece of smooth rope.[166]

According to Maslow, the fundamental dynamic constellation in individuals who suffer from *serious psychological disturbance* is characterized in part by feeling of worthlessness and helplessness, by resentment toward more powerful individuals, and by the fear of abandonment, humiliation, disapproval, condemnation, injury, and complete deprivation, which is potentially catastrophic in intensity. He differentiated this collection into two aspects; one is the insecurity feeling (the individual's general attitude about the world, particularly the people in it, his/her assumptions as to how this world feels towards him/her, whether it loves him/her or not, whether it accepts or rejects him/her, whether it helps or threatens him/her); the other is the feeling of self-evaluation or self-esteem (the individual's image and evaluation of him/herself; his/her own resources, his/her prestige, his/her strength, his/her worth, his/her body, his/her functions).[167]

For Carl Rogers, self-esteem is a central concept of his theory of personality. He called it positive self-regard, a feeling of worthiness coming from oneself, but originating in the positive regard of others. The basic tenet of his theory was that everyone has a need for positive regard. A person needs to get a lot of it from others, as a foundation for positive self-regard. Positive self-regard can function on its own when feeling of worthiness is well established from the acceptance, respect, sympathy, warmth and love of others. If this develops into fully autonomous and unconditional positive self-regard, then the person is in an optimal state for self-actualization.[168]

Inferiority Complex itself is projections of ones own self in the presence of the other. As such it is always transcendence and a way of choosing oneself. It is

165 Jung also used the skin response to reveal personality 'complexes'. The procedure he used was to read a list of words, and ask the subjects to respond to each by giving the first word that came to mind. A galvanometer was applied to the subject's hand during the word association test. The word arouses emotions and the instrument registers a higher current. Analyzing such responses Jung detected inferiority feeling as emotional tension. S. Stansfeld Sargent, *Basic Teaching of the Great Psychologists* (New York: Barnes & Noble, Inc., 1944), 131.

166 Ada P. Kahn, & Jan Fawcett, "Mental Health," *The Encyclopedia of Psychic Disorders,* Vol. III, (New Delhi: Viva Books Pvt Ltd, 2004), 64, 106.

167 A.H. Maslow, and Bela Mittelmann, *Principles of Abnormal Psychology* (New York: Harper & Brothers, 1941), 17.

168 Carl Rogers, *A Way of Being* (Boston: Houghton Mifflin, 1980), 108.

recognised by various 'patterns of failure behaviour'. Thus the inferiority complex is a free and global projection of oneself as inferior before others; it is the way in which one chooses to assume one's own being-for-others, the free solution which one gives to the Other's existence, that challenging humiliation. Thus, it is necessary to understand ones reactions of inferiority and one's failure behaviour in terms of the free outline of one's own inferiority as a choice of his/her own in the world.[169]

One can for social reasons and through a misunderstanding of his/her own choice of inferiority decide to cure oneself of stumbling. One can even succeed in it, yet without having ceased to feel or to will to be inferior. At all events the "inferiority complex" can arise only if it is founded on a free uneasiness of one's being-for-others. This being-for–others as a situation will act in the capacity of a cause, but all the same it must be discovered by a motive, which is nothing but one's own free projection. Thus inferiority which is felt and lived is the chosen instrument to make oneself comparable to a thing; that is, to make a person exist as a pure outside in the midst of the world. But it is evident that it must be lived in accordance with the nature, which is conferred on it by this choice – i.e., in shame, anger, and bitterness. Thus to choose inferiority does not mean to be pleasantly contented with an *aurea mediocritas*, which means to produce and assume the rebellion and despair which constitute the revelation of this inferiority. For instance, one can persist in manifesting oneself in a certain kind of employment because one feels inferior in it, whereas in some other field one could without difficulty show him/herself equal to the average. To choose to be an inferior artist is of necessity to wish to be a great artist; otherwise the inferiority would be neither suffered nor recognised. On the other side, the choice of inferiority implies the constant realization of a gap between the end pursued by the will and the end obtained.[170]

3.5. Contexual Issues and Inferiority Complex

The main reason for one to develop inferiority complex is because of the contextual issues in interpersonal relationship that has brought him or her to a lack of self-esteem or self-worth. The following contextual issues in life give an account of the rise of inferiority complex within the interpersonal relationship.

3.5.1. Ego Threat and Inferiority Complex

People with inferiority complex perceive social rejection even after they are told that they are personally accepted. The differences in interpersonal evaluations emerge when there is ego threat to the people with inferiority complex. They over generalize failure feedback by decreasing accessibility of personal strengths and increasing accessibility of personal flaws. They respond to threats with self-

169 Jean-Paul Sartre, *Being and Nothingness* (New York: Washington Square Press, 1966), 561-62.

170 Jean-Paul Sartre, *Being and Nothingness*, 577-78

degradation and sharp activation of social exclusion fears. They engage in indirect self-enhancement by rewarding a group with which they are affiliated. They seek out successful others to share in the reflected glory of their accomplishments. They do not feel good about their own performance and seek out successful others to share in the glory of their accomplishments. They are motivated to work primarily to gain interpersonal acceptance.[171]

3.5.2. Depression and Inferiority Complex

Persons who are depressed or low in esteem are less aggrandizing and exaggerating. Depression and low self-esteem are more strongly related to negative beliefs. The persons with low self-esteem may enhance themselves on positive unclear traits but have more difficulty disavowing the possession of negative unclear traits. Thus, the persons with low self-esteem may not exhibit more self-enhancement on unclear negative attributes. Persons with low self-esteem give less importance to positive information. They do believe that they have positive qualities but are too quick to acknowledge their negative attributes.[172]

Individuals with low self-esteem respond less adaptively to negative events and also feel worse after experiencing a negative event.[173] They are also less likely to engage in adaptive coping efforts; for example, after a failure, people with low self-esteem are less likely to make external attributions and may not work hard to improve their performance and are less likely to emphasize their strengths in domains unrelated to the failure.[174] In some cases, they respond in maladaptive ways by generalizing the negative implications of failure and are more apt to make internal, stable, and global attributions for negative life events.[175] Individuals with low self-esteem may be less motivated to use effective coping mechanisms after

---

171 Kathleen D. Vohs and Todd F. Heatherton, "Self-Esteem and Threats to Self: Implications for Self-Construals and Interpersonal Perceptions," *Journal of Personality and Social Psychology* 81, 5 (2001): 1103-04.

172 Jerry Suls, Katherine Lemos, and H. Lockett Stewart, "Self-Esteem, Construal, and Comparisons with the Self, Friends, and Peers." *Journal of Personality and Social Psychology* 82, 2 (2002): 252. Cited from J.D. Brown, "Evaluations of the self and others: Self-enhancement Biases in social Judgments," *Social Cognition* 4 (1986): 353-376.

173 J.D. Brown, & K.A. Dutton, "The Thrill of Victory, the Complexity of Defeat: Self-Esteem and People's Emotional Reactions to Success and Failure," *Journal of Personality and Psychology* 68 (1995): 712.

174 D.B. McFarlin, R.F. Baumeister, & J. Blascovich, "On Knowing When to Quit: Task Failure, Self-Esteem, Advice, and Nonproductive Persistence," *Journal of Personality* 52 (1984): 139.

175 Sara A. Heimpel, Joanne V. Wood, Margaret A. Marshall & Jonathon D. Brown, "Do People with Low Self-Esteem Really Want to Feel Better? Self-Esteem Differences in Motivation to Repair Negative Moods," *Journal of Personality and Social Psychology* 82, 1 (2002): 128.

negative events because they are less certain about their capacity to cope and restore or enhance their self-esteem.[176]

3.5.3. Negative Feedback and Inferiority Complex

For people with inferiority complex, negative feedback is consistent with a negative self-view and serves to confirm already-ingrained self-doubts. They lack the skills or resources to refute, discount, or negate negative feedback. They fail to regulate or counter a negative affective state; instead they recruit negatively lesser cognitions and over generalize negative feedback. Moreover, they automatically link personal failure with interpersonal rejection. The people with inferiority complex are predicted to focus on interpersonal relationships after threat and conceptualize the self as interdependent and connected to other. They show themselves as average and talk little about them. They don't emphasize personal qualities and accomplishments but emphasize their interpersonal qualities.[177]

3.5.4. Success and Inferiority Complex

Success is sublime. As it is well known, experiencing a major success brings joy, pride and pleasure in oneself and one feels 'on top of the world'. These reactions are universal. People with inferiority complex do not enjoy success because of the insecurities. They do not experience a boost to their feeling about themselves, instead experience anxiety and self-doubt. They believe in negative feedback more than positive. They aim for self-protection and rather than celebrating their talents, they try to avoid exposing their deficiencies and tend to fear failure and negative evaluation.[178] Their affective reactions also have a darker side, which is anxiety. Success promotes anxiety, because positive evaluations threaten their self-views. They get worried that their success will expose their weaknesses. Success generates negative self-thoughts in them. They remain in low self-esteem despite succeeding.[179]

3.5.5. Shame and Inferiority Complex

In shame, the self is perceived as small, inadequate, and lacking. This sense of felt inadequacy is often more prominent for people than any feeling of wrong-doing. The sense of not being good enough is often more deep-rooted and long

176 J.D. Campbell, "Self-Esteem and Clarity of the Self-Concept," *Journal of Personality and Social Psychology* 59 (1990): 538.

177 Kathleen D. Vohs and Todd F. Heatherton, "Self-Esteem and Threats to Self: Implications for Self-Construals and Interpersonal Perceptions," 1105.

178 R.F. Baumeister, D.M. Tice, and D. G. Hutton, "Self-Presentational Motivations and Personality Differences in Self-Esteem," *Journal of Personality* 57 (1989): 547.

179 Joanne V. Wood, Sara A. Heimpel, and Ian R. Newby-Clark, "Snatching Defeat from the Jaws of Victory: Self-Esteem Differences in the Experience and Anticipation of Success," *Journal of Personality and Social Psychology* 89, 5 (2005): 764-765.

standing than any awareness of not being good in terms of morality. Shame seems peculiarly social, inseparable from one's sense of 'face' and 'losing face'. To say that to be ashamed of one's self is to point to the connection of shame and one's identity. The family of shame related experiences includes embarrassment, humiliation, disgrace, mortification, shyness, modesty, pride, vanity, ridicule, dishonor, weakness and strength.[180]

3.5.6. Identity and Inferiority Complex

When self-esteem is threatened, people often become sad or depressed, or they may engage inactive attempts to minimize the damage to their identities, sometimes by adjusting cognitions or behavior and sometimes by responding with hostility towards the source of the threat.[181] Persons with inferiority complex store positive and negative information about close partners in a separate manner and do not feel accepted by others.[182] The individuals with inferiority complex bring conflicting motives to their relationships. One is an approach motive, to form and maintain relationships with flawless partners who reflect positively on them. The second one is avoidance motive, to protect themselves from rejection and embarrassment by withdrawing from persons who may reject or reflect poorly on them.[183] People with inferiority complex are likely to focus on current negative information about the other; they also are likely to remind themselves of additional negative information in the pursuit of self-protection. They may even experience and express hostility toward the other, defensively reacting to anticipated rejection.[184]

3.5.7. Marital Relationship and Inferiority Complex

People with inferiority complex have difficulty finding evidence of a partner's acceptance in more accommodating behavioral realities. They underestimate their partner's positive understanding of their specific traits and the love shown towards them. They are less satisfied in marital relationships, precisely because

---

180 C.R. Ridley, "Self-Esteem," 1161.

181 Vivian L. Vignoles, Jen Golledge, Eugenia Scabini, Camillo Regalia and Claudia Manzi, "Beyond Self-Esteem: Influence of Multiple Motives on Identity Construction," *Journal of Personality and Social Psychology* 90, 2 (2006): 308.

182 M. W. Baldwin, & L. Sinclair, "Self-Esteem and "if then" Contingencies of Interpersonal Acceptance," *Journal of Personality and Social Psychology* 71 (1996): 1130.

183 Steven M. Graham and Margaret S. Clark, "Self-Esteem and Organization of Valenced Information About Others: The "Jekyll and Hyde" – ing of Relationship Partners." *Journal of Personality and Social Psychology* 90, 4 (2006): 652.

184 G. Downey, A.L. Freitas, B. Michaelis, & H. Khouri, "The Self-fulfilling Prophecy in Close Relationships: Rejection Sensitivity and Rejection by Romantic Partners," *Journal of Personality and Social Psychology* 75 (1998): 545.

they needlessly question their partner's positive regard and acceptance.[185] They are unsure of themselves and moreover fearing of rejection see their partner's affection as weakening. They consequently try to protect themselves against the hurt posed by such feeling of vulnerability by devaluing their partner and thus downplaying the significance of what they stand to lose.[186]

Conclusion

In this chapter I have attempted to provide a wider understanding of inferiority complex in the light of certain theories of personality. The inferiority complex as a whole hangs very closely to low self-esteem and thus the concept of self-esteem was dealt with in detail. And also highlighting the contextual issues in interpersonal relationship, one's attitudes and behaviour to bring out the affectivity. This is mainly done keeping in mind the future of my research and it was helpful in choosing and designing the instruments and scales for my research. This chapter is very much needed to approach the subjects in my empirical research and address the problem of inferiority complex among employed dalits in Bangalore.

185 L.S. Murray, J.G. Holmes, & D. W. Griffin, "Self-Esteem and the Quest for Felt Security: How Perceived Regard Regulates Attachment Processes," *Journal of Personality and Social Psychology* 78 (2000): 478.

186 Sandra L. Murray, Paul Rose, Gina M. Bellavia, John G. Holmes, & Anna Garrett Kusche, "When Rejection Stings: How Self-Esteem Constrains Relationship-Enhancement Processes," *Journal of Personality and Social Psychology* 83, 3 (2002): 556-557.

Chapter 4

Analysis of Data and Discussion of Results

4.1. Introduction

The analysis of the data and discussion on the findings are presented in this chapter. As stated in Chapter 1, the main purpose of this study is to find out whether there is any Inferiority Complex among the Employed Dalits of Hindustan Aeronautical Limited, Graphite India Private Limited, and Karnataka State Government Services in Bangalore City, and if so to what extent. Analysis is done to explore the relationship between socio-demographic variables and Inferiority Complex in order to suggest guidelines to pastoral care based on the findings of the study.

The study has one dependent variable, namely, Inferiority Complex and five independent variables, namely, socio-demography, Questionnaire developed by the investigator, Rosenberg Self-Esteem Scale (RSE), Self Esteem Inventory (SEI), Social Distance Scale (SDS). The socio-demography consists of variables: such as gender, age, marital status, and people group, type of residence, employment, income, education, professional group, and length of service. The Questionnaire developed by the investigator consists of the following variables, such as Caste Identity, Due Respect, Restriction, Celebrating Festivals, Segregation, Inter-personal Relationship, Relationship with Superiors, Relationship with Subordinates, Relationship between Families, Relationship in the Canteen, Appreciation, Criticism, Competitions, Social Avoidance, Initiating Discussion, Freedom of self-expression, Suspicious Attitude, Sharing Food.

Statistical techniques used for analyzing the data are the Frequency and percentage (1= 0.833), measures of central tendency and measures of variability, such as Mean, and Standard Deviation. The Section 2-Questionnaire, Section 4-Self-Esteem Inventory and Section 5-Social Distance Scale are Likert Type 5 Point Scales with Never, Rarely, Sometimes, Frequently and Almost always. The highest score on the scale is 5 and lowest score is 1, whereas the Section

3-Rosenberg Self-Esteem Scale is a Likert Type 4 Point scale with Strongly Agree, Agree, Disagree and Strongly Disagree, and the highest score on this scale is 4 and the lowest score is 1 respectively. The unpaired't' test, was employed to measure the two-tailed P value and statistical significance, to assess the significance of the difference between two means and standard error of difference. One-Way Analysis of variance (ANOVA) was employed and the results were tested for significance using the Fisher's test at the 5% and 1% level of confidence. A relationship that is significant at the 5% level is considered to be significant and a relationship at the 1% level is considered to be highly significant.

4.2. Results and Discussion

The results and discussion is presented in the following sequence:

4.2.1. Relationship between Demographic Variables and Inferiority Complex

Table 1.0. Frequency and Percentage of the Demographic Variable (Gender) of the Employed Dalit and Non-Dalit Subjects.

Group	Gender	Frequency	Percentage
Dalit	Male	60	50
	Female	60	50
	Total	**120**	**100**
Non Dalit	Male	60	50
	Female	60	50
	Total	**120**	**100**

Table 1.0. shows the classification of the sample according to gender. Out of the total 240 subjects, 120 were Employed Dalits subjects and 120 Employed Non-Dalits subjects, of them were 60 Male and 60 Female in both the groups.

Table 2.0. Frequency and Percentage of Demographic Variable (Age) of the Employed Dalit and Non-Dalit Subjects.

Group	Age	Frequency	Percentage
Dalit	18-25	-	-
	26-35	14	11.66
	36-45	34	36.52
	46-60	69	46.48
	Total	**117**	**94.62**
Non Dalit	18-25	-	-
	26-35	17	14.16
	36-45	53	44.14
	46-60	50	41.65
	Total	**120**	**100**

Table 3.0. Frequency and Percentage of the Demographic Variables (Marital Status) of the Employed Dalit and Non-Dalit Subjects.

Group	Marital Status	Frequency	Percentage
Dalit	Married Unmarried Separated Total	114 5 1 **120**	94.96 4.16 0.833 **100**
Non Dalit	Married Unmarried Separated **Total**	102 11 2 **115**	84.96 9.16 1.66 **95.79**

Table 3.0. shows the classification of the sample according to marital status. The highest among Employed Dalits subjects 114 (94.96%) and 102 (84.96%) of Employed Non-Dalits subjects were married.

Table 4.0. Frequency and Percentage of the Demographic Variable (Employment) of the Employed Dalits and Non-Dalit Subjects.

Group	Employment	Frequency	Percentage
Dalit	State Govt. Public Sector Private Sector **Total**	40 40 40 **120**	33.32 33.32 33.32 **100**
Non Dalit	State Govt. Public Sector Private Sector **Total**	40 40 40 **120**	33.32 33.32 33.32 **100**

Table 4.0. shows the distribution of the sample according to the Employment. The table shows that 40 (33.32%) subjects each were chosen from State Government Services, Bangalore, Hindustan Aeronautical Limited, Bangalore for Public Sector and Graphite India Private Limited, Bangalore for Private Sector from among the Dalits 120 (100%) and Non-Dalits 120 (100%).

Table 5.0. Frequency and Percentage of Demographic Variable (Professional Group) of the Employed Dalits and Non-Dalit Subjects.

Group	Professional Group	Frequency	Percentage
Dalit	A	30	24.99
	B	30	24.99
	C	30	24.99
	D	30	24.99
	Total	**120**	**100**
Non Dalit	A	30	24.99
	B	30	24.99
	C	30	24.99
	D	30	24.99
	Total	**120**	**100**

Table 5.0. shows the distribution of the sample according to the Professional group. And out of the 120 (100%) subjects from Dalits and 120 (100%) subjects from the Non-Dalits, 30 (24.99%) each were chosen from the Professional group ABCD.

Table 6.0. Frequency and Percentage of the Demographic Variable (Length of Service) of the Employed Dalits and Non-Dalit Subjects.

Group	Length of Service	Frequency	Percentage
Dalit	1-20	69	57.47
	20-40	32	26.65
	40-60	-	
	Total	**101**	**84.13**
Non Dalit	1-20	80	66.64
	20-40	27	22.49
	40-60	-	
	Total	**107**	**89.13**

Table 6.0. shows the distribution of the sample according to the Length of Service. The highest 69 (57.47%) of Dalits and 80 (66.64%) of Non-Dalits were between 1-20 years in length of service.

Table 7.0. Frequency, Percentage, Mean and SD of the Demographic Variable (Type of Residence) of the Employed Dalits and Non-Dalits Subjects.

Group	Type of Residence	Frequency Percentage	Mean	SD
Dalit	Own Rented Company **Total**	75/62.47 27/22.49 16/13.32 **118/98.29**	0.625 0.225 0.13	0.0570 0.0205 0.0118
Non Dalit	Own Rented Company **Total**	68/56.64 31/25.82 20/16.66 **119/99.12**	0.56 0.2583 0.16	0.0511 0.0235 0.0146

Table 7.0. shows that 0.625 mean score or 75 (62.47%) of Employed Dalits subjects lived in their own houses, whereas 0.56 mean score or 68 (56.64%) of Employed Non-Dalits subjects lived in their own houses. It is observed that significantly higher number of Employed Dalits live in their own houses when compared to the Employed Non-Dalit subjects.

Table 8.0. Frequency, Percentage, Mean and SD of the Demographic Variable (Income) of the Employed Dalits and Non-Dalits Subjects.

Group	Income	Frequency Percentage	Mean	SD
Dalit	<5000 5001-10000 10001-15000 15001-20000 20000> **Total**	- 27/22.49 30/24.99 41/34.15 20/16.66 **118/98.29**	 0.225 0.25 0.3416 0.16	 0.0205 0.0228 0.0311 0.0146
Non Dalit	<5000 5001-10000 10001-15000 15001-20000 20000> **Total**	3/2.49 48/39.98 19/15.82 23/19.15 22/18.32 **114/94.96**	0.025 0.4 0.1583 0.1916 0.183	0.0022 0.0365 0.0144 0.0174 0.0167

Table 8.0. shows the highest mean score of 0.3416 or 41 (34.15%) among Employed Dalits subjects, whereas, 0.1916 of mean score or 23 (19.15%) among Employed Non-Dalits subjects were drawing salary between Rs. 15001-20000. It

is observed that Employed Dalits were drawing significantly higher salary when compared to the Employed Non-Dalits.

Table 9.0. Frequency, Percentage, Mean and SD of the Demographic Variable (Education) of the Employed Dalits and Non-Dalits Subjects.

Group	Education	Frequency Percentage	Mean	SD
Dalit	<7	9/7.49	0.075	0.0068
	8-10	27/22.49	0.225	0.0205
	PUC Pass	22/18.32	0.183	0.0167
	Graduation Completed	40/33.32	0.33	0.0301
	PG Completed	20/16.66	0.16	0.0146
	Any Other			
	Total	**118/98.29**		
Non Dalit	<7	13/10.82	0.1083	0.0098
	8-10	20/16.66	0.16	0.0146
	PUC Pass	23/19.15	0.1916	0.0174
	Graduation Completed	15/12.49	0.125	0.0114
	PG Completed	2/1.66	0.016	0.0014
	Total	**73/60.80**		

Table 9.0. shows the highest mean score of 0.33 or 40 (33.32%) of subjects among Employed Dalits subjects were graduates and whereas only 0.125 mean score or 15 (12.49%) were graduates among Employed Non-Dalits subjects. It is observed that graduates among Employed Dalits were significantly higher than the Employed Non-Dalits. It is also observed that 20 (16.66) of Dalits were post graduates. Though the Employed Dalits have better living conditions, higher education and income, still they are undergoing significantly higher level of Inferiority Complex as found in Table 17, 18, 19, and 20.

4.2.2. Observations in Relation to Questionnaire – Section 2

Table 10.0. Item Analysis of the Questionnaire – Section 2 of Employed Dalit Subjects. The items analysed are identity, due respect, restriction, celebrating festivals, segregation, relationship with superiors, appreciation, criticism, competitions, social avoidance, relationship with subordinates, initiating discussion, freedom of self-expression, interpersonal relationship, suspicious attitude, relationship between families, relationship in the canteen, and sharing food.

Sl.#	Item #	Variables	Mean	SD
1	18	Sharing Food (73-75)	3.62	2.0362
2	3	Restriction (15-16)	2.845	1.57685
3	1	Caste Identity (1-11)	3.70909	0.90059
4	8	Criticism (35-37)	3.53667	0.60011
5	6	Relationship with Superiors (28-29)	3.08	0.59397
6	16	Relationship between Families (54-65)	3.6325	0.57765
7	17	Relationship in the Canteen (66-72)	2.71714	0.47531
8	4	Celebrating Festivals (17-25)	3.25778	0.47265
9	14	Inter-personal Relationship (48-51)	2.985	0.45096
10	11	Relationship with Subordinates (43)	2.56	0.3304
11	2	Due Respect (12-14)	3.31	0.32909
12	9	Competitions (38-40)	3.16333	0.30238
13	13	Freedom of self-expression (47)	2.95	0.2692
14	5	Segregation (26-27)	3.575	0.23335
15	10	Social Avoidance (41-42)	3.76	0.15556
16	7	Appreciation (30-34)	3.498	0.14906
17	15	Suspicious Attitude (52-53)	3.685	0.09192
18	12	Initiating Discussion (44-46)	3.36667	0.08963

Table 10.0. shows the top ten SD scores among the Employed Dalit subjects in relationship to the Questionnaire-Section 2. Sharing food with others at work place is highly significant and tops the list with neither the Employed Dalits nor the Employed Non-Dalits sharing the food brought from their homes (SD Score 2.0362). It is observed that the Employed Dalit subjects were restricted from entering into some areas in the office and did not have access to all common places in their work place (Restriction, SD score of 1.57685). It was also found that the Employed Dalits felt lowly and intimidated when identified by their outcaste name; some colleagues behaved differently and even broke their friendship after knowing their outcaste (Caste Identity, SD score 0.90059). So the Employed Dalits felt it is good to conceal their outcaste identity because they did not feel welcome if they did so. Isaacs in his research also observed that many young people

hide their outcaste to get food and lodging, to win acceptance or at least to avoid rejection. At the work place, one's Dalit background was kept as a secret because friendship with colleagues were broken if the outcaste was known. Consequently, some Dalits went to great lengths to hide their outcaste background. Others tried to lead a non-Dalit life in public while living a Dalit private and family life. Yet others have chosen neither to hide nor to advertise their outcaste, "At almost any point of contact with the caste Hindu world, the satisfaction of a man's simplest needs often depended on his readiness to conceal his caste identity and, if need be, to falsify it."[187] Most of the parents faced the problem of how and when to tell their children about their outcaste, because most of them believed "that awareness of the past status was enough to instill "feelings of inferiority."[188] This was the main reason most of the parents delayed saying anything about it so that their children would not develop inferiority complex during their early years. Abdul Majeed Khan also observed that low caste membership or identity results in generating devalued structure or misidentified identity structure[189] about themselves, which is expressed in terms of low self-esteem, negative and poor self-image, low aspiration level, feeling of incompetence and inferiority, sense of powerlessness, alienation, loneliness and apathy conceptualized as the nucleus of 'Affective Syndrome'. Therefore, he suggests that the scheduled castes change their identity structure; that is a change in their behaviour along with the development of a positive social identity in order to escape from the suffering of inferiority complex.[190]

It is observed that the Employed Dalits do not take criticism with spirit at their work place and feel that their colleagues blame them for the mistakes that they are not responsible for and in turn the Employed Dalits blame themselves for the mistakes that they are not responsible for (Criticism, SD score 0.60011). Shaffer in his study observed that people with the attitude of inferiority learn to avoid competitions and criticisms and make no attempts to attack problems directly and substitute activities as satisfaction for their drives. They show a marked sensitivity to criticism and apply all criticism to themselves. They frequently cross streets to avoid meeting people and shun social groups. The attitude of inferiority is a generalised habit of reacting with a strong fear to all social situations, particularly to those involving competition or criticism. This attitude is acquired by a long sequence of experiences from the childhood. When inferiority is in the process of formation, the individual is learning to react with

187 H.R. Issacs, *India's Ex-Untouchables*, 143.

188 Ibid, 151.

189 Majeed observed that the misidentified identity structure is the root cause of inferiority complex.

190 Abdul Majeed Khan, *Affective Syndrome Crisis in Schedule Caste: A Fresh Look, Psychological Studies*, 1981, 358.

fear to criticism and to competition with others, thus leading to the persistent and intense defensive behaviour.[191]

Globally renowned spiritual master Deepak Chopra says that the essence of existence is relationship and every problem has its root in a failure of relationship.[192] The study reveals that the Employed Dalits are having significant problems in their relationship at work place which is serious according to Chopra (relationship with Superiors, SD score 0.59397; relationship between families, SD score 0.57765; relationship in the canteen, SD score, 0.47531; Inter-personal relationship, SD score, 0.45096; and relationship with subordinates takes tenth position with SD score, SD score 0.3304). They feel that neither their superiors nor their colleagues discuss with them clearly about the guidelines of the jobs to be done. There is a big gap in inter-family relationships. The Employed Dalits feel that neither the family members of their colleagues nor their subordinates visit their homes or attend their family functions. In some rare cases, the family members of the Employed Dalits do not feel at ease when the family members of their colleagues visit their homes. The Employed Dalits also feel that they are undeserving and unworthy to attend the family functions or visit the homes of the Employed Non-Dalits. The Employed Dalits in the canteen sit and eat with their own outcaste group silently. They feel that some Employed Non-Dalits change their seat because of different (or you may call it so called bad) eating habits. They also have inter-personal relationship problems arising out of losing friendship because their background has been revealed. Abdul Majeed Khan in his study observed that schedule caste individuals find themselves in an inferior state in the level of social hierarchy, marked by various social stigmas in the context of their inter-personal relationship with members of dominant high castes.[193] The study also revealed that the Employed Dalits feel shy to mingle and participate in the festivals, special programmes or public programmes (Celebrating Festivals, SD score, 0.47265). Their involvement in performing pooja and taking responsibilities during festivals and special programmes is very less because they feel that they are avoided and not accepted. Shaffer also observed that the attitude of inferiority is a generalised habit of reacting with a strong fear to all social situations thus leading to the persistent and intense defensive behaviour.[194]

4.2.3. Effect of Inferiority Complex in Relation to Section 2 Questionnaire, 3 Rosenberg Self-Esteem Scale (RSE), 4 Self-Esteem Inventory, & 5 Social Distance Scale

191 L.F. Shaffer, *The Psychology of Adjustment* (New York: Hougton Mifflin Co., 1936), 150-151.

192 Deepak Chopra, "We are the world, let's heal ourselves" *Times of India*, 14/2/06, 1 & 9.

193 Abdul Majeed Khan, *Affective Syndrome Crisis in Schedule Caste: A Fresh Look, Psychological Studies*, 1981, 358.

194 L.F. Shaffer, *The Psychology of Adjustment* (New York: Hougton Mifflin Co., 1936), 150-151.

Table 11.0. Mean, SD, Mean Difference, and T-Value of Male and Female Employed Dalit Subjects in Relationship to Section 2 Questionnaire, 3 Rosenberg Self-Esteem Scale (RSE), 4 Self-Esteem Inventory, & 5 Social Distance Scale.

Dalits - Male & Female				
		Mean	**SD**	**MEAN DIFF**
Sec – 2 Questionnaire	Male Female	3.783 3.864	29.3055 29.9359	 -0.081
Sec 3 - Rosenberg Self-Esteem Scale (RSE)	Male Female	0.37683 0.37666	2.9189 2.9176	0.00017
Sec 4 - Self-Esteem Inventory	Male Female	1.4883 1.5585	23.0571 12.0720	 -0.0702
Sec 5 - Social Distance Scale	Male Female	0.3771 0.3746	2.9215 2.9021	0.0025
Total	Male Female	6.02523 6.17376	58.203 47.8276	 -0.14853*

The Table 11.0. shows that the Employed Dalit Female subjects are effected by the Inferiority Complex according to the Questionaire, and Self-Esteem Inventory and the Employed Dalit Male subjects are effected by the Inferiority Complex according to the Rosenberg Self-Esteem Scale, and Social Distance Scale.

Table 12.0. The Mean, SD, Mean Difference, T-Value, Degree of freedom, and P Value of Employed Dalits Male and Female of Section 2 Questionnaire, Section 3 Rosenberg Self-Esteem Scale (RSE), Section 4 Self-Esteem Inventory, & Section 5 Social Distance Scale.

DALIT – Male and Female							
		MEAN N=60	**SD**	**MEAN DIFF**	**T - value**	**Df**	**Sig. Level**
Sec – 2 Questionnaire	M F	3.783 3.864	29.3055 29.9359	 -0.081	 0.0150	118	 0.9881
Sec - 3 Rosenberg Self-Esteem Scale (RSE)	M F	0.37683 0.37666	2.9189 2.9176	0.00017	0.0003	118	0.9997
Sec - 4 Self-Esteem Inventory	M F	1.4883 1.5585	23.0571 12.0720	 -0.0702	 0.0209	118	 0.9834
Sec - 5 Social Distance Scale	M F	0.3771 0.3746	2.9215 2.9021	0.0025	0.0047	118	0.9963
TOTAL	M F	6.02523 6.17376	58.203 47.8276	 -0.14853	 0.0153	118	 0.9878*

*Significant

Table 12.0. shows the effect of Inferiority Complex among Male and Female Employed Dalit subjects. The results show that there is increase in Mean level in relation to section 2 Questionnaire, and section 4 Self-Esteem Inventory, and significantly higher level of Mean among Employed Male subjects of section 5 Social Distance Scale. The results also show that there is increase in Mean level in relation to sections 2 Questionnaire and section 4 Self-Esteem Inventory of Employed Dalit Female subjects, and significantly higher level of Mean among Employed Dalit Female subjects of section 2 Questionnaire. Table also shows an overall increase of Mean level among Employed Dalit Female subjects.

Table 13.0. The Mean, SD, Mean Difference, of Dalit and Non-Dalit Subjects in Relationship to Section 2- Questionnaire, Section – 3 Rosenberg Self-Esteem Scale (RSE), Section – 4 Self-Esteem Inventory, & Section – 5 Social Distance Scale.

The Effect of Inferiority Complex among Dalits & Non-Dalits				
		MEAN N=120	SD	MEAN DIFF
Sec – 2 Questionnaire	Dalit Non Dalit	2.4953 1.3105	20.944 14.355	1.1848
Sec - 3 Rosenberg Self-Esteem Scale (RSE)	Dalit Non Dalit	0.1884 0.1863	2.0638 2.0410	0.0021
Sec - 4 Self-Esteem Inventory	Dalit Non Dalit	0.7616 0.4933	8.34 5.40	0.2683
Sec - 5 Social Distance Scale	Dalit Non Dalit	0.187 0.094	2.0592 1.0338	0.093
TOTAL	Dalit Non Dalit	**3.6323** **2.08441**	**33.407** **22.8298**	**1.5482***

Table 13.0. shows the level of Mean, SD, Mean Difference among Dalit and Non-Dalit Subjects in Relationship to Section 2 - Questionnaire, Section – 3 Rosenberg Self-Esteem Scale (RSE), Section – 4 Self-Esteem Inventory, & Section – 5 Social Distance Scale. The table shows that there is higher level of Mean score among the Employed Dalits than compared to Non-Dalits.

Table 14.0. The Mean, SD, Mean Difference, and T-Value, Degree of freedom, and P alue of Dalit and Non-Dalit Subjects in Relationship to Section 2-Questionnaire, Section – 3 Rosenberg Self-Esteem Scale (RSE), Section – 4 Self-Esteem Inventory, & Section – 5 Social Distance Scale.

DALIT & NON-DALIT						
		MEAN N=120	SD	T – value MEAN DIFF	df	Sig. Level
Section 2 Questionnaire	Dalit Non-Dalit	2.4953 1.3105	20.944 14.355	1.1848	0.5111	238
Section 3 (RSE)	Dalit Non-Dalit	0.1884 0.1863	2.0638 2.0410	0.0021	0.0079	238
Section 4 (SEI)	Dalit Non-Dalit	0.7616 0.4933	8.34 5.40	0.2683	0.2957	238
Section 5 (SDS)	Dalit Non-Dalit	0.187 0.094	2.0592 1.0338	0.093	0.4421	238
TOTAL	Dalit Non-Dalit	3.6323 2.08441	33.407 22.8298	1.5482	0.4191	238

* Significant ** Highly Significant

Table 14.0. shows the effect of Inferiority Complex among Employed Dalits and Non-Dalit subjects. The results show that there is significant increase in Mean level and high significance level *(p)* in relation to sections Section 2 - Questionnaire, Section – 3 Rosenberg Self-Esteem Scale (RSE), Section – 4 Self-Esteem Inventory, & Section – 5 Social Distance Scale.

4.2.4. Effect of Inferiority Complex in Relation to Professional Group A, B, C, & D

Table 15.0. The Mean, SD, Mean Difference, of Employed Dalit Subjects in Relationship to Professional Group A B C D.

The Effect of Inferiority Complex among Employed Dalits				
		MEAN N=30	SD	MEAN DIFF
A	Male Female	22.946 22.921	88.8720 88.7739	0.025**
B	Male Female	23.64 24.64	91.5573 95.4638	-1.000
C	Male Female	24.582 25.728	95.2056 99.6466	-1.146**
D	Male Female	25.24 25.49	97.7540 98.7507	-0.25
TOTAL	Male Female	96.408 98.779	373.3889 382.635	-2.371**

Table 15.0. shows the Mean, SD, and Mean Difference among the Employed Dalits. The table shows that there is an overall higher level of Inferiority Complex among the Employed Female Dalits than compared to the Employed Male Dalits. The table also shows that in Group A the males are having higher level of Inferiority Complex than the females. In the group B, C, and D, the female are having higher level of Inferiority Complex than the males.

Table 16.0. The Mean, SD, Mean Difference, T-Value, Degree of freedom and P Value of Employed Dalit Subjects in Relationship to Professional Group A B C D.

DALIT							
		MEAN N=30	SD	MEAN DIFF	T -value	df	Sig. Level
A	Male	22.946	88.8720	0.025	0.0008	28	0.9994**
	Female	22.921	88.7739				
B	Male	23.64	91.5573			28	
	Female	24.64	95.4638	-1.000	0.0293		0.9768
C	Male	24.582	95.2056			28	
	Female	25.728	99.6466	-1.146	0.0322		0.9745**
D	Male	25.24	97.7540			28	
	Female	25.49	98.7507	-0.25	0.0070		0.9945
TOTAL	Male	96.408	373.3889			118	
	Female	98.779	382.635	-2.371	0.0344		0.9727**

* Significant ** Highly Significant

Table 16.0. shows the effect of Inferiority Complex among Male and Female Employed Dalit subjects in relation to their professional group ABCD. The results show that there is significant increase in Mean level among Employed Dalit Male subjects starting with group DCBA. The results also show that there is significant increase in Mean level in relation to professional groups starting with C, D, B, and A of Employed Dalit Female subjects. The table also shows that group C Employed Dalit Females and group D Employed Dalit Males had significantly higher level of Mean. The table also shows that in Group A the males are having higher level of Inferiority Complex than the females. In the group B, C, and D, the female are having higher level of Inferiority Complex than the males. The results show that there is an overall higher mean level among the Employed Dalit Female Dalit subjects in relation to professional group.

Table 17.0. The Mean, SD, Mean Difference, and T-Value of Dalit and Non-Dalit Subjects in Relationship to Professional Group A B C D.

DALIT & NON-DALIT							
		MEAN N=30	SD	MEAN DIFF	T - value	df	Sig. Level
A	Dalit Non-Dalit	11.46 8.73	62.80 47.81	2.73	0.1894	58	0.8504
B	Dalit Non-Dalit	12.07 8.07	66.12 44.21	4.00	0.2755	58	0.7839
C	Dalit Non-Dalit	12.57 8.27	68.89 45.29	4.3	0.2857	58	0.7761
D	Dalit Non-Dalit	12.68 8.281	69.47 45.35	4.399	0.2905	58	0.7724**
TOTAL	Dalit Non-Dalit	48.78 33.351	267.28 182.66	15.429	0.5221	238	0.6021**

* Significant ** Highly Significant

Table 17.0. shows the effect of Inferiority Complex among Employed Dalit and Non-Dalit subjects in relation to their professional group ABCD. The results show that there is increase in Mean level among Employed Dalit subjects of group starting with D, C, B, A and significantly higher level of Mean among group D of Employed Dalit subjects. The results show that there is an overall higher Mean level among Employed Dalits subjects in relation to professional group.

Table 18.0. The Mean, SD, Mean Difference, and T-Value of Employed Dalit and Non-Dalit Subjects.

MEAN, SD, MEAN DIFF, T, OF A B C D							
		MEAN N=60	**SD**	**MEAN DIFF**	**T - value**	**df**	**Sig. Level**
DALIT	M F	6.0258 6.1746	46.67 47.82	-0.1488	0.0172	118	0.9863**
NON – DALIT	M F	4.1555 4.1826	32.1883 32.3987	0.0271	0.0046	118	0.9963
TOTAL	Dalit Non Dalit	12.2004 8.3381	94.49 64.587	3.8623	0.3697	238	0.7120**

* Significant ** Highly Significant

Table 18.0. shows the effect of Inferiority Complex among Employed Dalit and Non-Dalit subjects in relation to their professional group ABCD. The results show that there is a significantly higher level of Mean among Employed Dalit Female subjects. The results show that there is an overall higher Mean level among Employed Dalits subjects in relation to professional group.

Table 19.0. ANOVA: Inferiority Complex of Employed Dalit and Non-Dalit Male and Female Subjects.

ANOVA : ABCD OF DALIT AND NON-DALIT MALE AND FEMALE						
	Source	**Sum of squares**	**df**	**Mean square**	**F. Value**	**Sig. P. Value**
DALIT MALE	Between groups Within groups Total	46.128 488,610.544 488,656.673	3 56 59	15.376 8,725.188	0.002	1.000*
DALIT FEMALE	Between groups Within groups Total	72.893 513,446.048 513,518.941	3 56 59	24.298 9,168.679	0.003	1.000**
NON DALIT MALE	Between groups Within groups Total	17.065 232,314.393 232,331.458	3 56 59	5.688 4,148.471	0.001	1.000
NON DALIT FEMALE	Between groups Within groups Total	11.398 235,289.304 235,300.702	3 56 59	3.799 4,201.595	0.001	1.000

* Significant ** Highly Significant

Table 19.0. shows the effect of Inferiority Complex among Male and Female of Employed Dalit subjects in relation to their professional group ABCD. The results show significantly higher level of Mean among Employed Dalit Female subjects.

Table 20.0. ANOVA: Inferiority Complex of Employed Dalit and Non-Dalit.

ANOVA :ABCD OF DALIT AND NON-DALIT						
	Source	Sum of squares	Df	Mean square	F. Value	Sig. P. Value
DALIT	Between groups Within groups Total	27.951 518,740.615 518,768.566	3 116 119	9.317 4,471.902	0.002	1.000**
NON DALIT	Between groups Within groups Total	6.969 242,095.677 242,102.646	3 116 119	2.323 2,087.032	0.001	1.000

* Significant ** Highly Significant

Table 20.0. shows the effect of Inferiority Complex among Employed Dalit and Non-Dalit subjects in relation to their professional group ABCD. The results show that there is significantly higher level of Inferiority Complex among Employed Dalit subjects than Employed Non-Dalits.[195]

4.3. Review of Major Findings

The major findings of the study are reviewed in order to draw its implications for pastoral care.

4.3.1. The investigation revealed that 69(57.47%) of Employed Dalits whose length of service is between 1-20 years are significantly affected by inferiority complex.

4.3.2. The investigation revealed that 75(62.47%) of Dalit subjects lived in their own houses, in comparison to 68(56.64%) of Non-Dalit subjects. It is observed that Employed Dalits were significantly well placed by owning a house compared to the Employed Non-Dalits. But inspite of good economic status they are still experiencing higher level of Inferiority Complex compared to Employed Non-Dalits.

4.3.3. The investigation revealed that the highest 40(33.32%) of subjects among Employed Dalits were graduates in comparison to 15(12.49%) among Employed Non-Dalit subjects. It is observed that graduate level educated

195 Rath and Sircar reported that lower caste had lower self esteem about themselves in comparison to high caste groups. (Rath and Sircar, "Intercaste relation as reflected in the study of attitudes and opinions of six Hindu Caste groups," *The Journal of Social Psychology*, 51, 25, (1960).

is higher in number among the Employed Dalit subjects compared to the Employed Non-Dalit subjects. Inspite of having good educational status they are still experiencing higher level of Inferiority Complex compared to Employed Non-Dalit subjects.

4.3.4. The investigation revealed that 41(34.15%) among Employed Dalit subjects are drawing salary between Rs. 15001.00 to Rs. 20000.00 in comparison to 23(19.15%) among Non-Dalit subjects. It is observed that Employed Dalit subjects are drawing higher salary compared to the Employed Dalit subjects. But inspite of being in good financial position, they still experience higher level of Inferiority Complex compared to the Employed Non-Dalit subjects. It is evident from the finding that having good service in employment, good education and salary, or possessing an own house does not create a passage to escape from the suffering of Inferiority Complex.

4.3.5. Sharing food with others at work place is highly significant and tops the list with neither the Employed Dalits nor the Employed Non-Dalits sharing the food brought from their homes.

4.3.6. It is observed that the Employed Dalit subjects were restricted from entering into some areas in the office and did not have access to all common places in their work place.

4.3.7. It was also found that the Employed Dalits felt lowly and intimidated when identified by their outcaste name; some colleagues behaved differently and even broke their friendship after knowing their outcaste backgrounds.

4.3.8. It is observed that the Employed Dalits do not take criticism positively at their work place and feel that their colleagues blame them for the mistakes that they are not responsible for and in turn the Employed Dalits blame themselves for the mistakes that they are not responsible for.

4.3.9. The study revealed that Employed Dalits are having significant problems in their relationship at work place. They feel that neither their superiors nor their colleagues discuss with them clearly about the guidelines of the jobs to be done.

4.3.10. The study revealed that there are significant relationship problems between the families. The Employed Dalits feel that neither the family members of their colleagues nor their subordinates visit their homes or attend their family functions. In some rare cases, the family members of the Employed Dalits do not feel at ease when the family members visit their homes.

4.3.11. The Employed Dalits also feel that they are undeserving and unworthy to attend the family functions or visit the homes of the Employed Non-Dalits. The Employed Dalits in the canteen sit and eat with their own outcaste group silently. They feel that some Employed Non-Dalits change their seat because of the bad eating habits.

4.3.12. They also have inter-personal relationship problems because of loosing friendship due to their background.

4.3.13. The study also revealed that the Employed Dalits feel shy to mingle and participate in the festival, special or public Programmes.

4.3.14. The investigation revealed that there is increase in Mean level in relation to sections 3 Rosenberg Self-Esteem Scale and section 5 Social Distance Scale, and significantly higher level of Mean among Employed Dalit Male subjects of section 5 Socail Distance Scale. The investigation reveals that there is significant effect of Inferiority Complex among Employed Dalit Female subjects.

4.3.15. The investigation reveals that there is significant increase in Mean level and high significance level *(p)* in relation to sections 2 Questionnaire, section 3 Rosenberg Self-Esteem Sclae, section 4 Self-Esteem Inventory and section 5 Social Distance Scale among Employed Dalit subjects.

4.3.16. The results show that there is significant increase in Mean level among Employed Dalit Male subjects of group D and Employed Dalit Female subjects of group C. The results also show that there is an overall higher Mean level among the Employed Dalit Female subjects starting with C D B and A, and among Employed Dalit Males starting from D C B and A in relation to professional group.

4.3.17. The investigation reveals that there is significant effect of Inferiority Complex among Employed Dalit subjects and significantly higher among group D.

4.3.18. The investigation reveals that there is significant effect of Inferiority Complex among Males and Females of Employed Dalits and highly significant among Employed Dalit Female subjects.

4.3.19. The investigation reveals that there is significantly higher level of Inferiority Complex among Employed Dalit subjects.

Chapter 5

Implications for Pastoral Care

5.1. Introduction

The oppression of Dalits has affected them not only physically, but also socially, culturally, and religiously. This multi-sided suffering has given them an inferior social status and made them economically poor and politically powerless. These factors gave them a multi-faceted identity that they are outcaste, untouchables and slaves. In such state they chose a name for themselves as 'Dalits', a positive assertion of pride which led them to become conscious of their historical captivity and a sign to liberate them by rejecting oppression.[196] This chapter provides the implications for the Pastoral Care by using the finding presented in the previous chapter as useful tools based on the Theological and Biblical insights. The researcher has suggested a model with four essential functions of pastoral care, which are imperative. They are: pastoral Caregiver as Liberator, Shepherd, Therapon, and Counsellor (LSTC).

5.2. Theological Basis

The Dalits are always in search of religions or cults, which propagate anti-caste, egalitarian, monotheistic ideals and practices. James Massey, one of the prominent Dalit theologians observed that the term Dalit as been used widely. He expresses that "Dalit is thus not a mere descriptive name or title, but an expression of hope for the recovery of their past identity. The struggle of these 'outcasts' has given the term 'Dalit' a positive meaning. The very realization of the Dalits themselves as 'Dalit', and their very acceptance of the state of 'dalitness' is the first

196 James Massey, "An Analysis of the Dalit Situation with Special Reference to Dalit Christians and Dalit Theology," *Religion and Society* 52, 3-4 (Sep-Dec 2007): 61.

step towards their transformation into full and liberated human being."[197] This name has also helped the Dalits not only to establish their common identity, but also it is recognition of their present state into which they have been pushed.[198] Dalit protest and resistance movements seem to have gone through numerous phases. Bhakti movement within Hinduism between the fourteenth and sixteenth centuries symbolized 'low' castes' desire for an egalitarian society and religion. The Bhakti movement stood for transformation of Hindu society and used religious resources to push forward the basic theology that all people were equal before God. On the other hand, the dominant castes co-opted it and transformed it into a reform movement within Hinduism.[199]

The Bible also affirms that all human beings are created in the image of God, and no one is less than the other. The Dalits are created in the image of God, as all other human beings. M.E. Prabhakar affirms that the source and the process of Dalit theology lay in the agony and sufferings of Dalits in their search for self-identity, equality and community. All the experiences and expressions of Dalits in their search for a meaningful life in community is Dalit theology.[200] One of the main sources of doing Dalit theology is Dalit experience of suffering and pain. The Narration of the story of their pathos and their protest has a primary place in doing Dalit theology. Dalit theology helps the Dalits to bring out their anger and pain. V. Devasahayam, a prominent Dalit theologian asserts that the Dalit pathos as the starting point and basic assumption of Dalit theology.[201] The Employed Dalits with all their experiences are in search of a meaningful life in the work place and community. They are in search of positive self-image, self-identity and equality in their living experiences. For James Massey, theology begins from the experiences of the lowliest people. It is built on the living experiences of the people.[202] God created us to use our gifts and talents to enhance the life of another, to enhance the life of the community. The most central is a belief that our God is a personal God, who knows and loves each one of us. Genuine self-esteem comes when we discover ourselves, as God knows us, which means we discover ourselves as God values us. That discovery is made through a genuine relationship with God and the same should reflect in the human relationship caring with concern for one another, that we care about what one another are thinking and feeling and

---

197 James Massey, "Down Trodden: The Struggle of India's Dalits for Identity, Solidarity, and Liberation," (Geneva: WCC, 1997), 3.

198 James Massey, "Dalits and Human Rights", *Religion and Society* 49, 2 & 3 (June-Sep 2004): 2.

199 D. Nirula, *Dalits: A Bruised Dignity* (New Delhi: A.P.H. Publishing House, 2005), 84.

200 M.E. Prabhakar, "Introduction", *Towards a Dalit Theology*, M.E. Prabhakar(ed.), (Delhi: ISPCK, 1988), 1.

201 V. Devasahayam, "Doing Dalit Theology: Basic Assumption," *Frontiers of Dalit Theology*, V. Devasahayam, (ed.), (Delhi: ISPCK, 1997), 273.

202 James Massey, "Ingredients for a Dalit Theology," *Towards a Dalit Theology* M.E. Prabhakar (ed.), (Delhi: ISPCK, 1988), 60.

doing. The implication of such relationship between Divine and human is that our thoughts and actions matter to God who is intimately present to us and in us.[203] The primary assertion of Dalit theology is that it is a theology about Dalits, for Dalits and originated in Dalits, "the theology which they themselves would like to expound."[204] Dalit theology is one of the responses of the Dalit issues; it is based on the assumption that they themselves are the makers of their history, which means that they are the 'subjects' of their history. Dalit theology like other liberation theologies, is a theological expression, born out of the historical experience of oppressed people who call themselves Dalits, and on the other hand, with their encounter with the God in Jesus Christ whom they found in the Bible, as taking the side of the oppressed people.[205]

Nirmal, also believes that Jesus Christ is a perfect example of a Dalit. He asserts that Jesus' life was similar to a Dalit; Jesus was weak, down-trodden, crushed, oppressed and marginalized, but God's glory is manifested and displayed in Him.[206] Nirmal continues to say that "to speak of a Servant-God, therefore, is to recognise and identify him as a truly Dalit deity."[207] The cross has a special meaning in Dalit theology, Nirmal further asserts the dalitness of Jesus when he says "on the cross, he was the broken, the crushed, the split, the torn, the driven-asunder man."[208] The high point of Dalit experience and Jesus' experience on the cross is the experience of God forsaking Jesus. The Son of God felt forsaken and He affirmed the same by saying, "My God, My God, why hast thou forsaken me". And this is the way of suffering for millions of Dalits in India.

Azaraiah strengthens Nirmal by saying that the historical Jesus of Nazareth deliberately chose to side with 'the sinners and the publicans', with 'the oppressed and the downtrodden', with 'the lost' (Luke 15, Luke 19:1-10), and 'the least' (Matt 25).[209] Wilson continues and takes us one step further from Azaraiah in understanding the mission of God in the world and the gospel of Jesus Christ, as the humanization of man, which involves three vital steps: 1) revelation of one's real self, 2) revolution in one's life's situation, and 3) revaluation of the value

203 Carroll Saussy, "Faith and Self-Esteem," *Journal of Pastoral Care* XLII, 2 (Summer 1988): 125-137.

204 George Oomen: "The Emerging Dalit Theology: A Historical Appraisal", *Indian Church History Review* XXXIV, 1 (June 2000): 31.

205 James Massey, "An Analysis of the Dalit Situation with Special Reference to Dalit Christians and Dalit Theology," 83.

206 A.P. Nirmal, "Towards a Christian Dalit Theology", *A Reader in Dalit Theology*, A.P. Nirmal (ed.), (Madras: GLTCRI, 2000), 54-55.

207 Ibid., 35.

208 Ibid., 39.

209 M. Azaraiah, *Mission in Christ's Way in India Today* (Madras: CLS, 1989), 6.

system to bring about a new culture. He goes on to say that this new culture is a human culture, and negates whatever comes in the way.[210]

Humans' deepest need is for self-esteem and so the enhancement of self-esteem should be among our highest concerns as human beings. Glasser, proponent of Reality therapy maintains that persons have only two essential personality needs, to love and to be loved, and to feel that one is worthwhile to oneself and others. His reality therapy assumes that it is impossible to maintain self esteem if one is living irresponsibly. He declares "Moral, standards, values, or right and wrong behaviour are all intimately related to the fulfillment of our need for self-worth."[211] A Theology of self-esteem requires the believer to esteem their neighbor as themselves. When Christ said that the whole law could be summed up in two commandments, which is love for God and love for one's neighbor. (Matt. 22: 34-40). Some Christian psychiatrists add a third commandment 'love yourself.'[212] They claim that unless one first learns to love him or herself properly he or she will never learn to love his or her neighbor, for Christ distinctly commands, 'Love your neighbor as yourself.'[213] So at this juncture it becomes necessary for the Christian counsellor to help people to develop their self-worth, self-respect, and self-esteem that is appropriate to the human condition that God intended.

5.3. Biblical Basis

The biblical basis and the greatest model of pastoral care is the person and work of Jesus Christ. Jesus listened to many people with understanding love and had reflected deeply on what he heard. Pastoral care is listening to the stories of the people. As people tell their stories to the pastoral caregiver, they gain insight into their experience. So the pastoral caregiver should develop adequate listening skills and help the members of the community to reflect on their experience.[214] The living relationship of a Christian pastor and the people is called as being, and this quality of being is understood as a quality in the eternal nature of God. In this living relationship there are reconciliation, forgiveness, and healing, which form the very core of the human being.[215] The gospels are the complete revelation of the meaning of pastoral care because they reveal the Spirit of Jesus in relation to persons and their needs. The Spirit is the manifestation of the Spirit of God. Jesus Christ dedicated Himself to showing forth the love of God in His own love for the people. As told in the gospel according to John 20:21, "As the Father has sent me,

210 K. Wilson, "An Approach to Christian Dalit Theology," *Towards a Dalit Theology*, M.E. Prabhakar (ed.), (New Delhi: ISPCK, 1988), 50-56.

211 William Glasser, *Reality Therapy* (New York: Harper & Row, 1965), 11.

212 Richard Peace, *Learning to Love Ourselves* (Downers Grove: InterVarsity Press, 1970). 48.

213 Jay E. Adams, *The Christian Counselor's Manual* (Michigan: Baker Book House, 1973), 142.

214 Brid Long, "Theological Reflection in the Supervision of Pastoral Care," *Journal of Pastoral Care* 52, 2 (1998): 123-128.

215 Carroll A. Wise, *The Meaning of Pastoral Care* (New York: Harper and Row, 1966), 1.

so send I you" was how Jesus gave the charge to His disciples. The development of Christian concept of pastoral care in the New Testament is demonstrated in Jesus giving charge to His disciples prior to sending them out on a mission (Matt. 9:35-10:16). They were given the power to heal the sick, raise the dead, cleanse the lepers and cast out demons.[216] They were to deal with the profound needs of human beings as Jesus did. The disciples had received freely and were to give freely. The pastor cannot give unless he first received, and infact, giving and receiving are mutual experience and pastoral care is a deeply mutual undertaking.[217]

The other biblical basis is found in 2 Corinthians 5, where we see pastoral care as the experience of reconciliation. It is also a redemptive ministry to persons. Jesus saw this as the fulfillment of the law and the prophets, but opposed applications of the law when they interfered with the needs of persons. Jesus broke the Sabbath in order to heal people. For Him, helping people was far more important than Sabbath. He mingled with publicans and sinners, and forgave harlots. Jesus loved the unlovable and showed an example of the ministry of reconciliation. God reconciled us through Christ and has given us the ministry of reconciliation. The aim of psychotherapy is to help persons resolve their inner conflict and become reconciled to themselves and to others. Wise stresses that the goal of reconciliation as fundamental to pastoral care.[218]

For Wise, gospel is simply the good news of God's redeeming love as revealed in Jesus Christ. In other words, Gospel is Jesus Christ Himself, and the reconciling relationship with God is offered in relationship to Jesus. This new relationship is a new sense of being, which enables a person to move toward discovering and becoming the person according to the persons potential. This is further strengthened by Pauline statement, 'God was in Christ reconciling the world unto himself (2 Cor. 5:19) and (in John 1:14) it is said that, 'The Word became flesh and dwelt among us'.[219] God's message to man concerning His redemptive love is communicated effectively through the incarnation of Jesus Christ. And the most deepest and effective form of communication is the Spirit of Christ that incarnates in human beings. This level of communication is the essence of pastoral care and the pastor is called to continue the work of Christ by loving people in a finite way and thus leading to the redemptive love of God.[220]

Pastoral care is a ministry directed towards the healing, sustaining, guiding and reconciling of troubled persons leading them to find ultimate meaning in life which is associated with the cure of souls.[221] The root word for soul in Hebrew

216 Ibid., 4.

217 Carroll A. Wise, *The Meaning of Pastoral Care*, 2.

218 Ibid., 5.

219 Carroll A. Wise, *The Meaning of Pastoral Care*, 9.

220 Ibid., 12-13.

221 W. Clebsch and C. Jaekle, *Pastoral Care in Historical Perspective* (Englewood Cliffs, NJ: Prentice Hall, Inc., 1964), 4.

'nephesh' means 'appetite', which means our souls are appetitive and so to care for the soul of our people is to be attentive to their deepest hungers and thirst, which are sometimes corporate and communal as well as individual. The task of pastoral care is to help persons become new beings in Christ, so that they are enabled to live in shalom with God, neighbour, self and all creation.[222] Pastoral care also refers to a type of care, wisdom, value sharing and intense concern usually demonstrated by the representatives (ordained or non-ordained) of the church. The communities and individuals are affected by the contemporary social issues and so pastoral care takes place in the midst of changing social circumstances. There is an urgent need for the church to address these social issues in order to impact the lives of its members.[223] In the light of the theological and biblical basis, an attempt is made in this chapter to present the implications for pastoral care based on the major finding of the study.

5.4. Pastoral Care Model (LSTC - Pastoral Caregiver as Liberator, Shepherd, Therapon, and Counsellor) to Work with Employed Dalits

The major findings of the study are summarised in order to draw its implications for pastoral care and the following suggestions are based on the findings. The finding in (4.3.1.) revealed that 69(57.47%) of Employed Dalits whose length of service is between 1-20 years are significantly affected by inferiority complex. So it is important for the Pastoral Caregiver to concentrate more on the Employed Dalits whose service is in the period of 1-20 years and help them to come out of the inferiority complex. The finding in (4.3.2) revealed that 75(62.47%) of Dalit subjects lived in their own houses, in comparison to 68(56.64%) of Non-Dalit subjects. It is observed that Employed Dalits were significantly well placed by owning a house compared to the Employed Non-Dalits. But inspite of good economic status they are still experiencing higher level of Inferiority Complex compared to Employed Non-Dalits. The finding in (4.3.3) revealed that the highest 40(33.32%) of subjects among Employed Dalits were graduates in comparison to 15(12.49%) among Employed Non-Dalit subjects. It is observed that graduate level educated is higher in number among the Employed Dalit subjects compared to the Employed Non-Dalit subjects. Inspite of having good educational status they are still experiencing higher level of Inferiority Complex compared to Employed Non-Dalit subjects. The finding in (4.3.4) revealed that 41(34.15%) among Employed Dalit subjects are drawing salary between Rs. 15001.00 to Rs. 20000.00 in comparison to 23(19.15%) among Non-Dalit subjects. It is observed that Employed Dalit subjects are drawing higher salary compared to the Employed Dalit subjects. But inspite of being in good financial

222 Brita L. Gill-Austern, "Rediscovering Hidden Treasures for Pastoral Care," *Pastoral Psychology* 43, 4 (1995): 235.

223 Horace L. Graffin, "Revisioning Christian Ethical Discourse on Homosexuality: A Challenge for Pastoral Care in the 21st Century," *The Journal of Pastoral Care* 53, 2 (1999): 209.

position, they still experience higher level of Inferiority Complex compared to the Employed Non-Dalit subjects. It is evident from the finding that having good service in employment, good education and salary, or possessing an own house does not create a passage to escape from the suffering of Inferiority Complex. So it is suggested that the Pastoral Caregiver give attention also to the Employed Dalits with good economic and educational status and help them to come out of their inferiority complex.

The finding in (4.3.5) revealed that sharing food with others at work place is highly significant and tops the list with neither the Employed Dalits nor the Employed Non-Dalits sharing the food brought from their homes. So it is suggested not to insist very much insharing their food. The finding in (4.3.6) revealed that the Employed Dalit subjects were restricted from entering into some areas in the office and did not have access to all common places in their work place. So it is suggested that the Pastoral Caregivers to make ways for the Employed Dalits to have access to all common places in their office and work place. The finding in (4.3.7) revealed that the Employed Dalits felt lowly and intimidated when identified by their outcaste name; some colleagues behaved differently and even broke their friendship after knowing their outcaste backgrounds. The finding in (4.3.8) revealed that the Employed Dalits do not take criticism positively at their work place and feel that their colleagues blame them for the mistakes that they are not responsible for and in turn the Employed Dalits blame themselves for the mistakes that they are not responsible for. So it is suggested not to call the Employed Dalits by their outcaste name since it makes them lowly and intimidated and also not to blame the Employed Dalits for the mistakes that they are not responsible and not to pass unnecessary criticism because they do not take criticism positively.

The finding in (4.3.9) revealed that Employed Dalits are having significant problems in their relationship at work place. They feel that neither their superiors nor their colleagues discuss with them clearly about the guidelines of the jobs to be done. There are also significant relationship problems between the families. The finding (4.3.10) revealed that the Employed Dalits feel that neither the family members of their colleagues nor their subordinates visit their homes or attend their family functions. In some rare cases, the family members of the Employed Dalits do not feel at ease when the family members visit their homes. The finding (4.3.11) revealed that the Employed Dalits also feel that they are undeserving and unworthy to attend the family functions or visit the homes of the Employed Non-Dalits. The Employed Dalits in the canteen sit and eat with their own outcaste group silently. They feel that some Employed Non-Dalits change their seat because of the bad eating habits. The finding in (4.3.12) revealed that they also have inter-personal relationship problems because of loosing friendship due to their background. So it is suggested that the superiors and colleagues working with the Employed Dalits discuss clearly about the guidelines of the jobs to be done. It is also suggested not to compel them to attend the family functions or visit the Emploued Non Dalits because it makes them feel that they are undeserving and unworthy.

The finding in (4.3.13) revealed that the Employed Dalits feel shy to mingle and participate in the festival, special or public Programmes, so it is suggested to encourage them to get over their shyness and participate in the events. There is increase in Mean level in relation to sections 3 Rosenberg Self-Esteem Scale and section 5 Social Distance Scale, and significantly higher level of Mean among Employed Dalit Male subjects of section 5 Social Distance Scale. The study reveals that there is significant effect of Inferiority Complex among Employed Dalit Female subjects. So it is suggested that the Pastoral Caregivers give more attention to the Employed Dalit Female subjects and help them to come out of the inferiority complex. There is significant increase in Mean level and high significance level *(p)* in relation to sections 2 Questionnaire, section 3 Rosenberg Self-Esteem Scale, section 4 Self-Esteem Inventory and section 5 Social Distance Scale among Employed Dalit subjects. The results show that there is significant increase in Mean level among Employed Dalit Male subjects of group D and Employed Dalit Female subjects of group C. The results also show that there is an overall higher Mean level among the Employed Dalit Female subjects starting with C D B and A, and among Employed Dalit Males starting from D C B and A in relation to professional group. The study reveals that there is significant effect of Inferiority Complex among Employed Dalit subjects and significantly higher among group D. There is significant effect of Inferiority Complex among Males and Females of Employed Dalits and highly significant among Employed Dalit Female subjects. On the whole the investigation reveals that there is significantly higher level of Inferiority Complex among Employed Dalit subjects. So it is suggested that the Pastoral Caregivers give more importance and attention to the Employed Dalits and help them to over come the inferiority complex. In particular, it is suggested to give more importance to group D Employed Dalits, and when it comes to male, it is Group D, and among females it is Group C. And it is to be noted not to neglect the others groups because they are also affected by the inferiority complex. The Pastoral Caregivers needs to give top priority to Emlpoyed Male Dalits belonging Group D, C, B and then A in order and among the Employed Female Dalits the top priority should be given to the following order, that is Group C, D, B and Then A, and help them to over come the inferiority complex. The Pastoral Caregivers working with the Employed Dalits in order to help them to overcome their inferiority complex can use the following Pastoral Care Model, which **is** Pastoral Caregiver as Liberator, Shepherd, Therapon, and Counsellor (LSTC). This Pastoral Care Model (LSTC) is suggested in the light of the Major Findings, Theological and Biblical basis.

5.4.1. Pastoral Caregiver as Liberator

The need of the hour demands that pastoral care widen its horizons towards a social and political context, and make contribution to justice and human liberation, especially where there is oppression. Dalit is a label applied to members of those outcastes which have borne the stigma of untouchability because of the extreme impurity and pollution connected with their traditional occupations. Dalit liberation has meant liberation from this kind of religiously imposed and religiously sanctioned degradation.[224] Dalit theology is a 'movement theology', a counter theology, a theology of identity. Its location is within an ongoing movement of oppressed people yearning and struggle for liberation. It seeks to provide a theological interpretation of that movement as well as to discern God's active presence in it and purpose through it. It also redefines what the church's mission should be and how to carry it out as an integral part of the movement. Its overall aim has been to serve those on the movement in the conviction that God has taken the side of the Dalits. In carrying out this theological task, Dalit theology has looked primarily to Jesus Christ Himself as well as to the Biblical witness to Him as the interpretative key for this Christian perspective on Dalit liberation.[225]

The experiences of the Employed Dalits are parallel to the rejection and sorrow experienced by Jesus as He lived among the Jewish community. Jesus was compassionate and it is the responsibility of the church to liberate those who are suffering at the hands of social discrimination and oppression.[226] The pastoral caregivers are called to offer their contributions towards protecting the fundamental rights of Employed Dalits and promoting social ethics, inspired by the Biblical basis of pastoral care, thus creating conditions of life that safeguard a respectful relationship within the work environment, so that it may provide health and welfare which is the core of Holistic Pastoral Care and Counselling.

Pastoral caregivers as liberators can use the concept of empowerment in the context of therapy to recognize the cause of many problems, experienced by Employed Dalits, as lying in their 'powerlessness'. Moreover, individual powerlessness is often related with social oppression. Empowerment implies recognising and where ever possible, challenging oppressive aspects of existing power relationships. The concept of 'empowerment' highlights the positive dimension of power and suggests that a capacity of the therapeutic relationship is to enhance a client's power. Powerlessness is a source of real suffering, which has psychological and sometimes physical effects.[227] The pastoral caregiver should

224 John C. B. Webster, *Religion and Dalit Liberation: An Examination of Perspectives* (New Delhi: Manohar, 1999), 11-12.

225 Ibid., 72.

226 Charles Gerkin, *Prophetic Pastoral Practice,* (Nashville, TN: Abingdon Press, 1991), 27.

227 Colin Feltham (ed.), *Controversies in Psychotherapy and Counselling* (New Delhi: Sage Publications, 1999), 294-299.

empower the Employed Dalits, so that they can become powerful psychologically and physically.

5.4.2. Pastoral Caregiver as Shepherd

Jesus in His parables described the characteristics of the good shepherd. The shepherd knows his sheep by name and the sheep recognize His voice. The shepherd rejoices more in finding the lost, outcast and abandoned, like the sheep without a shepherd.[228] The pastoral caregiver as shepherd should represent the position of an advocate who is motivated to defend, nurture, and support the Employed Dalits. Shepherding degenerates into the rescuer role. The qualities of advocacy, such as generosity, helpfulness, and caring for the needs, are essential to help the Employed Dalits overcome Inferiority Complex. The pastoral caregiver as shepherd should serve to reassure the Employed Dalits, that they are not alone in the midst of the threat of non-being. The shepherd should surround the Employed Dalits with appropriate protection, encouragement, and direction. The durability and reliability of the pastoral caregiver as shepherd builds the assurance in Employed Dalits that someone will be there in the inevitable times of vulnerability and need. By giving sanctuary to the Employed Dalits, the shepherd creates places of refuge and safety which can be viewed as emotional spaces of shelter and security. All these attributes are found in the Biblical image of the good shepherd.[229]

Hiltner uses the ancient metaphor of shepherding as a focal concept concerning ways of bringing the gospel to the particular needs of people in their problems and their sin. He views shepherding as a perspective and dominant factor only under particular circumstances. The ultimate aim and goal of shepherding is to relate the gospel to the need and condition of people.[230] All shepherding moves in the direction of healing, in a sense to restoration of functional wholeness that has been impaired in a person. The aim of shepherding is to help the Employed Dalits move in the direction of healing. The healing may not happen always but some shepherding is a matter of sustaining, without power to bring about restoration, just as an injured sheep might die despite all the tender care of the shepherd.[231] According to narrative approach, healing and transformation take place when an individual is given space to free herself or himself from the pathology of low self-esteem to a state of peace, experiencing God's love, care and presence in her or his life.[232]

228 Felipe Gomez, "Christology and Pastoral Practice from below," *East Asian Pastoral Review*, 1982/1, 9-10.

229 Cathy Hasty, "Using a Modification of the Classic Drama Triangle to Enhance Pastoral Care," *Journal of Pastoral Care*, 2001, Vol. 55, No. 2, 152.

230 Seward Hiltner, *The Christian Shepherd* (Nashville: Abingdon Press, 1959), 14.

231 Ibid., 19.

232 Larry Graham Kent., 24.

The basic operating principles of Christian shepherding can be understood by examining the actual shepherding situation. Hiltner does this in the light of theological understanding and also with the help of sciences such as psychiatry, clinical psychology, and social work.[233] The first operating principle of Christian shepherding is concern and acceptance. The shepherd needs both to feel, and to express appropriately his own genuine concern for the Employed Dalits and accept them as they are. Accepting a person means to accept his/her negative feelings but it does not mean an agreement. It is accepting the very feeling that threatens the relationship. The acceptance of such negative feeling usually results in emergence of positive feeling. Concern and acceptance are closely linked with love and understanding.[234] The second basic principle of Christian shepherding is clarification and judgment. The genuine acceptance in the shepherding relationship helps to diminish the anxiety and then the forces may emerge and be ready for clarification. Judgment in a Christian sense is something that comes from within and not from without and means good news rather than bad news.[235] The pastoral caregiver by showing genuine acceptance in the shepherding relationship to the Employed Dalits helps to diminish the anxiety in them and by that there can emerge clarification.

5.4.3. Pastoral Caregiver as Therapon

A Therapon is one who helps, serves, and heals and it emerges from the well known term 'Therapist' and it comes from the Greek root word ' therapeia' which means helping, serving, healing relationship. The Latin translation for therapon is 'ministerium' from which the word 'minister' comes and it means helper and servant. In providing pastoral care to the Employed Dalits, the pastor strives as therapon to restore their estranged relationship into a healing relationship. There are three factors that are essential to be successful in securing a healing relationship.

5.4.3.1. Accurate Empathy

The fundamental condition for a caring relationship is the capacity for accurate, empathic listening, where one enters into the emotive sphere of reference of another, willing to participate attentively to what is here and now occurring inwardly. This human empathy has characteristically been understood in correspondence with divine empathy. This is considered as a great analogy in Christian tradition between the human capacity to enter into the experience of another and God's empathic engagement in human experience in the incarnation.

Empathy is a type of understanding, a capacity to penetrate the understanding of another from within, to read something inwardly, or view the other person as ones own self, to see from the inside. Empathy is seeking to grasp the other

233 Ibid.

234 Ibid., 28.

235 Ibid., 35.

person's developing experience in its here and now complexity and sensitivity from within the other person's unique frame.[236]

The pastoral caregiver should enter the emotive sphere of reference of the Employed Dalits by having the capacity for accurate, empathic listening, willing to participate attentively to what is here and now occurring in them inwardly. The pastoral caregiver should have an empathic understanding.[237] The pastoral caregiver should sense the feeling and personal meaning which the client is experiencing in that moment and then perceive them from the client's point of view and communicate successfully. This is called as empathic understanding. This takes place very rarely but if the pastoral caregiver can grasp the moment to moment experiences occurring in the inner world of the client, as the client sees and feels it, without losing the separateness of his own identity in this empathic process, then the change is likely to occur.[238]

5.4.3.2. Self-congruence

The pastoral caregiver is termed as congruent, when he/she is thoroughly open to his or her own experience, aware of what is occurring emotively within. Being open to one's own feeling process is regarded as one of the necessary conditions of a relationship of constructive behavioural change.[239] The pastoral caregiver in his/her relationship with Employed Dalits should be thoroughly open to his/her own feeling process in order to see a constructive behavioural change in them.[240] In order to facilitate change in the client, the therapist in his relationship has to remain as what he is, genuine, without front or facade openly the feelings and attitudes, which at that moment are following in him. This is called as congruence and it means that the feelings the therapist is experiencing are available to him, available to his awareness, and he is able to live these feelings, be them, and able to communicate them. This is a difficult condition to achieve, but if the therapist is able to listen acceptantly to what is going on within himself, then that is the higher degree of congruence. The more genuine and congruent the therapist in relationship, there will be more probability of personality change in the client.[241]

---

236 Thomas Oden, *Classical Pastoral Care*, 8-10.

237 For a more comprehensive understanding of these conditions please refer to the article of Carl Rogers, What we know about Psychotherapy, *Pastoral Psychology*, Vol.12, No.113, April 1961, 31-33.

238 Carl Rogers, *On Becoming a Person,* 282.

239 Thomas Oden, *Classical Pastoral Care*, Vol. 3 (Secunderabad: OM Books, 2005), 14.

240 Carl R. Rogers, *On Becoming a Person*, 282.

241 Ibid., 282.

5.4.3.3. Unconditional Acceptance

According to Rogers,[242] one of the necessary conditions to facilitate effective therapeutic change in the client is 'unconditional positive regard'.[243] When the therapist is experiencing a warm, positive, and acceptant attitude towards what is in the client, this facilitates change. This involves the therapist's genuine willingness for the client to be whatever feeling is going on in him at that moment, such as fear, confusion, pain, pride, anger, hatred, love, or courage. This means that the therapist cares for the client in a non-possessive way, accepting his behavior without reservations and evaluation. This is called as 'unconditional positive regard'. The more this happens between the therapist and the client, the more the success will be in therapy.[244] In such environment, a client perceives the pastoral caregiver as non-judgemental, open-minded, and as treating them as persons, despite of exhibiting problems and feeling of unworthiness. The clients will experience compassion and respect, which are the core of their humanity. So every act of pastoral care to the Employed Dalits should be deeply grounded in unconditional love.[245] The concept of unconditional love occurs when the therapist is experiencing a warm, positive, and acceptant attitude towards what is in the client, this facilitates change. The therapist must guard the autonomy, the psychological independence and the integrity of the client by deliberately refraining from interfering with the activity occurring in the client. The client himself must achieve the therapeutic insight spontaneously. This is the concept of unconditional love, which is the most important for Rogers. The more this happens between the therapist and the client, the more success there will be in therapy. The pastoral caregiver needs to view accurate empathy, self-congruence and unconditional acceptance as 'necessary and sufficient conditions for Employed Dalits to overcome Inferiority Complex.

According to Rogers, every pastoral caregiver should have the unconditional positive regard towards the Employed Dalits in order to help them overcome the Inferiority Complex. The pastoral caregiver should be non-judgemental, open-minded, and treat them as persons, despite of exhibiting problems and feeling of unworthiness, that is Inferiority Complex. So every act of pastoral care to the Employed Dalits should be deeply grounded in unconditional love.[246] The concept of unconditional love can be experienced by the Employed Dalits, if the Pastoral caregiver exhibits a warm, positive, and acceptant attitude towards the Employed Dalits.

242 Carl Rogers, The necessary and sufficient conditions of therapeutic personality change. *Journal of Consulting Psychology,* 1957, 21, 95-103.

243 Carl Rogers, *On Becoming a Person,* 282.

244 Carl Rogers, *On Becoming a Person,* 282.

245 Thomas Oden, *Classical Pastoral Care,* Vol. 3 (Secunderabad: OM Books, 2005), 28.

246 Ibid.

5.4.4. Pastoral Caregiver as Counsellor

Pastoral Counselling takes place within a faith context that strengthens the counselling relationship. In Christian Counselling, Holy Spirit is an active agent of change and is between the human spirit and Holy Spirit. Holy Spirit acts as an agent of creativity, providing discernment and guiding the counsellor's sensitivity to timing, verbal and body language, and other nuances that enhance the counseling endeavor. The power of the Holy Spirit addresses the human spirit to free from all constrains. In this way pastoral counselling seeks to point beyond itself to God who is a Counsellor Himself (Isa. 9. 8). The Holy Spirit uses human resources for the betterment of human life. In this way, the Triune God is actively engaged in redeeming human interpersonal relationships.

Counselling is a psychological process and all counselling approaches are aimed at changing how people think and feel. Counselling is a movement within and between the minds of client and counsellor. The researcher suggests few counselling therapies from the humanistic-existential and cognitive-behavioural school, and Skilled Client Counselling Model and Solution Focused Counselling that can be of help while counselling Employed Dalits to overcome the Inferiority Complex. The researcher also feels that Employee Assistant Programmes and Teaching Special Social Skills can be useful tools to the Counsellor in helping Employed Dalits to overcome Inferiority Complex.

5.4.4.1. Humanistic-Existential Therapies

The humanistic therapies are based on humanism, a system of values and beliefs that emphasize the superior qualities of humankind and people's abilities to develop their human potential. Humanistic counsellors and therapists emphasize enhancing clients' abilities to experience their feelings and thereby think and act in harmony with their underlying tendencies to actualize themselves as unique individuals. Existential approaches to counselling and therapy stress peoples' capacity to choose how they create their existence. The prominent counselling approaches within the humanistic-existential school that are relevant to work with Employed Dalits are Person-Centered therapy, Reality Counselling and Maslow's Hierarchy of Human Needs.

5.4.4.2. Person-Centered Counseling

Rogers' basic assumption is that both counselor and client are trustworthy, and all individuals move instinctively towards the realization of their inherent potential. The way they define and perceive themselves becomes their subjective self-concept[247] and single motivating drive is their inherent actualizing tendency to maintain and enhance themselves. Blockages to the actualizing tendency are

247 Behaviour can be observed from the point of view of outsiders, that is the external frame of reference or from the view of the behavers themselves, which is internal or subjective or perceptual frame of reference. Carl Rogers.

the cause of all psychological problems and the purpose of the counseling should aim at clearing such blockages. The self concept starts to develop from a very early age in life, based on one's own valuing process. There are other self-conceptions which reflect internalized conditions of worth or the values of others, which are treated as though they are based on the individual's own valuing process. The self-actualising, fully functioning people have the following attributes, openness to experience, rationality, personal responsibility, self-regard, a capacity for good personal relations, and ethical living. Counsellors must be genuine, accepting and empathic.[248]

The self-actualising, fully functioning person according to Rogers will have the following attributes: [249]

- Openness to experience: This attribute allows an individual to develop more efficient behaviour because it encourages a wider perceptual field and a tendency to behave from choice rather than necessity.
- Rationality: is a feature of openness to experience. An individual who is rational can maintain and enhance his/her actualising tendency.
- Personal responsibility: is taking responsibility of one's own self-actualisation, and not putting the responsibility on others. It is trusting in one's own organismic valuing process, trusting the authority within themselves, accepting responsibility for their own behaviour and for being different from others. By this there is increased personal autonomy.
- Self-regard: The fully functioning people have a high degree of self-acceptance and unconditional self-regard, which is based on their own organismic valuing process and does not need the praise of others.
- A capacity for good personal relationship: means that others are seen as unique and worthy to relate with openly and freely. One has the capacity to communicate a strong and fruitful self-awareness. Such relationship is characterized by mutual concern for self-actualisation of persons, authenticity, attentive listening and appropriate self-disclosure. The important factors in this relationship are congruence, and genuineness. The most important factor is empathy.

According to Rogers the Employed Dalits are basically trustworthy and move towards the realization of their inherent potential. Pastoral caregiver as counsellor should help the Employed Dalits to maintain and enhance themselves and motivate them to move towards the actualising tendency and help them to clear if there are any blockages. The Pastoral Caregiver as Counsellor should help the Employed Dalits to have the following attributes, such as openness to

---

248 Ray Colledge, *Mastering Counselling Theory* (New York: Palgrave MacMillan, 2002), 129.

249 Ibid.

experience, rationality, personal responsibility, self-regard, a capacity for good personal relations, and ethical living which make them as fully functioning people.[250]

Pastoral caregivers as counsellors must be able to relate to the Employed Dalits in such a way as to reassure them of their dependability and trustworthiness. They must not resort to psychological labeling and diagnosis or to interpretive insights. This might hinder the development of Employed Dalits' trust in their inner resources. Counsellors must have a high degree of personal acceptance if they are to offer acceptance of the feeling of the Employed Dalits. Counsellors must be genuine, accepting and empathic in caring for the Employed Dalits to overcome Inferiority Complex.[251]

5.4.4.3. Maslow's Hierarchy of Human Needs

Maslow called Self-actualisation as the greatest drive and this can be attained by satisfying the lower motivations, including hunger and thirst, safety and belonging.[252] Basic physiological needs are those which must be met to stay alive, including food, water, action, rest, etc. Once these needs are satisfied a new set of needs emerge: protection from danger, which includes security, shelter, stability, structure and boundaries, and security from job loss which includes a safe working environment. The need of 'belongingness' is our need for affectionate relationship with others. Maslow points out, human beings need to be liked, loved, respected and cherished in their own right if they are to avoid social anxiety, alienation and loneliness. According Maslow, failure to secure these needs usually manifests in maladjustment or sever psychopathology.

There are two esteem needs. Higher esteem is the self-esteem generated by our own sense of achievement, self-respect, self-sufficiency and independence. Lower esteem comes from the respect of others for what we achieve and includes attention, status, appreciation and dominance. Cognitive needs involve curiosity, exploration and the search for meaning and knowledge and self-actualisation need is the realization of one's full potential. Aesthetic needs are the final set of needs for order and beauty which are higher aspirations of human beings. Maslow's theories have been of particular importance to the psychology of motivation in the workplace and the needs of employees beyond the reward of earning money.

According to Maslow, the Pastoral Caregiver should help the Employed Dalits to satisfy their lower motivations, which includes hunger and thirst, safety and security, so that they can move towards the Self-actualisation. The Pastoral Caregiver should help the Employed Dalits to avoid social anxiety, alienation and loneliness, so that they will automatically overcome Inferiority Complex which

250 Ray Colledge, *Mastering Counselling Theory* (New York: Palgrave MacMillan, 2002), 129.

251 Ray Colledge, *Mastering Counselling Theory* (New York: Palgrave MacMillan, 2002), 129.

252 Ibid.

they are subjected to at present. The Pastoral Caregiver as Counsellor should help the Employed Dalits to attain their full potential. [253]

5.4.4.4. Cognitive-Behavioural Therapies

Behavioural therapies mainly focus on changing observable behaviours by providing different rewarding or reinforcing consequences. The cognitive-behavioural incorporates the contribution of how people think in creating, sustaining and changing their problems. In cognitive-behavioural approaches, counsellors and therapists assess clients and then intervene to help them to change specific ways of thinking and behaving that sustain them and help them to cope with their problems. One of the prominent counselling approaches from within the cognitive-behavioural school, which can be of help to work with the Employed Dalits with Inferiority Complex, is Rational Emotive Therapy (RET).

Behavioural therapies can help the Pastoral Caregiver to understand how Employed Dalits think in creating, sustaining and changing their problems. The pastoral caregiver can intervene with Employed Dalits and help them to change specific ways of thinking and behaving in relation to their problems.

5.4.4.5. Rational Emotive Therapy

RET is a decidedly non-religious cognitive therapy that focuses on the individual's responsibility for his or her own feeling. The profounder of RET thinks that religion burdens individuals with moral commandments but believes that RET can play a good role in pastoral counselling.[254] Some scholars believe that RET can be most helpful in therapy with strongly religious clients, and does not invalidate religious faith.[255] RET focuses on the individual's responsibility for his or her own path through life. The primary goal of RET is to bring pleasure to the individual's life; enjoyment and survival are the main goals in life.

There are three vital human goals: to survive, to be relatively free from pain, and to be reasonably content or satisfied. In addition there are six primary goals that relate to human happiness: people want to be happy when alone, people want to be happy with others, people want to be intimate with a selected few, people want to be informational and educational, people want to be economical and vocational, people want to be recreational.[256]

---

253 Ray Colledge, *Mastering Counselling Theory* (New York: Palgrave MacMillan, 2002), 129.

254 Gordon F. West, "The Applicability of Selected Rational-Emotive Therapy Principles for Pastoral Counselling," *The Journal of Pastoral Care,* 1997, Vol. 51, No. 2, 187-189. Albert Ellis is the founder of RET and he views religion as dictatorial, irrational and unnecessary. Albert Ellis was born in 1913 in Pittsburgh, Pennsylvania, but grew up in the city of New York.

255 H. Young, "Practicising RET with Bible-Belt Christians," *British Journal of Cognitive Psychotherapy,* 1984, Vol. 2, 60-76.

256 Ray Colledge, *Mastering Counselling Theory* (New York: Palgrave MacMillan, 2002), 228.

Rational Emotive Therapy is based on three primary hypotheses:[257]

- Thinking and emotions are closely related.
- They are very closely related in such a way that they affect relationships, so that thinking becomes emotion and emotion becomes thought.
- Thinking and emotion take the form of internalised sentences or self-talk that becomes a person's thoughts or emotions. These internalised thoughts generate and modify emotions.

The main techniques used in the Rational Emotive Behavioural Counselling (REBC) is uncovering and disputing irrational beliefs. The goal of REBC is to help individuals to become fully functioning, self-actualising and happier. In the counselling process, the individual are helped to overcome that which is blocking or disturbing them to become fully functioning, self-actualising and happier. It also helps individual to gain profound philosophical changes by putting an end to rigid primary thinking and replacing it with preferential thinking. The main focus is on changing thoughts, emotions and behaviour in order to act more effectively to reach primary and fundamental goals.[258]

The characteristics of self-actualised people are:[259]

- Self-interest: They value their own interests but sometimes compromise for the sake of their loved ones.
- Self-direction and responsibility: They take primary responsibility for directing their lives. They take responsibility for some problems and will not blame others or social conditions.
- Social interest: They show interest in social survival and for the needs of others.
- Flexibility: They are flexible in thinking, open to change, have no rigid rules for themselves or for others.
- Tolerance: They dislike certain behaviours, but tolerate if such behaviour is seen in other people.
- Acceptance of uncertainty: The uncertainty in this world is accepted and enjoyed.
- Self-acceptance: They do not measure their worth by what other people think about them and unconditionally accept themselves.
- Commitment: They are committed to things outside themselves, and believe that utmost fulfillment and happiness can be achieved by pursuing a long-term, absorbing interest.

257 Ibid., 229.

258 Ray Colledge, 335-336.

259 Ibid., 336-37.

- Scientific thinking: They are objective and rational in thinking and apply logic and scientific methods.
- Creativity and originality: They are innovative and creative in ordinary and artistic problems.
- Acceptance of human animality: They accept the animal nature present in humans (themselves and others).

The Rational Emotive Behavioural Counselling can be of help to the Pastoral Caregiver to help the Employed Dalits in uncovering and disputing irrational beliefs. REBC can help the Employed Dalits to become fully functioning, self-actualising and happier. In the counselling process, the Employed Dalits are helped to overcome that which is blocking or disturbing them to become fully functioning, self-actualising and happier. It also can help the Employed Dalits to gain profound philosophical change by putting an end to rigid primary thinking and replacing it with preferential thinking. The main focus is on changing thoughts, emotions and behaviour in order to act more effectively to reach primary and fundamental goals. [260]

5.4.4.6. Skilled Client Counselling

The main aim of the Skilled Client Model is to enable clients to become more skilled in their own right. There are three stages with a main task, presented in the Model, which is relating, understanding, and changing. And in each stage there are three different phases. In stage one, the main task is 'to form a collaborative working relationship and the three phases are pre-counselling stage, starting the initial session and facilitating client disclosure. In stage two, the main task is 'to assess and agree on a shared definition of the client's problems' and the three phases are reconnaissance, detecting and deciding, agreeing on a shared definition of the client's problems. In stage three, the main task is 'to achieve client change and the maintenance of change' and the three phases are intervening, terminating, and client self-helping.[261]

The Pastoral Caregiver as Counsellor can use Skilled Client Counselling in order to enable the Employed Dalits to become more skilled in their own right. The Pastoral Caregiver can use the three stages that are presented in the model that is relating, understanding, and changing. The Pastoral Caregiver as Counsellor can help the Employed Dalits to form a collaborative working relationship by starting the initial session and facilitating their disclosure. In stage two, the Pastoral Caregiver can help them to assess and agree on a shared definition of

---

260 Ray Colledge, 336-37.

261 Richard Nelson-Jones, *Essential Counselling and Therapy Skills* (New Delhi: Sage Publication, 2002), 27.

their problems and in stage three, help them to achieve and maintain the change, such as intervening, terminating, and self-helping.[262]

5.4.4.7. Solution-Focused Counselling (SFC)

A solution-focused model for counseling helps the counselees find their solutions to their problems in the available time. SFC is used as a general term for short-term counseling, solution-focused brief therapy, brief pastoral counselling and solution-focused pastoral counseling. All these are called solution-oriented approaches to counseling. Solution-focused counseling method draws upon counselees' existing abilities that have helped them to establish working goals, identify a hopeful outcome, and measure the effectiveness of behavioral change. SFC encourages and supports the counsellees to discover their own inner strengths and capabilities, resources that will facilitate personal recovery and long-term working outcomes. Even when there is limited time, solutions remain the focus of effective counseling. SFC enables troubled people to move forward from their old way of acting to a new way of life.[263]

5.4.4.8. Employee Assistance Programme

Pastoral Caregiver as Counsellor can start Employee Assistance Programmes. The employee counselling and employee assisting programmes are designed to deal directly with problems that Employed Dalits face in the context of organization. The EAP can provide confidential and professional service and benefit the Employed Dalits by extending in-company resources in the constructive and supportive management with concern for their work and personal life. The EAP can provide leadership and motivation in a non-judgmental manner with professional standard. The EAP can offer service delivery advantages such as independence, perceived confidentiality and a creative, original approach.[264]

5.4.4.9. Holistic Counselling

The main focus of the Holistic Counselling is to give importance to the whole being and well-being rather than just focusing particularly on physical, mental or emotional state. The Holistic Counselling helps individual to cultivate self-empowerment, take responsibility for themselves, accept themselves, and to develop courage to change them. This is very much useful for the Employed Dalits, because they feel lost and think that they no longer have control over their lives and have become victims of the external circumstances. And so the advantage of the Holistic Counselling is to help the Employed Dalits to have

262 Ibid.

263 Jim R. Sharp, "Solution-Focused Counseling: A Model for Parish Ministry," *The Journal of Pastoral Care,* spring 1999, Vol. 53, No.1, 72-79.

264 Colin Feltham (ed.), *Controveries in Psychotherapy and Counselling* (New Delhi: Sage Publications, 1999), 257.

the feeling of self-empowerment, so that they can take responsibility, accept themselves, and find courage to change their lives. Holistic counseling involves stress management techniques, listening and communication skills, relaxation exercises, and sometimes even meditation to help individuals in realizing their full potential in all aspects of their lives. And on the whole, the Holistic Counselling helps individuals to experience life with greater joy and self-awareness.[265]

5.4.4.10. Teaching Special Social Skills

Pastoral Caregiver as Counsellor can teach special social skills to the Employed Dalits. The Employed Dalits tend to seek out fewer social events and interpersonal contacts, and perform less skillfully in interpersonal and social interchanges. They are less comfortable in social situations, often sensitive to being ignored or rejected. So the Counsellors task is to help Employed Dalits learn social skills and develop assertiveness. Along with that the Counsellor should motivate them to be involved in activities. Active participation and improved performance in activities and interpersonal relationships will lead to improved self-esteem and self-evaluation. The Employed Dalits should be motivated to be part of interpersonal activities, which will make them feel appreciated, accepted, valued, esteemed, and liked. They should be motivated in activities, which can demonstrate competence, independence, and adequacy. They also should be motivated to participate in fun activities that contain intrinsic pleasure.[266]

5.5. Summary of Implications

The following is a summary of implications for pastoral care. The findings of the study are useful tools for pastoral caregivers and the Employers to help the Employed Dalits overcome the Inferiority Complex. In the light of the major findings, the researcher suggested four essential functions of pastoral care as imperative. They are: pastor as Liberator, Shepherd, Therapon, and Counsellor.

Pastoral caregiver as liberator should make contribution to justice and human liberation, specially where there is oppression. They need to take the responsibility to liberate those who are suffering at the hands of social discrimination and oppression by empowering the powerless. They are called to offer their contributions towards protecting the fundamental rights of employed Dalits and promoting social ethics, inspired by the biblical basis of pastoral care, thus creating conditions of life that safeguard a respectful relationship within the work environment, so that it may provide health and welfare.

Pastoral caregiver as Shepherd should take the role of a rescuer, should defend, nurture, and support the Employed Dalits. Pastoral caregiver should possess the qualities such as generosity, helpfulness, and caring for their needs. The pastoral caregiver as Good Shepherd should provide protection,

265 www.selfdirections.com.au/counselling.htm, Issi Aaron, issi@self-healing.com.au

266 Ibid.

encouragement, and direction to the Employed Dalits. He/she should create places of refuge and safety in the world, emotional spaces of shelter and security. All shepherding moves in the direction of healing, in a sense to restoration of functional wholeness that has been impaired in the Employed Dalits by the Inferiority Complex.

Pastor as Therapon should strive to restore the estranged relationship into a healing relationship by way of helping and serving. There are three factors that are essential to be successful in securing a healing relationship. *Accurate Empathy:* The pastoral caregiver should enter the emotive sphere of the reference of the Employed Dalits by having the capacity for accurate, empathic listening, willing to participate attentively to what is here and now occurring in them inwardly. The pastoral caregiver should have an empathic understanding, so that he/she can have a capacity to penetrate the understanding of Employed Dalits from within, to read something inwardly, or view them as ones own self, to see from the inside. *Self-congruence:* The pastoral caregiver is termed as congruent, when he/she is thoroughly open to his or her own experience, aware of what is occurring emotively within. The pastoral caregiver in his/her relationship with Employed Dalits should be thoroughly open to his/her own feeling process in order to see a constructive behavioural change in them. *Unconditional acceptance:* According to Rogers, one of the necessary conditions to facilitate effective therapeutic change in the client is 'unconditional positive regard'. In such environment, clients perceive the pastoral caregivers as non-judgmental, open-minded, and as treating them as persons, despite exhibiting problems and feeling of unworthiness. The pastoral caregiver needs to view accurate empathy, self-congruence and unconditional acceptance as necessary and sufficient conditions for Employed Dalits to overcome Inferiority Complex.

Pastoral caregiver as Counsellor is encouraged to use different counselling models such as Rogers' person-centered counselling therapy and Maslow's hierarchy of human needs therapy from the humanistic-existential school and rational emotive therapy from the cognitive-behavioural school and two other therapies such as the 'Skilled Client Counselling Model', Holistic Counselling and 'Solution Focused Counselling' that can be of help while counselling Employed Dalits to overcome Inferiority Complex. Pastoral caregiver also can start Employees Assistance Programmes in Churches and work places and also can teach them special social skills in order to develop self assertiveness and thereby overcome the inferiority complex in work environment.

Conclusion

The multiplicity of theoretical ideas leaves the pastoral caregiver a wealth of options to choose from in working with the Employed Dalits. This wealth may be confusing to the learner in pastoral care. Identifying common factors found in most theories and practices can be helpful as pastoral caregivers weave their way through the numerous therapeutic possibilities. The above implications suggest reinforcing the existence of commonalities among theories. Recognising those commonalities may help the pastoral caregiver to gain confidence in integrating theories and practices to meet specific needs of Employed Dalits.

Chapter 6

Conclusion

6.1. Introduction

The study "Inferiority Complex among Employed Dalits in Bangalore: Implications for Pastoral Care" was undertaken in the context of the persistent deprivation and oppression of Dalits due to continued existence of a solid core of the phenomenon of caste. The old caste hierarchies sway inspite of the legal abolition of untouchability and the discrimination policy in post-Independent India. Inspite of the positive change for Dalits, in terms of their educational achievement, occupational improvement, political assertion and influence, they are still unable to get rid of the stigma of untouchability and thus suffer from psychosocial problems. Education is seen as the key to fundamental change in social structures and social attitudes. Indeed, education has been the only avenue available to Dalit masses in rising up from positions of degradation, gaining self-respect and employment. As a result the Employed Dalits have considerably improved their standards of lifestyle and there has been a shift from ascribed status to achieved status. However it is not very clear, whether this has helped them to improve their self-image. Hence, this study was undertaken with a purpose to find whether there are any psychosocial problems, particular, 'the Inferiority Complex among Employed Dalits in Bangalore'.

In order to understand the research problem, the theoretical framework was built around the subject, 'Caste and Identity', and Personality Theories and Contextual issues in relation to Inferiority Complex. The second chapter provided insights into the research problem by dealing with the meaning, definition and characteristics of caste and untouchability. It also traces the origin of caste and untouchability from different viewpoints with special references to Ambedkar and Gandhi. The later part elaborates on how the Dalits asserted and claimed their identity demanding their Constitutional Rights with the help of

Dalit Movement before and after Ambedkar. The third provided insights in the concept of inferiority complex and it was well understood in the light of different personality theories, focussing mainly on the interpersonal relationship, which were essential and necessary to do the present Empirical research on Inferiority Complex among Employed Dalits in Bangalore.

This is an Empirical study with a Quantitative approach. The locale of the study was Bangalore and the sample consisted of 240 subjects, 120 Employed Dalits as the experimental group of which 60 subjects were male and 60 subjects were female and 120 Non-Employed Dalits as control group of which 60 subjects were male and 60 subjects were female. Purposive Sampling Method was used to draw subjects from Hindustan Aeronautical Limited (HAL), Graphite India Private Limited (GIPL), and Karnataka State Government Services (KSGS) in Bangalore city with the help of the records of the Employees Associations. The background information was gathered using demographical sheet, and questionnaire developed by the researcher. Rosenberg Self-Esteem Scale (RSE), Self Esteem Inventory, Social Distance Scale were used to find out the inferiority complex among Employed Dalits in Bangalore. Statistical tests employed in this study were unpaired t-test, 'T' test, Analysis of Variance, and the results were tested for significance using the Fisher's test at the 5% and 1% level of confidence. This chapter presents the summary of the finding and testing of hypothesis, suggestions for future research and summary of implications.

6.2. Summary of Finding and Testing of Hypothesis

- The investigation reveals that there is significant effect of Inferiority Complex among Employed Dalit subjects and significantly higher among Employed Dalit Female subjects. The investigation also revealed that there is significantly higher level of Inferiority Complex among group D Male Employed Dalits, and group C among Employed Dalit Female subjects. The Employed Dalit subjects belonging to group D were the most affected by Inferiority Complex on the whole. Thus, the hypothesis 4.1. that Employed Dalits in urban settings seemingly develop a higher level of inferiority complex when compared to the Non-Dalits in the same context is accepted.
- The investigation revealed that there is significant effect of Inferiority Complex among Employed Dalits in spite of being well placed in the society by having good education, own housing facility, and economic conditions. The investigation also revealed the major ways of how Employed Dalits are affected by Inferiority Complex. They are affected by Inferiority Complex when sharing food with others at work place, topping the list, followed by restriction, caste identity, criticism, and relationship with superiors, relationship between families, relationship in the canteen, celebrating festivals, inter-personal relationship, and lastly relationship with subordinates. Therefore, hypothesis 4.2. that in spite of their educational and

economic development the Employed Dalits experience inferiority complex that is seemingly caused by the stigma of untouchability is accepted.

- The investigation revealed that there is significant effect of Inferiority Complex among group D Male Employed Dalits, and group C among Employed Dalit Female subjects. The investigation also revealed that 69(57.47%) of Employed Dalits whose length of service is between 1-20 years were significantly affected by inferiority complex. The study found that 75(62.47%) of Dalits subjects lived in their own houses, in comparison to 68(56.64%) of Non-Dalit subjects and the highest 40(33.32%) of subjects among Employed Dalits were graduates in comparison to 15(12.49%) among Non-Dalits. It is also found that 41(34.15%) among Employed Dalit subjects were drawing salary between Rs. 15001.00 to Rs. 20000.00 in comparison to 23(19.15%) among Non-Dalit subjects. Thus, hypothesis 4.3. that there seems to be a link between the level of inferiority complex and the level of socio-economic achievements is accepted.

6.3. Suggestions for Future Research

Based on the findings of this study, the following suggestions are made for future research.

- Similar studies can be done comparing the Employed Dalits and Unemployed Dalits, comparing the Employed Dalits and Self-Employed Dalits, both in rural and urban setting.
- Similar studies also can be done comparing professional groups exclusively, such as Group A of Employed Dalits and Group A of Employed Non-Dalits.
- Similar studies can also be done comparing the Employed Dalit Christians and Employed non-Christian Dalits.
- Studies can also include topics like high self-esteem, depression, stress, which are pertinent and relevant issues faced by the Dalits.
- If the researcher is developing his own scale, it is suggested to have less number of items. The reason for this is the time factor. The employees are busy with their work and other personal things and have less time to give for the research work. If the scale has more items, one can expect non-cooperation from the participants. For this reason, it is suggested to employ minimum number of items and scales in the study and to have smaller size in sample.

Conclusion

The outcome of this research significantly indicates that Employed Dalits are suffering from Inferiority Complex as compared to the Employed Non-Dalits. The following hypotheses have been tested and were found to be true. The Employed Dalits in urban settings seemingly develop a higher level of inferiority complex when compared to the Non-Dalits in the same context. In spite of their educational and economic development the Employed Dalits experience inferiority complex that is seemingly caused by the stigma of untouchability. There seems to be a link between the level of inferiority complex and the level of socio-economic achievements.

These hypotheses were guidelines for the researcher to develop a relevant questionnaire and collect data from the Sample group. The implications for Pastoral Care were made based on the findings of the research to technically address the issue of Inferiority Complex. The researcher has suggested several methods derived from a variety of schools in pastoral care and counselling for the treatment of Inferiority Complex among Employed Dalits. The list of methods presented herein is in no way complete, and no pastoral caregiver would ever use all of these methods. The researcher suggests that the pastoral caregiver choose from the methods available and use the ones that appear most beneficial for the Employed Dalits or people they encounter with inferiority complex.

Appendices

Appendix 1

The Constitution of India, which safeguarded the rights of Scheduled Castes.

1. Equality before Law: Article 14 provides that the state shall not deny to any person equality before the law or equal protection of the laws.
2. Prohibition of discrimination on grounds of religion, race, caste, sex or birth: Article 15 provides that the State shall discriminate against any citizen on these grounds. No citizens shall on these grounds be subject to any disability or restriction with regard to access to shops, public restaurants, hotels and bathing ghats, roads and places of public resorts maintained wholly or partly out of State funds or dedicated to the use of general public. Article 15(4) also provides that nothing in this article shall prevent the State from making any special provision for the advancement of any socially and educationally backwards classes of citizens or for the Scheduled Castes and Tribes.
3. Equality of opportunity in matters of public employment: Article 16 provides that no citizen shall on grounds only of religion, race, caste, sex, descent, place of birth, residence or any of them, be ineligible for, or discriminated against in respect of, any employment or office under the State. Article 16(4) also provides that nothing in this article shall prevent the State from making any provision for the reservation of appointments or posts in favour of any backward class of citizens which, in the opinion of the State, is not adequately represented in the services under the state.
4. Abolition of Untouchability: Article 17 provides that "Untouchability" is abolished and its practice in any form is forbidden and enforcement of any disability arising out of "Untouchability" shall be an offence punishable in accordance with law.
5. Freedom of Religion: Article 25 provides that all persons are equally entitled to freedom of conscience and the right freely to profess, practice and

propagate religion. Article 25(2) provides that nothing in this article shall affect the operation of any existing law or prevent the State from making any law providing for social welfare and reform or the throwing open of Hindu religious institutions of public character to all classes and sections of Hindus. Explanation II to Article 25(2) provides that the reference to Hindus shall be construed as including a reference to persons professing the Sikh, Jaina, or Buddhist religion, and the reference to Hindu religious institutions shall be construed accordingly.

6. Welfare State: Article 38 provides that the State shall strive to promote the welfare of the people by securing and protecting as effectively as it any a social order in which justice, social, economic and political, shall inform all the institutions of the national life.
7. Protection from Injustice: Article 46 provides that the State shall promote with special care the educational and economic interests of the weaker sections of the people and in particular of the Scheduled Castes and Tribes, and shall protect them from social injustice and all forms of exploitation.
8. Welfare of Tribals: Article 164 provides that in the states of Bihar, Madhya Pradesh and Orissa, there shall be a minister in-charge of tribal welfare who may in addition be in charge of the Scheduled Castes and backward classes or any other work.
9. Right to Vote: Article 325 provides that there shall be one general electoral role for every constituency for election to either House of Parliament or either House of the Legislature of a State and no person shall be ineligible for exclusion in such roll or claim to be included in any special electoral role for any such constituency on grounds only of religion, race, caste, sex or any of them.
10. Adult Suffrage: Article 326 provides that the elections to the House of the people and to the Legislative Assemblies of State shall be on the basis of adult suffrage.
11. Reservation of seats for Scheduled Castes: Article 330 provides that seats shall be reserved in the House of the People for the Scheduled Castes and the Scheduled Tribes as nearly as may be in proportion to their population as ascertained at the last preceding census of which the relevant figures have been published. Article 332 makes similar provisions in the Legislative Assemblies of the States.
12. Reservation for Elections to be Temporary: Article 334 provides that the reservation of seats for the Scheduled Castes and Scheduled Tribes shall cease on the expiry of 10 years. (However, this provision has been amended from time to time and now provides for reservations to cease on the expiry of 50 years).
13. Reservations in Services and Posts: Article 335 provides that the claims of the members of the Scheduled Castes and Scheduled Tribes shall be

taken into consideration, consistently with the maintenance of efficiency of administration, in the making of appointments to services and posts in connection with the affairs of the Union or States.

14. Special Officer for Scheduled Castes and Tribes: Article 338 provides that there shall be a special officer for the Scheduled Castes and Tribes to be appointed by the President. It shall be the duty of the special officer to investigate all matters relating to the safeguards provided for the Scheduled Castes and Tribes under the Constitution and report to the president on the working of those safeguards at such intervals as the president may direct, and the President shall cause all such reports to be laid before each House of Parliament.
15. Scheduled Castes and Tribes: Article 341 and 342 provides that the president after due procedure any by public notification specify the Castes, races or tribes which shall be deemed to be Scheduled Castes or Tribes as the case may be. Parliament may by law include in or exclude from the list of Scheduled Castes and Tribes specifies in a notification any caste, race or tribe. Article 366 defines Scheduled Castes and Tribes to means such castes, races or tribes or parts of or groups within such castes, races or tribes as deemed under article 341 and 342 to be Scheduled Castes and Tribes. The Fifth Schedule also provides for the administration and control of Scheduled Tribes in certain areas through Tribes Advisory Councils.

Appendix 2

The text of the Poona Pact is as follows: Source; Found in the Publisher's note to the book, Dr. Ambedkar on Poona Pact, by L.R. Balley.

1. There shall be seats reserved for the Depressed Classes out of general electorate seats in the provincial Legislatures as follows: Madras 30; Bombay with Sind 15; Punjab 8; Bihar and Orissa 18; Central Provinces 20; Assam 7; Bengal 30; United Provinces 20; Total 148. These figures are based on the total strength of the Provincial Councils, announced in the Prime Minister's decision.
2. Election to these seats shall be by joint electorates subjects, however, to the following procedure: All the members of the Depressed Classes, registered in the general electoral roll in a constituency, will form an electoral college, which will elect a panel of four candidates belonging to the Depressed Classes for each of such reserved seats, by the method of the single vote; the four persons getting the highest number of votes in such primary election, shall be candidates for election by the general electorate.
3. Representation of the Depressed Classes in the Central Legislature shall likewise be on the principle of joint electorates and reserved seats by the method of primary election in the manner provided for in Clause 2 above, for their representation in the provincial Legislatures.
4. In the Central Legislature, eighteen percent, of the seats allotted to the general electorate for British India in the said legislature shall be reserved for the Depressed Classes.
5. The system of primary election to a panel of candidates for election to the Central Provincial Legislatures, as hereinbefore mentioned, shall come to an end after the first ten year, unless terminated sooner by mutual agreement under the provision of Next Clause.
6. The system of representation of the Depressed Classes by reserved seats in the provincial and central Legislatures as provided for in Clauses 1 and 4 shall continue until determined by mutual agreement between the communities concerned in the settlement.

7. Franchise for the Central and Provincial Legislature for the Depressed Classes shall be as indicated in the Lothian Committee Report.
8. There shall be no disabilities attaching to any one on the ground of his being a member of the Depressed Classes in regard to any elections to local bodies or appointment to the Public Services. Every endeavor shall be made to secure fair representation for the Depressed Classes in these respects, subject to such educational qualifications as may be laid down for appointment to the Public Services.
9. In every province out of the educational grant, an adequate sum shall be earmarked for providing educational facilities to the Members of the Depressed Classes.

Appendix 3

Characteristics of People with High and Low Self-esteem

The following are characteristics of people with		
	High Self-esteem	Low Self-esteem
1	Talk about ideas	Talk about self or others
2	Caring attitude	Critical attitude
3	Humility	Arrogance
4	Respect authority	Rebel against authority
5	Courage of convictions	Go along to get along
6	Confidence	Confusion
7	Concerned about character	Concerned about reputation
8	Assertive	Aggressive
9	Accept responsibility	Blame the whole world
10	Self-interest	Selfish
11	Optimistic	Fatalistic
12	Willing to learn	Know it all
13	Sensitive	Touchy
14	Discuss	Argue
15	Discipline	Distorted sense of freedom
16	Internally driven	Externally driven
17	Respect others	Look down on others
18	Enjoy decency	Enjoy vulgarity
19	Know limit	Every thing goes
20	Giver	Taker

Source: Anitha J. kumplunkal H.C., *Indian Currents,* 4 – 10 May 2009, p.38.

Appendix 4

Questionnaire

Each one belongs to a particular order in the social hierarchy. Most of the time, we are identified with our social status and people relate to us accordingly. The way people perceive, interact and work, differs greatly resulting specific psycho-social experiences. Every environment has its own impact and influence on the persons around, and work environment is one of them. This study is intended to explore, your psycho-social experiences within the work environment in Bangalore. There is no right or wrong answers in this questionnaire. You are requested to read carefully and answer all questions. All the information provided will be treated as confidential. Thank you.

Section 1 - Demographical Details

The purpose of this section is to get background information about you and your family's social, educational and economic status. Indicate your response / choice by marking a tick [ ] in the appropriate box.

1. Your name: (Optional) ....
2. Your Age
   ☐ 18 – 25
   ☐ 26 – 35
   ☐ 36 – 45
   ☐ 46 – 60
3. Your Marital Status
   ☐ Married
   ☐ Unmarried / Single
   ☐ Separated / Divorced / Widowed
4. According to your original certificate and employment record, you belong to:
   ☐ Dalit (SC)
   ☐ Non-Dalit (Non SC)

5. Type of residence?
   ☐ Own House
   ☐ Rented House
   ☐ Company House / Quarters
   ☐ Any Other? ....
6. Where do you work?
   ☐ HAL, Bangalore
   ☐ Graphite India, Bangalore
   ☐ State Government Services, Bangalore
7. What is your monthly income
   ☐ Below 5000
   ☐ 5001 to 10000
   ☐ 10001 to 15000
   ☐ 15001 to 20000
   ☐ Above 20001
8. What is your educational qualification
   ☐ Below 7th Standard
   ☐ 8th Std - 10th Standard
   ☐ PUC Pass
   ☐ Completed Graduation
   ☐ Completed Post-Graduation
   ☐ Any Other, specify ....
9. What is your Professional Group / Class / Grade? Give designation...............
   ☐ Group A / Class 1 / Grade 1
   ☐ Group B / Class II / Grade II
   ☐ Group C / Class III / Grade III
   ☐ Group D / Class IV / Grade IV
10. What is your length of service in your employment ....

Section – 2 Questionnaire

Directions: Indicate your response / choice by marking a tick [ ] in the appropriate box.

1. I like to be referred by my caste name in my work place. (Reverse)
☐ Never ☐ Rarely ☐ Sometimes ☐ Frequently ☐ Almost always
2. I feel welcome at my work place despite my caste membership.
☐ Never ☐ Rarely ☐ Sometimes ☐ Frequently ☐ Almost always
3. My colleagues have broken friendship with me after knowing that I belong to a particular caste.
☐ Never ☐ Rarely ☐ Sometimes ☐ Frequently ☐ Almost always
4. I think it is good to conceal my caste identity at my work place.
☐ Never ☐ Rarely ☐ Sometimes ☐ Frequently ☐ Almost always
5. I feel lowly when people call me by my caste name at my work place.
☐ Never ☐ Rarely ☐ Sometimes ☐ Frequently ☐ Almost always
6. I feel that identifying my caste is intimidating at my work place.
☐ Never ☐ Rarely ☐ Sometimes ☐ Frequently ☐ Almost always
7. I like people at my work place to call me by some other caste name rather than my own.
☐ Never ☐ Rarely ☐ Sometimes ☐ Frequently ☐ Almost always
8. I think that people at my work place behave with me differently when they know my caste name.
☐ Never ☐ Rarely ☐ Sometimes ☐ Frequently ☐ Almost always
9. I think that caste consciousness is powerful at my work place.
☐ Never ☐ Rarely ☐ Sometimes ☐ Frequently ☐ Almost always
10. I discuss caste issues in my department.
☐ Never ☐ Rarely ☐ Sometimes ☐ Frequently ☐ Almost always
11. I withdraw myself from a group when caste issues are discussed.
☐ Never ☐ Rarely ☐ Sometimes ☐ Frequently ☐ Almost always
12. People at my work place call me by derogatory names in relation to caste.
☐ Never ☐ Rarely ☐ Sometimes ☐ Frequently ☐ Almost always
13. I get due respect like any other caste people at my work place. (Reverse)
☐ Never ☐ Rarely ☐ Sometimes ☐ Frequently ☐ Almost always
14. I think that other caste people receive more respect than me at my work place.
☐ Never ☐ Rarely ☐ Sometimes ☐ Frequently ☐ Almost always
15. I am restricted from entering into some areas in the office because of my caste background.
☐ Never ☐ Rarely ☐ Sometimes ☐ Frequently ☐ Almost always

16. I have access to all common / public places at my work place.
☐ Never ☐ Rarely ☐ Sometimes ☐ Frequently ☐ Almost always
17. I participate in celebrating festivals and special functions at my work place. (Reverse)
☐ Never ☐ Rarely ☐ Sometimes ☐ Frequently ☐ Almost always
18. I mingle with people during the celebration of festivals and special programmes at my work place. (Reverse)
☐ Never ☐ Rarely ☐ Sometimes ☐ Frequently ☐ Almost always
19. I feel shy to mingle with people during the festivals and public programmes at my work place.
☐ Never ☐ Rarely ☐ Sometimes ☐ Frequently ☐ Almost always
20. I involve in performing pooja during festivals at my work place. (Reverse)
☐ Never ☐ Rarely ☐ Sometimes ☐ Frequently ☐ Almost always
21. Though I come from a different caste background, I am given important responsibilities during the celebrations of festivals and special programmes. (Reverse)
☐ Never ☐ Rarely ☐ Sometimes ☐ Frequently ☐ Almost always
22. I think that people avoid me during festivals and special programmes because of my caste background.
☐ Never ☐ Rarely ☐ Sometimes ☐ Frequently ☐ Almost always
23. People accept parsadam from me during festivals at my work place.
☐ Never ☐ Rarely ☐ Sometimes ☐ Frequently ☐ Almost always
24. Caste plays an important role during festivals and special programmes at my work place.
☐ Never ☐ Rarely ☐ Sometimes ☐ Frequently ☐ Almost always
25. I am treated with due respect in the department during festival and special programmes. (Reverse)
☐ Never ☐ Rarely ☐ Sometimes ☐ Frequently ☐ Almost always
26. I think that some people from certain castes are segregated at my work place.
☐ Never ☐ Rarely ☐ Sometimes ☐ Frequently ☐ Almost always
27. We come together as a caste group at my work place.
☐ Never ☐ Rarely ☐ Sometimes ☐ Frequently ☐ Almost always
28. My superiors discuss with me clearly about the guidelines of the jobs to be done. (Reverse)
☐ Never ☐ Rarely ☐ Sometimes ☐ Frequently ☐ Almost always
29. My colleagues help me to understand the given job description.
☐ Never ☐ Rarely ☐ Sometimes ☐ Frequently ☐ Almost always
30. My work in the department is underestimated because of my caste identity.
☐ Never ☐ Rarely ☐ Sometimes ☐ Frequently ☐ Almost always

31. My successful job performances are appreciated in the department. (Reverve)
☐ Never ☐ Rarely ☐ Sometimes ☐ Frequently ☐ Almost always
32. I think that the successful job performances of other caste people in my department is more appreciated?
☐ Never ☐ Rarely ☐ Sometimes ☐ Frequently ☐ Almost always
33. The staff working under my supervision feels that I am not fit for the position because of my caste background.
☐ Never ☐ Rarely ☐ Sometimes ☐ Frequently ☐ Almost always
34. I feel proud of my work accomplishments in the department. (Reverse)
☐ Never ☐ Rarely ☐ Sometimes ☐ Frequently ☐ Almost always
35. I take criticism with right spirit in the work place. (Reverse)
☐ Never ☐ Rarely ☐ Sometimes ☐ Frequently ☐ Almost always
36. Just because I am from a different caste background, my colleagues blame me for mistakes that I am not responsible.
☐ Never ☐ Rarely ☐ Sometimes ☐ Frequently ☐ Almost always
37. I blame myself for the mistakes that I am not responsible.
☐ Never ☐ Rarely ☐ Sometimes ☐ Frequently ☐ Almost always
38. I have work competitions in my department.
☐ Never ☐ Rarely ☐ Sometimes ☐ Frequently ☐ Almost always
39. I react with fear to competitions at my work place.
☐ Never ☐ Rarely ☐ Sometimes ☐ Frequently ☐ Almost always
40. Reacting with fear to competitions is there from my childhood.
☐ Never Rarely Sometimes Frequently Almost always
41. I avoid meeting people at my work place.
☐ Never ☐ Rarely ☐ Sometimes ☐ Frequently ☐ Almost always
42. I try to avoid social groups at my work place.
☐ Never ☐ Rarely ☐ Sometimes ☐ Frequently ☐ Almost always
43. Though I am from a different caste background, my subordinates listen to what I say. (Reverse)
☐ Never ☐ Rarely ☐ Sometimes ☐ Frequently ☐ Almost always
44. I initiate discussion in the department. (Reverse)
☐ Never ☐ Rarely ☐ Sometimes ☐ Frequently ☐ Almost always
45. I feel undeserving to initiate discussion in my department.
☐ Never ☐ Rarely ☐ Sometimes ☐ Frequently ☐ Almost always
46. I am ashamed to initiate discussion in the department because of my caste background.
☐ Never ☐ Rarely ☐ Sometimes ☐ Frequently ☐ Almost always
47. I have freedom of self-expression in my department. (Reverse)
☐ Never ☐ Rarely ☐ Sometimes ☐ Frequently ☐ Almost always

48. I lose friendly relationships in the department because of my caste background.
☐ Never ☐ Rarely ☐ Sometimes ☐ Frequently ☐ Almost always
49. Though I am from a different caste background, people from other castes like my friendship. (Reverse)
☐ Never ☐ Rarely ☐ Sometimes ☐ Frequently ☐ Almost always
50. I enjoy playing fun with my colleagues in the department.
☐ Never ☐ Rarely ☐ Sometimes ☐ Frequently ☐ Almost always
51. I get along well with the other caste groups in my work place. (Reverse)
☐ Never ☐ Rarely ☐ Sometimes ☐ Frequently ☐ Almost always
52. I am suspicious about favours done to me by my colleagues at the work place.
☐ Never ☐ Rarely ☐ Sometimes ☐ Frequently ☐ Almost always
53. This suspicious attitude is there from my childhood.
☐ Never ☐ Rarely ☐ Sometimes ☐ Frequently ☐ Almost always
54. Though I come from a different caste background, my colleagues invite me to their homes.
☐ Never ☐ Rarely ☐ Sometimes ☐ Frequently ☐ Almost always
55. Though I come from a different caste background, my colleagues visit my home. (Reverse)
☐ Never ☐ Rarely ☐ Sometimes ☐ Frequently ☐ Almost always
56. Though I come from a different caste background, my subordinates of other castes accept my invitation to attend my family functions. (Reverse)
☐ Never ☐ Rarely ☐ Sometimes ☐ Frequently ☐ Almost always
57. Though I come from a different caste background, my superiors belonging to other castes invite me to attend their family functions. (Reverse)
☐ Never ☐ Rarely ☐ Sometimes ☐ Frequently ☐ Almost always
58. Though I come from a different caste background, my colleagues belonging to other castes invite me to attend their family functions. (Reverse)
☐ Never ☐ Rarely ☐ Sometimes ☐ Frequently ☐ Almost always
59. Though I hold an high office in my department, I feel unworthy to attend family functions of my subordinate colleagues.
☐ Never ☐ Rarely ☐ Sometimes ☐ Frequently ☐ Almost always
60. Since I come from a particular caste background, I feel undeserving to attend family functions of my friends from other caste background.
☐ Never ☐ Rarely ☐ Sometimes ☐ Frequently ☐ Almost always
61. Caste plays an important role when it comes to the family functions.
☐ Never ☐ Rarely ☐ Sometimes ☐ Frequently ☐ Almost always
62. Though I come from a different caste background, my colleagues belonging to other castes eat with my family. (Reverse)
☐ Never ☐ Rarely ☐ Sometimes ☐ Frequently ☐ Almost always

63. With my family, I visit homes of friends / colleagues belonging to other castes. (Reverse)
☐ Never ☐ Rarely ☐ Sometimes ☐ Frequently ☐ Almost always
64. My family members feel at ease when we visit homes of friends / colleagues from other castes. (Reverse)
☐ Never ☐ Rarely ☐ Sometimes ☐ Frequently ☐ Almost always
65. My family members feel at ease when my colleagues and their family visit my home. (Reverse)
☐ Never ☐ Rarely ☐ Sometimes ☐ Frequently ☐ Almost always
66. People belonging to other caste sit and eat with me in the canteen / other eating places. (Reverse)
☐ Never ☐ Rarely ☐ Sometimes ☐ Frequently ☐ Almost always
67. I feel uncomfortable to eat with others because I do not have good eating habits.
☐ Never ☐ Rarely ☐ Sometimes ☐ Frequently ☐ Almost always
68. My friends while eating in the canteen like me because I have good eating habits.
☐ Never ☐ Rarely ☐ Sometimes ☐ Frequently ☐ Almost always
69. I sit and eat with my own caste group in the canteen / other eating places.
☐ Never ☐ Rarely ☐ Sometimes ☐ Frequently ☐ Almost always
70. Other caste people in my work place change their seat if I join them for eating?
☐ Never ☐ Rarely ☐ Sometimes ☐ Frequently ☐ Almost always
71. I maintain silence when other caste people sit with me to eat.
☐ Never ☐ Rarely ☐ Sometimes ☐ Frequently ☐ Almost always
72. I mix well with people of other caste background in the canteen / other eating places. (Reverse)
☐ Never ☐ Rarely ☐ Sometimes ☐ Frequently ☐ Almost always
73. Though I come from a different caste background, my colleagues share the food I bring from home. (Reverse)
☐ Never ☐ Rarely ☐ Sometimes ☐ Frequently ☐ Almost always
74. I like to share my food while eating with others in the department.
☐ Never ☐ Rarely ☐ Sometimes ☐ Frequently ☐ Almost always
75. I like to share the food that others bring from their homes?
☐ Never ☐ Rarely ☐ Sometimes ☐ Frequently ☐ Almost always

Section 3 - Rosenberg Self-Esteem Scale (RSE)

Directions: For the statements below, indicate your response / choice by marking a tick [ ] in the appropriate box.

Item I:

a) I feel that I am a person of worth, at least on an equal basis with others.
Strongly Agree ☐ Agree ☐ Disagree ☐ Strongly Disagree ☐

b) I feel that I have a number of good qualities
Strongly Agree ☐ Agree ☐ Disagree ☐ Strongly Disagree ☐

c) All in all, I am inclined to feel that I am a failure.
Strongly Agree ☐ Agree ☐ Disagree ☐ Strongly Disagree ☐

Item II:

a) I am able to do things as well as most other people.
Strongly Agree ☐ Agree ☐ Disagree ☐ Strongly Disagree ☐

b) I feel I do not have much to be proud of.
Strongly Agree ☐ Agree ☐ Disagree ☐ Strongly Disagree ☐

Item III:

a) I take a positive attitude towards myself.
Strongly Agree ☐ Agree ☐ Disagree ☐ Strongly Disagree ☐

Item IV:

a) On the whole, I am satisfied with myself.
Strongly Agree ☐ Agree ☐ Disagree ☐ Strongly Disagree ☐

Item V:

a) I wish I could have more respect for myself.
Strongly Agree ☐ Agree ☐ Disagree ☐ Strongly Disagree ☐

Item VI:

a) I certainly feel useless at times.
Strongly Agree ☐ Agree ☐ Disagree ☐ Strongly Disagree ☐

b) At times I think I am no good at all.
Strongly Agree ☐ Agree ☐ Disagree ☐ Strongly Disagree ☐

Section 4 - Self-Esteem Inventory

Directions: For the statements below, indicate your response / choice by marking a tick [ ] in the appropriate box which is most true of your level of exhibiting these behaviors in your life.

1. I seek approval and affirmation from others, and I am afraid of criticism.
☐ Never ☐ Rarely ☐ Sometimes ☐ Frequently ☐ Almost always
2. I guess at what normal behavior is, and I usually feel as if I am different from other people.
☐ Never ☐ Rarely ☐ Sometimes ☐ Frequently ☐ Almost always
3. I isolate myself from and I am afraid of people in authority roles.
☐ Never ☐ Rarely ☐ Sometimes ☐ Frequently ☐ Almost always
4. I am not able to appreciate my own accomplishments and good deeds.
☐ Never ☐ Rarely ☐ Sometimes ☐ Frequently ☐ Almost always
5. I tend to have difficulty following a project through from beginning to end.
☐ Never ☐ Rarely ☐ Sometimes ☐ Frequently ☐ Almost always
6. I get frightened or stressed when I am in the company of an angry person.
☐ Never ☐ Rarely ☐ Sometimes ☐ Frequently ☐ Almost always
7. In order to avoid a conflict, I find it easier to lie than tell the truth.
☐ Never ☐ Rarely ☐ Sometimes ☐ Frequently ☐ Almost always
8. I have problems with my own compulsive behavior, e.g. drinking, drug use, gambling, overeating, smoking, use of sex, shopping, etc.
☐ Never ☐ Rarely ☐ Sometimes ☐ Frequently ☐ Almost always
9. I judge myself without mercy. I am my own worst critic, and I am harder on myself than I am on others.
☐ Never ☐ Rarely ☐ Sometimes ☐ Frequently ☐ Almost always
10. I feel more alive in the midst of a crisis, and I am uneasy when my life is going smoothly; I am continually anticipating problems.
☐ Never ☐ Rarely ☐ Sometimes ☐ Frequently ☐ Almost always
11. I have difficulty having fun. I don't seem to know how to play for fun and relaxation.
☐ Never ☐ Rarely ☐ Sometimes ☐ Frequently ☐ Almost always
12. I am attracted to others when I perceive to have been victims, and I develop close relationship with them. In this way I confuse love with pity, and can pity and rescue.
☐ Never ☐ Rarely ☐ Sometimes ☐ Frequently ☐ Almost always
13. I need perfection in my life at home and work, and I expect perfection from others in my life.
☐ Never ☐ Rarely ☐ Sometimes ☐ Frequently ☐ Almost always

14. I seek out novelty, excitement, and the challenge of newness in my life with little concern given to the consequences of such action.
☐ Never ☐ Rarely ☐ Sometimes ☐ Frequently ☐ Almost always
15. I take myself very seriously, and I view all of my relationships just as seriously.
☐ Never ☐ Rarely ☐ Sometimes ☐ Frequently ☐ Almost always
16. I have problems developing and maintaining intimate relationships.
☐ Never ☐ Rarely ☐ Sometimes ☐ Frequently ☐ Almost always
17. I feel guilty when I stand up for myself or take care of my needs first, instead of giving in or taking care of others' needs first.
☐ Never ☐ Rarely ☐ Sometimes ☐ Frequently ☐ Almost always
18. I seek and or attract people who have compulsive behaviors. (e.g., alcohol, drugs, gambling, food, shopping, sex, smoking, overworking, or seeking excitement.)
☐ Never ☐ Rarely ☐ Sometimes ☐ Frequently ☐ Almost always
19. I feel responsible for others and find it easier to have concern for others than for myself.
☐ Never ☐ Rarely ☐ Sometimes ☐ Frequently ☐ Almost always
20. I am loyal to people for whom I care, even in the face of evidence that the loyalty is underserved.
☐ Never ☐ Rarely ☐ Sometimes ☐ Frequently ☐ Almost always
21. I cling to and will do anything to hold on to relationships because I am afraid of being alone and fearful of being abandoned.
☐ Never ☐ Rarely ☐ Sometimes ☐ Frequently ☐ Almost always
22. I am impulsive and act too quickly, before considering alternative actions or possible consequences.
☐ Never ☐ Rarely ☐ Sometimes ☐ Frequently ☐ Almost always
23. I have difficulty in being able to feel or to express feeling, I feel out of touch with my feeling.
☐ Never ☐ Rarely ☐ Sometimes ☐ Frequently ☐ Almost always
24. I mistrust my feeling and the feeling expressed by others.
☐ Never ☐ Rarely ☐ Sometimes ☐ Frequently ☐ Almost always
25. I isolate myself from other people, and I am initially shy and withdrawn in new social setting.
☐ Never ☐ Rarely ☐ Sometimes ☐ Frequently ☐ Almost always
26. I feel that I am being taken advantage of by individuals and society in general; I often feel victimized.
☐ Never ☐ Rarely ☐ Sometimes ☐ Frequently ☐ Almost always
27. I can be over responsible much of the time, but I can be extremely irresponsible at other times.
☐ Never ☐ Rarely ☐ Sometimes ☐ Frequently ☐ Almost always

28. I feel confused and angry at myself and not in control of my environment or my life when stresses are great.
    ☐ Never ☐ Rarely ☐ Sometimes ☐ Frequently ☐ Almost always
29. I spend a lot of time and energy rectifying or cleaning up messes and the negative consequences of ill-thought-out of impulsive actions for which I am responsible.
    ☐ Never ☐ Rarely ☐ Sometimes ☐ Frequently ☐ Almost always
30. I deny that my current problems stem from my past. I deny that I have stuffed-in feeling from the past which are impeding my current life.
    ☐ Never ☐ Rarely ☐ Sometimes ☐ Frequently ☐ Almost always

Section 5 - Social Distance Scale

A Modified form of Bogardus Social Distance Scale by Prof. Kuppaswamy, further modified by Rev. Epratha Sarathy to suit the population of the present research.

Directions: Indicate your response / choice by marking a tick [ ] in the appropriate box.

1. It is possible for me to establish kinship by marriage with other caste members.
   ☐ Never ☐ Rarely ☐ Sometimes ☐ Frequently ☐ Almost always
2. It is possible for me to take food with other caste members in their dinning room.
   ☐ Never ☐ Rarely ☐ Sometimes ☐ Frequently ☐ Almost always
3. It is possible for me to cultivate intimate friendship with other caste members.
   ☐ Never ☐ Rarely ☐ Sometimes ☐ Frequently ☐ Almost always
4. It is possible to take other caste members as guests in my home.
   ☐ Never ☐ Rarely ☐ Sometimes ☐ Frequently ☐ Almost always
5. It is possible for me to be accepted as neighbour by other caste members.
   ☐ Never ☐ Rarely ☐ Sometimes ☐ Frequently ☐ Almost always
6. It is possible for me to have casual acquaintance with other caste members.
   ☐ Never ☐ Rarely ☐ Sometimes ☐ Frequently ☐ Almost always

Thank you for your cooperation in taking time to answer the questions.

Epratha Sarathy

Appendix 5

Questionnaire

ಪ್ರಶ್ನಾವಳಿ

ಪ್ರತಿಯೊಬ್ಬ ಮನುಷ್ಯ ಒಂದು ವಿಶೇಷವಾದ ಸಾಮಾಜಿಕ , ಪುರೋಹಿತ ಕ್ರಮಕ್ಕೆ ಸೇರಿರುತ್ತಾರೆ. ಅನೇಕ ಸಮಯಗಳು ಜನರು ನಮ್ಮನ್ನು , ನಮ್ಮ ಸಾಮಾಜಿಕ ಅಂತಸ್ತು ಗುರ್ತಿಸಿ ಅದರ ಪ್ರಕಾರವಾಗಿ ಸಂಬಂಧ ಬೆಳಸುತ್ತಾರೆ. ಜನರು ಗ್ರಹಿಸುವ ರೀತಿ, ಪರಸ್ಪರ ಕ್ರಿಯೆ, ಮತ್ತು ಕೆಲಸ ಮಾಡುವ ರೀತಿಯಲ್ಲಿ ಬಹಳವಾಗಿ ವ್ಯತ್ಯಾಸ ಇರುವುದರಿಂದ ನಿರ್ದಿಷ್ಟ

ಮಾನಸಿಕ ಮತ್ತು ಸಾಮಾಜಿಕ ಅನುಭವ ಪರಿಣಾಮವಾಗುವುದು. ಪ್ರತಿಯೊಂದು ಸನ್ನಿವೇಶ ಸುತ್ತ ಮುತ್ತಲಿನಲ್ಲಿರುವ ಜನರ ಮೇಲೆ ಒತ್ತು ತರುವ ಪರಿಣಾಮ ಇರುತ್ತದೆ. ಅದೇ

ರೀತಿಯಾದದ್ದು ಕೆಲಸ ಮಾಡುವ ಸನ್ನಿವೇಶ. ಬೆಂಗಳೂರು ಪರಿದಿಯಲ್ಲಿ ನೀವು ಕೆಲಸ ಮಾಡುವ ಸನ್ನಿವೇಶದಲ್ಲಿ, ನಿಮಗೆ ಉಂಟಾಗುವ ಮಾನಸಿಕ, ಮತ್ತು ಸಾಮಾಜಿಕ ಅನುಭವಗಳನ್ನು

ಪರಿಶೋಧನೆ ಮಾಡುವುದೇ ಈ ವ್ಯಾಸಂಗದ ಉದ್ದೇಶ. ಈ ಪ್ರಶ್ನಾವಳಿಯಲ್ಲಿ ಯಾವುದೇ ತಪ್ಪಾದ ಅಥವಾ ಸರಿಯಾದ ಉತ್ತರಗಳಿಲ್ಲ. ದಯವಿಟ್ಟು ಶ್ರದ್ಧೆಯಿಂದ ಓದಿ ಎಲ್ಲಾ ಪ್ರಶ್ನೆಗಳಿಗೆ

ಉತ್ತರ ನೀಡಿ. ನೀವು ನೀಡುವ ಎಲ್ಲಾ ವಿಷಯಗಳನ್ನು ಗುಪ್ತವಾಗಿ ಇಡುತ್ತೇವೆ.

ವಂದನೆಗಳು.

ಭಾಗ ಒಂದು:೧. ಜನಾಂಗ ಸ್ಥಿತಿ ವಿವರಣೆ

ನಿಮ್ಮ ಮತ್ತು ನಿಮ್ಮ ಕುಟುಂಬದ ಬಗ್ಗೆ ಪ್ರಾಧಾನ್ಯತೆ ಕೊಡುವಂತ ಸಾಮಾಜಿಕ, ಆರ್ಥಿಕ ಮತ್ತು ವಿಧ್ಯಾಭ್ಯಾಸದ ವಿಷಯಗಳನ್ನು ಪಡೆಯುವುದೇ ಈ ಭಾಗದ ಉದ್ದೇಶವಾಗಿದೆ.

ನಿಮ್ಮ ಆಯ್ಕೆ ಅಥವಾ ಉತ್ತರವನ್ನು ಸರಿಯಾದ ಪೆಟ್ಟಿಗೆಯಲ್ಲಿ ( ) ಗುರುತು ಹಾಕಿ ಸೂಚಿಸಿರಿ.

೧) ನಿಮ್ಮ ಹೆಸರು

೨) ಲಿಂಗ : ಸ್ತ್ರೀ/ಪುರುಷ

೩) ನಿಮ್ಮ ವಯಸ್ಸು ಸರಿಯಾಗಿ

- ☐ ೧೮-೨೫ ವರ್ಷಗಳು
- ☐ ೨೬-೩೫ ವರ್ಷಗಳು
- ☐ ೩೬-೪೫ ವರ್ಷಗಳು
- ☐ ೪೬-೬೦ ವರ್ಷಗಳು

೪) ನಿಮ್ಮ ವೈವಾಹಿಕ ಸ್ಥಿತಿ

- ☐ ವಿವಾಹಿತರು
- ☐ ಅವಿವಾಹಿತರು / ಒಂಟಿಗರು
- ☐ ದಾಂಪತ್ಯ ಜೀವಿತದಿಂದ ಬೇರ್ಪಡಿ / ವಿವಾಹ ವಿಚ್ಛೇಧನೆಗೊಳಗಾಗಿರುವಿರೇ / ವಿಧವೆ ಅಥವಾ ವಿಧುರರೆ.

೫) ನಿಮ್ಮ ಮೂಲ ದಾಖಲೆ ಮತ್ತು ಕೆಲಸದ ದಾಖಲೆಗಳ ಪ್ರಕಾರ ನೀವು

- ☐ ದಲಿತರೇ (ಪರಿಶಿಷ್ಟ ಜಾತಿ ಎಸ್.ಸಿ.)
- ☐ ದಲಿತರಲ್ಲ (ಪರಿಶಿಷ್ಟ ಜಾತಿಯಲ್ಲ ನಾನ್ ಎಸ್.ಸಿ.)

೬) ನಿಮ್ಮ ವಾಸ ಸ್ಥಳದ ಸ್ಥಿತಿ?

- ☐ ಸ್ವಂತದ್ದು
- ☐ ಬಾಡಿಗೆ ಮನೆ
- ☐ ಸಂಸ್ಥೆಯ ವಸತಿ ಮನೆಯೇ
- ☐ ಇತರೆ

೭) ನೀವು ಉದ್ಯೋಗ ಎಲ್ಲಿ ಮಾಡುತ್ತಿರುವಿರಿ?

- ☐ ಎಚ್.ಎ.ಎಲ್.ಬೆಂಗಳೂರು
- ☐ ಗ್ರಾಫೈಟ್ ಇಂಡಿಯಾ, ಬೆಂಗಳೂರು
- ☐ ಕರ್ನಾಟಕ ರಾಜ್ಯ ಸರ್ಕಾರ ಸೇವೆಗಳು, ಬೆಂಗಳೂರು

೮) ನಿಮ್ಮ ತಿಂಗಳ ವರಮಾನ ಎಷ್ಟು?

- ☐ ೫೦೦೦ ರೂ. ಕೆಳಗೆ
- ☐ ೫೦೦೧ ರಿಂದ ೧೦,೦೦೦ ವರೆಗೆ
- ☐ ೧೦,೦೦೧ ರಿಂದ ೧೫,೦೦೦ ವರೆಗೆ
- ☐ ೧೫,೦೦೧ ರಿಂದ ೨೦,೦೦೦ ವರೆಗೆ
- ☐ ೨೦,೦೦೦ ಮೇಲೆ

೯) ನೆಮ್ಮ ವೆದ್ಯಾಭ್ಯಾಸದ ಅರ್ಹತೆ ಕೆಳಕಂಡಂತೆ.

- ☐ ೭ನೇ ತರಗತೆ ಕೆಳಗೆ
- ☐ ೮ ನೇ -೧೦ನೇ ತರಗತೆ
- ☐ ಪೆ.ಯು.ಸೆ. ಉತ್ತೀರ್ಣ
- ☐ ಪಧವೀಧರರೆ
- ☐ ಸ್ನಾತಕೋತ್ತರ ಶೆಕ್ಷಣ
- ☐ ಇನ್ನೆತರೆ

೧೦) ನೆಮ್ಮ ಕಸುಬೆನ ಗುಂಪು ಏನು / ದರ್ಜೆ / ವರ್ಗ / ಉದ್ಯೋಗವನ್ನು ತೆಳೆಸೆ

- ☐ ಗುಂಪು ಎ / ದರ್ಜೆ ಒಂದು / ವರ್ಗ ಒಂದು
- ☐ ಗುಂಪು ಬೆ / ದರ್ಜೆ ಎರಡು / ವರ್ಗ ಎರಡು
- ☐ ಗುಂಪು ಸೆ / ದರ್ಜೆ ಮೂರು / ವರ್ಗ ಮೂರು
- ☐ ಗುಂಪು ಡೆ / ದರ್ಜೆ ನಾಲ್ಕು / ವರ್ಗ ನಾಲ್ಕು

೧೧) ಎಷ್ಟು ವರ್ಷದೆಂದ ಉದ್ಯೋಗದಲ್ಲೆರುವೆರೆ? ____________________

ಭಾಗ-ಎರಡು

ಸೂಚನೆ : ನೆಮ್ಮ ಆಯ್ಕೆ / ಉತ್ತರವನ್ನು ಪೆಟ್ಟೆಗೆಯಲ್ಲೆ ( ) ಗುರುತು ಹಾಕೆ ಸೂಚೆಸೆರೆ

೧) ನನ್ನ ಕೆಲಸದ ಸ್ಥಳದಲ್ಲೆ ನನ್ನನ್ನು ನನ್ನ ಜಾತೆಯ ಹೆಸರೆನೆಂದ ಗುರುತೆಸುಮದು ನನಗೆ ಇಷ್ಟವಾಗೆದೆ.

☐ ಇಲ್ಲವೇ ಇಲ್ಲ ☐ ಅಪರೂಪವಾಗೆ ☐ ಕೆಲವೊಮ್ಮೆ

☐ ಪದೇ ಪದೇ ☐ ಪ್ರತೆಸಾರೆ

೨) ನಾನು ಈ ಜಾತೆಗೆ ಸೇರೆದಾಗ್ಯೂ ನನ್ನ ಕೆಲಸದ ಸ್ಥಳದಲ್ಲೆ ನನ್ನನ್ನು ಸ್ವಾಗತೆಸುತ್ತಾರೆ.

☐ ಇಲ್ಲವೇ ಇಲ್ಲ ☐ ಅಪರೂಪವಾಗೆ ☐ ಕೆಲವೊಮ್ಮೆ

☐ ಪದೇ ಪದೇ ☐ ಪ್ರತೆಸಾರೆ

೩) ನಾನು ಈ ಜಾತೆಗೆ ಸೇರೆದವನೆಂದು ನನ್ನ ಸಹೋದ್ಯೋಗೆಗಳೆಗೆ ಗೂತ್ತಾದ ಮೇಲೆ ನನ್ನ ಸ್ನೇಹವನ್ನು ಬೆಟ್ಟು ಬೆಟ್ಟರು.

☐ ಇಲ್ಲವೇ ಇಲ್ಲ ☐ ಅಪರೂಪವಾಗೆ ☐ ಕೆಲವೊಮ್ಮೆ

☐ ಪದೇ ಪದೇ ☐ ಪ್ರತೆಸಾರೆ

೪) ನನ್ನ ಕೆಲಸದ ಸ್ಥಳದಲ್ಲಿ ನನ್ನ ಜಾತಿಯ ಗುರುತನ್ನು ಗುಟ್ಟಾಗಿ ಇಡುಮದು ಒಳ್ಳೆಯದು ಎಂದು ನೆನಸುತ್ತೇನೆ.

☐ ಇಲ್ಲವೇ ಇಲ್ಲ ☐ ಅಪರೂಪವಾಗಿ ☐ ಕೆಲವೊಮ್ಮೆ

☐ ಪದೇ ಪದೇ ☐ ಪ್ರತಿಸಾರಿ

೫) ನನ್ನ ಕೆಲಸದ ಸ್ಥಳದಲ್ಲಿ ಜನರು ನನ್ನ ಜಾತಿ ಹೆಸರಿನಿಂದ ಕರೆಯುವಾಗ ನನ್ನಲ್ಲಿ ದೀನ ಭಾವನೆ ಉಂಟಾಗುತ್ತದೆ.

☐ ಇಲ್ಲವೇ ಇಲ್ಲ ☐ ಅಪರೂಪವಾಗಿ ☐ ಕೆಲವೊಮ್ಮೆ

☐ ಪದೇ ಪದೇ ☐ ಪ್ರತಿಸಾರಿ

೬) ನನ್ನ ಕೆಲಸದ ಸ್ಥಳದಲ್ಲಿ ನನ್ನ ಜಾತಿಯನ್ನು ಹೇಳಲು ನನಗೆ ಹೆದರಿಕೆಯಾಗುಮದು.

☐ ಇಲ್ಲವೇ ಇಲ್ಲ ☐ ಅಪರೂಪವಾಗಿ ☐ ಕೆಲವೊಮ್ಮೆ

☐ ಪದೇ ಪದೇ ☐ ಪ್ರತಿಸಾರಿ

೭) ನನ್ನ ಕೆಲಸದ ಸ್ಥಳದಲ್ಲಿ ನನ್ನ ಜನರು ನನ್ನನ್ನು ನನ್ನದಲ್ಲದ ಬೇರೆ ಜಾತಿಯ ಹೆಸರಿನಿಂದ ಕರೆಯುಮದು ನನಗೆ ಇಷ್ಟ .

☐ ಇಲ್ಲವೇ ಇಲ್ಲ ☐ ಅಪರೂಪವಾಗಿ ☐ ಕೆಲವೊಮ್ಮೆ

☐ ಪದೇ ಪದೇ ☐ ಪ್ರತಿಸಾರಿ

೮) ನನ್ನ ಕೆಲಸದ ಸ್ಥಳದಲ್ಲಿ ಜನರಿಗೆ ನನ್ನ ಜಾತಿಯ ಬಗ್ಗೆ ಗೊತ್ತಾದ ಮೇಲೆ ನನ್ನೊಡನೆ ಭಿನ್ನವಾಗಿ ವರ್ತಿಸುತ್ತಾರೆ.

☐ ಇಲ್ಲವೇ ಇಲ್ಲ ☐ ಅಪರೂಪವಾಗಿ ☐ ಕೆಲವೊಮ್ಮೆ

☐ ಪದೇ ಪದೇ ☐ ಪ್ರತಿಸಾರಿ

೯) ನನ್ನ ಕೆಲಸದ ಸ್ಥಳದಲ್ಲಿ ಜಾತಿಯ ಮನೋಭಾವ ಬಲವಾಗಿದೆಯೆಂದು ನೆನೆಸುತ್ತೇನೆ.

☐ ಇಲ್ಲವೇ ಇಲ್ಲ ☐ ಅಪರೂಪವಾಗಿ ☐ ಕೆಲವೊಮ್ಮೆ

☐ ಪದೇ ಪದೇ ☐ ಪ್ರತಿಸಾರಿ

೧೦) ನನ್ನ ಇಲಾಖೆಯಲ್ಲಿ ನಾನು ಜಾತಿಯ ವಿಷಯಗಳನ್ನು ಚರ್ಚಿಸುತ್ತೇನೆ.

☐ ಇಲ್ಲವೇ ಇಲ್ಲ ☐ ಅಪರೂಪವಾಗಿ ☐ ಕೆಲವೊಮ್ಮೆ

☐ ಪದೇ ಪದೇ ☐ ಪ್ರತಿಸಾರಿ

೧೧) ಜಾತಿಯ ವಿಷಯಗಳನ್ನು ಚರ್ಚಿಸುವಾಗ ನಾನು ಗುಂಪಿನಿಂದ ಹಿಂದೆ ಹೋಗುತ್ತೇನೆ.

☐ ಇಲ್ಲವೇ ಇಲ್ಲ ☐ ಅಪರೂಪವಾಗಿ ☐ ಕೆಲವೊಮ್ಮೆ

☐ ಪದೇ ಪದೇ ☐ ಪ್ರತಿಸಾರಿ

೧೨) ನನ್ನ ಕೆಲಸದ ಸ್ಥಳದಲ್ಲಿ ಜನರು ನನ್ನನ್ನು ಜಾತಿಗೆ ಸಂಬಂಧಿಸಿದಂತ ಅವಮಾನವಾಗುವ ಹೆಸರುಗಳನ್ನು ಕರೆಯುತ್ತಾರೆ.

☐ ಇಲ್ಲವೇ ಇಲ್ಲ ☐ ಅಪರೂಪವಾಗಿ ☐ ಕೆಲವೊಮ್ಮೆ

☐ ಪದೇ ಪದೇ ☐ ಪ್ರತಿಸಾರಿ

೧೩) ನನ್ನ ಕೆಲಸದ ಸ್ಥಳದಲ್ಲಿ ಬೇರೆ ಜಾತಿಯ ಜನರ ಹಾಗೆ ನನಗೂ ತಕ್ಕ ಮರ್ಯಾದೆ ಸಿಗುತ್ತದೆ.

☐ ಇಲ್ಲವೇ ಇಲ್ಲ ☐ ಅಪರೂಪವಾಗಿ ☐ ಕೆಲವೊಮ್ಮೆ

☐ ಪದೇ ಪದೇ ☐ ಪ್ರತಿಸಾರಿ

೧೪) ನನ್ನ ಕೆಲಸದ ಸ್ಥಳದಲ್ಲಿ ನನಗಿಂತ ಬೇರೆ ಜಾತಿ ಜನರಿಗೆ ಹೆಚ್ಚಿನ ಮರ್ಯಾದೆ ಸಿಗುತ್ತದೆ ಎಂದು ನೆನೆಸುತ್ತೇನೆ.

☐ ಇಲ್ಲವೇ ಇಲ್ಲ ☐ ಅಪರೂಪವಾಗಿ ☐ ಕೆಲವೊಮ್ಮೆ

☐ ಪದೇ ಪದೇ ☐ ಪ್ರತಿಸಾರಿ

೧೫) ನನ್ನ ಜಾತಿಯ ಹಿನ್ನಲೆ ಕುರಿತಾಗಿ ಇಲಾಖೆಯಲ್ಲಿ ನನಗೆ ಕೆಲವು ಪ್ರದೇಶಗಳಲ್ಲಿ ಪ್ರವೇಶ ನಿಷೇಧಿಸಿದೆ.

☐ ಇಲ್ಲವೇ ಇಲ್ಲ ☐ ಅಪರೂಪವಾಗಿ ☐ ಕೆಲವೊಮ್ಮೆ

☐ ಪದೇ ಪದೇ ☐ ಪ್ರತಿಸಾರಿ

೧೬) ನನ್ನ ಕೆಲಸದ ಸ್ಥಳದಲ್ಲಿ ಎಲ್ಲಾ ಸಾಮಾನ್ಯ ಅಥವಾ ಸರ್ವ ಜನರ ಸ್ಥಳಗಳಿಗೆ ನನಗೆ ಪ್ರವೇಶ ಇದೆ.

☐ ಇಲ್ಲವೇ ಇಲ್ಲ ☐ ಅಪರೂಪವಾಗಿ ☐ ಕೆಲವೊಮ್ಮೆ

☐ ಪದೇ ಪದೇ ☐ ಪ್ರತಿಸಾರಿ

೧೭) ನನ್ನ ಕೆಲಸದ ಸ್ಥಳದಲ್ಲಿ ವಿಶೇಷ ಕಾರ್ಯಕ್ರಮಗಳು ಮತ್ತು ಹಬ್ಬಗಳಲ್ಲಿ ನಾನು ಭಾಗವಹಿಸುತ್ತೇನೆ.

☐ ಇಲ್ಲವೇ ಇಲ್ಲ ☐ ಅಪರೂಪವಾಗಿ ☐ ಕೆಲವೊಮ್ಮೆ

☐ ಪದೇ ಪದೇ ☐ ಪ್ರತಿಸಾರಿ

೧೮) ನನ್ನ ಕಲಸದ ಸ್ಥಳದಲ್ಲಿ ಕಾರ್ಯಕ್ರಮಗಳು ಮತ್ತು ಹಬ್ಬಗಳು ನಡೆಯುವಾಗ ನಾನು ಜನರೊಡನೆ ಸೇರುತ್ತೇನೆ.

☐ ಇಲ್ಲವೇ ಇಲ್ಲ ☐ ಅಪರೂಪವಾಗಿ ☐ ಕೆಲವೊಮ್ಮೆ

☐ ಪದೇ ಪದೇ ☐ ಪ್ರತಿಸಾರಿ

೧೯) ನನ್ನ ಕೆಲಸದ ಸ್ಥಳದಲ್ಲಿ ಸಾರ್ವಜನಿಕ ಕಾರ್ಯಕ್ರಮಗಳು ಮತ್ತು ಹಬ್ಬಗಳು ನಡೆಯುವಾಗ ನನಗೆ ಜನರೊಡನೆ ಸೇರುವುದಕ್ಕೆ ನಾಚಿಕೆಯಾಗುತ್ತದೆ.

☐ ಇಲ್ಲವೇ ಇಲ್ಲ ☐ ಅಪರೂಪವಾಗಿ ☐ ಕೆಲವೊಮ್ಮೆ

☐ ಪದೇ ಪದೇ ☐ ಪ್ರತಿಸಾರಿ

೨೦) ನನ್ನ ಕೆಲಸದ ಸ್ಥಳದಲ್ಲಿ ನಡೆಯುವ ಹಬ್ಬಗಳ ಪೂಜೆಯಲ್ಲಿ ನಾನು ಭಾಗವಹಿಸುತ್ತೇನೆ.

☐ ಇಲ್ಲವೇ ಇಲ್ಲ ☐ ಅಪರೂಪವಾಗಿ ☐ ಕೆಲವೊಮ್ಮೆ

☐ ಪದೇ ಪದೇ ☐ ಪ್ರತಿಸಾರಿ

೨೧) ನಾನು ಬೇರೆ ಜಾತಿಯ ಹಿನ್ನೆಲೆಯಿಂದ ಬಂದವನಾದರೂ ಹಬ್ಬಗಳು ಮತ್ತು ವಿಶೇಷ ಕಾರ್ಯಕ್ರಮಗಳು ನಡೆಯುವಾಗ ನನಗೆ ಮುಖ್ಯವಾದ ಪಾತ್ರಗಳನ್ನು ನೀಡುತ್ತಾರೆ.

☐ ಇಲ್ಲವೇ ಇಲ್ಲ ☐ ಅಪರೂಪವಾಗಿ ☐ ಕೆಲವೊಮ್ಮೆ

☐ ಪದೇ ಪದೇ ☐ ಪ್ರತಿಸಾರಿ

೨೨) ನನ್ನ ಜಾತಿಯ ಹಿನ್ನೆಲೆ ಕಾರಣದಿಂದ ಹಬ್ಬಗಳು ಮತ್ತು ವಿಶೇಷ ಕಾರ್ಯಕ್ರಮಗಳಿಂದ ಜನರು ನನ್ನನ್ನು ದೂರವಿಡುತ್ತಾರೆಂದು ನಾನು ಯೋಚಿಸುತ್ತೇನೆ.

☐ ಇಲ್ಲವೇ ಇಲ್ಲ ☐ ಅಪರೂಪವಾಗಿ ☐ ಕೆಲವೊಮ್ಮೆ

☐ ಪದೇ ಪದೇ ☐ ಪ್ರತಿಸಾರಿ

೨೩) ನನ್ನ ಕೆಲಸದ ಸ್ಥಳದಲ್ಲಿ ಹಬ್ಬಗಳು ನಡೆಯುವಾಗ ಜನರು ನನ್ನಿಂದ ಪ್ರಸಾದವನ್ನು ಸ್ವೀಕರಿಸುತ್ತಾರೆ.

☐ ಇಲ್ಲವೇ ಇಲ್ಲ ☐ ಅಪರೂಪವಾಗಿ ☐ ಕೆಲವೊಮ್ಮೆ

☐ ಪದೇ ಪದೇ ☐ ಪ್ರತಿಸಾರಿ

೨೪) ನನ್ನ ಕಲಸದ ಸ್ಥಳದಲ್ಲಿ ಹಬ್ಬಗಳು ಮತ್ತು ವಿಶೇಷ ಕಾರ್ಯಕ್ರಮಗಳು ನಡೆಯುವಾಗ ಜಾತಿ ಮುಖ್ಯವಾದ ಪಾತ್ರ ವಹಿಸುತ್ತದೆ.

☐ ಇಲ್ಲವೇ ಇಲ್ಲ ☐ ಅಪರೂಪವಾಗಿ ☐ ಕೆಲವೊಮ್ಮೆ

☐ ಪದೇ ಪದೇ ☐ ಪ್ರತಿಸಾರಿ

೧೫) ಇಲಾಖೆಯಲ್ಲಿ ಹಬ್ಬಗಳು ಮತ್ತು ವಿಶೇಷ ಕಾರ್ಯಕ್ರಮಗಳು ನಡೆಯುವಾಗ ನನಗೆ ತಕ್ಕ ಗೌರವ ಕೊಡುತ್ತಾರೆ.

☐ ಇಲ್ಲವೇ ಇಲ್ಲ ☐ ಅಪರೂಪವಾಗಿ ☐ ಕೆಲವೊಮ್ಮೆ

☐ ಪದೇ ಪದೇ ☐ ಪ್ರತಿಸಾರಿ

೧೬) ನನ್ನ ಕಲಸದ ಸ್ಥಳದಲ್ಲಿ ಕೆಲವು ಜಾತಿಗೆ ಸೇರಿದ ಜನರನ್ನು ಬೇರ್ಪಡಿಸುತ್ತಾರೆಂದು ನನ್ನ ಭಾವನೆ.

☐ ಇಲ್ಲವೇ ಇಲ್ಲ ☐ ಅಪರೂಪವಾಗಿ ☐ ಕೆಲವೊಮ್ಮೆ

☐ ಪದೇ ಪದೇ ☐ ಪ್ರತಿಸಾರಿ

೧೭) ನನ್ನ ಕಲಸದ ಸ್ಥಳದಲ್ಲಿ ನಾವು ಒಂದು ಜಾತಿ ಗುಂಪಾಗಿ ಸೇರಿ ಬರುತ್ತೇವೆ.

☐ ಇಲ್ಲವೇ ಇಲ್ಲ ☐ ಅಪರೂಪವಾಗಿ ☐ ಕೆಲವೊಮ್ಮೆ

☐ ಪದೇ ಪದೇ ☐ ಪ್ರತಿಸಾರಿ

೧೮) ನನ್ನ ಮೇಲಾಧಿಕಾರಿಗಳು ನನ್ನೊಡನೆ ಸ್ಪಷ್ಟವಾಗಿ ಚರ್ಚಿಸಿ ಮಾಡಬೇಕಾದ ಕೆಲಸಗಳಿಗೆ ಮಾರ್ಗದರ್ಶನ ನೀಡುತ್ತಾರೆ.

☐ ಇಲ್ಲವೇ ಇಲ್ಲ ☐ ಅಪರೂಪವಾಗಿ ☐ ಕೆಲವೊಮ್ಮೆ

☐ ಪದೇ ಪದೇ ☐ ಪ್ರತಿಸಾರಿ

೧೯) ನನ್ನ ಸಹೋದ್ಯೋಗಿಗಳು ನನಗೆ ಕೊಡಲ್ಪಟ್ಟ ಕಲಸದ ವಿವರಣೆ ಅರ್ಥ ಮಾಡಿಕೊಳ್ಳಲು ಸಹಾಯ ಮಾಡುತ್ತಾರೆ.

☐ ಇಲ್ಲವೇ ಇಲ್ಲ ☐ ಅಪರೂಪವಾಗಿ ☐ ಕೆಲವೊಮ್ಮೆ

☐ ಪದೇ ಪದೇ ☐ ಪ್ರತಿಸಾರಿ

೨೦) ನನ್ನ ಜಾತಿಯ ಗುರುತಿನ ಕಾರಣದಿಂದ ನನ್ನ ಕೆಲಸವನ್ನು ಇಲಾಖೆಯಲ್ಲಿ ಕೀಳಾಗಿ ಭಾವಿಸುತ್ತಾರೆ.

☐ ಇಲ್ಲವೇ ಇಲ್ಲ ☐ ಅಪರೂಪವಾಗಿ ☐ ಕೆಲವೊಮ್ಮೆ

☐ ಪದೇ ಪದೇ ☐ ಪ್ರತಿಸಾರಿ

೨೧) ಇಲಾಖೆಯಲ್ಲಿ ನನ್ನ ಕೆಲಸದ ಸಾಧನೆಗಳನ್ನು ಮೆಚ್ಚಿಕೊಳ್ಳುತ್ತಾರೆ.

☐ ಇಲ್ಲವೇ ಇಲ್ಲ ☐ ಅಪರೂಪವಾಗಿ ☐ ಕೆಲವೊಮ್ಮೆ

☐ ಪದೇ ಪದೇ ☐ ಪ್ರತಿಸಾರಿ

೩೧) ನನ್ನ ಇಲಾಖೆಯಲ್ಲಿ ಬೇರೆ ಜಾತಿಯ ಜನರ ಕೆಲಸದ ಸಾಧನೆಗಳನ್ನು ಹೆಚ್ಚಾಗಿ ಮೆಚ್ಚಿಕೊಳ್ಳುತ್ತಾರೆಂದು ನೆನೆಸುತ್ತೇನೆ .

☐ ಇಲ್ಲವೇ ಇಲ್ಲ ☐ ಅಪರೂಪವಾಗಿ ☐ ಕೆಲವೊಮ್ಮೆ

☐ ಪದೇ ಪದೇ ☐ ಪ್ರತಿಸಾರಿ

೩೨) ನನ್ನ ಮೇಲ್ವಿಚಾರಣೆಯ ಕೆಳಗೆ ಕೆಲಸ ಮಾಡುವ ನೌಕರರು ನನ್ನ ಜಾತಿಯ ಹಿನ್ನಲೆ ಕಾರಣದಿಂದ ನಾನು ಆ ಸ್ಥಾನಕ್ಕೆ

ಸರಿಯಾದವನಲ್ಲವೆಂದು ಭಾವಿಸುತ್ತಾರೆ.

☐ ಇಲ್ಲವೇ ಇಲ್ಲ ☐ ಅಪರೂಪವಾಗಿ ☐ ಕೆಲವೊಮ್ಮೆ

☐ ಪದೇ ಪದೇ ☐ ಪ್ರತಿಸಾರಿ

೩೪) ಇಲಾಖೆಯಲ್ಲಿ ನನ್ನ ಕೆಲಸದ ಸಾಧನೆಗಳ ಕುರಿತಾಗಿ ನಾನು ಹೆಮ್ಮೆಪಡುತ್ತೇನೆ.

☐ ಇಲ್ಲವೇ ಇಲ್ಲ ☐ ಅಪರೂಪವಾಗಿ ☐ ಕೆಲವೊಮ್ಮೆ

☐ ಪದೇ ಪದೇ ☐ ಪ್ರತಿಸಾರಿ

೩೫) ನನ್ನ ಕೆಲಸದ ಸ್ಥಳದಲ್ಲಿ ವಿಮರ್ಶೆಯನ್ನು ಒಳ್ಳೆಯ ಮನಸ್ಸಿನಿಂದ ತೆಗೆದುಕೊಳ್ಳುತ್ತೇನೆ.

☐ ಇಲ್ಲವೇ ಇಲ್ಲ ☐ ಅಪರೂಪವಾಗಿ ☐ ಕೆಲವೊಮ್ಮೆ

☐ ಪದೇ ಪದೇ ☐ ಪ್ರತಿಸಾರಿ

೩೬) ನಾನು ಕೇವಲ ಬೇರೆ ಜಾತಿ ಹಿನ್ನಲೆಯಿಂದ ಬಂದವನೆಂಬ ಕಾರಣದಿಂದ ನನ್ನ ಸಹೋದ್ಯೋಗಿಗಳು ನನ್ನ ಜವಾಬ್ದಾರಿಯಲ್ಲಿ ನಡೆಯದ ತಪ್ಪುಗಳಿಗೆ ನನ್ನನ್ನು ನಿಂದಿಸುತ್ತಾರೆ.

☐ ಇಲ್ಲವೇ ಇಲ್ಲ ☐ ಅಪರೂಪವಾಗಿ ☐ ಕೆಲವೊಮ್ಮೆ

☐ ಪದೇ ಪದೇ ☐ ಪ್ರತಿಸಾರಿ

೩೭) ನನ್ನ ಜವಾಬ್ದಾರಿಯಲ್ಲಿ ನಡೆಯದ ತಪ್ಪುಗಳಿಗೆ ನಾನು ನನ್ನನ್ನೇ ನಿಂದಿಸುತ್ತೇನೆ.

☐ ಇಲ್ಲವೇ ಇಲ್ಲ ☐ ಅಪರೂಪವಾಗಿ ☐ ಕೆಲವೊಮ್ಮೆ

☐ ಪದೇ ಪದೇ ☐ ಪ್ರತಿಸಾರಿ

೩೮) ನನ್ನ ಇಲಾಖೆಯಲ್ಲಿ ಕೆಲಸದ ಪೈಪೋಟಿ ನನಗಿದೆ.

☐ ಇಲ್ಲವೇ ಇಲ್ಲ ☐ ಅಪರೂಪವಾಗಿ ☐ ಕೆಲವೊಮ್ಮೆ

☐ ಪದೇ ಪದೇ ☐ ಪ್ರತಿಸಾರಿ

೩೯) ನನ್ನ ಕೆಲಸದ ಸ್ಥಳದಲ್ಲಿ ಪೈಪೋಟಿಗೆ ಭಯದಿಂದ ವರ್ತಿಸುತ್ತೇನೆ.

☐ ಇಲ್ಲವೇ ಇಲ್ಲ ☐ ಅಪರೂಪವಾಗಿ ☐ ಕೆಲವೊಮ್ಮೆ

☐ ಪದೇ ಪದೇ ☐ ಪ್ರತಿಸಾರಿ

೪೦) ಪೈಪೋಟಿಗಳಿಗೆ ಭಯದಿಂದ ವರ್ತಿಸುವುದು ನನಗೆ ಬಾಲ್ಯದೆಸೆಯಿಂದ ಇದೆ.

☐ ಇಲ್ಲವೇ ಇಲ್ಲ ☐ ಅಪರೂಪವಾಗಿ ☐ ಕೆಲವೊಮ್ಮೆ

☐ ಪದೇ ಪದೇ ☐ ಪ್ರತಿಸಾರಿ

೪೧) ನನ್ನ ಕೆಲಸದ ಸ್ಥಳದಲ್ಲಿ ನಾನು ಜನರನ್ನು ಸಂಧಿಸದೆ ತಪ್ಪಿಸಿಕೊಳ್ಳುತ್ತೇನೆ.

☐ ಇಲ್ಲವೇ ಇಲ್ಲ ☐ ಅಪರೂಪವಾಗಿ ☐ ಕೆಲವೊಮ್ಮೆ

☐ ಪದೇ ಪದೇ ☐ ಪ್ರತಿಸಾರಿ

೪೨) ನನ್ನ ಕೆಲಸದ ಸ್ಥಳದಲ್ಲಿ ಸಾಮಾಜಿಕ ಗುಂಪುಗಳಿಂದ ತಪ್ಪಿಸಿಕೊಳ್ಳಲು ನಾನು ಪ್ರಯತ್ನಿಸುತ್ತೇನೆ.

☐ ಇಲ್ಲವೇ ಇಲ್ಲ ☐ ಅಪರೂಪವಾಗಿ ☐ ಕೆಲವೊಮ್ಮೆ

☐ ಪದೇ ಪದೇ ☐ ಪ್ರತಿಸಾರಿ

೪೩) ನಾನು ಬೇರೆ ಜಾತಿ ಹಿನ್ನೆಲೆಯಿಂದ ಬಂದವನಾದರೂ ನನ್ನ ಕೈಕೆಳಗಿನವರು ನಾನು ಹೇಳಿದ್ದನ್ನು ಕೇಳುತ್ತಾರೆ.

☐ ಇಲ್ಲವೇ ಇಲ್ಲ ☐ ಅಪರೂಪವಾಗಿ ☐ ಕೆಲವೊಮ್ಮೆ

☐ ಪದೇ ಪದೇ ☐ ಪ್ರತಿಸಾರಿ

೪೪) ಇಲಾಖೆಯಲ್ಲಿ ಚರ್ಚೆಗಳನ್ನು ನಾನು ಆರಂಭಿಸುತ್ತೇನೆ.

☐ ಇಲ್ಲವೇ ಇಲ್ಲ ☐ ಅಪರೂಪವಾಗಿ ☐ ಕೆಲವೊಮ್ಮೆ

☐ ಪದೇ ಪದೇ ☐ ಪ್ರತಿಸಾರಿ

೪೫) ಇಲಾಖೆಯಲ್ಲಿ ಚರ್ಚೆಗಳನ್ನು ಆರಂಭಿಸಲು ನಾನು ಅರ್ಹನಲ್ಲ ಎಂದು ಭಾವಿಸುತ್ತೇನೆ.

☐ ಇಲ್ಲವೇ ಇಲ್ಲ ☐ ಅಪರೂಪವಾಗಿ ☐ ಕೆಲವೊಮ್ಮೆ

☐ ಪದೇ ಪದೇ ☐ ಪ್ರತಿಸಾರಿ

೪೬) ನನ್ನ ಜಾತಿ ಹಿನ್ನೆಲೆ ಕಾರಣದಿಂದ ಇಲಾಖೆಯಲ್ಲಿ ಚರ್ಚೆಗಳನ್ನು ಆರಂಭಿಸಲು ನನಗೆ ನಾಚಿಕೆ ಆಗುತ್ತದೆ.

☐ ಇಲ್ಲವೇ ಇಲ್ಲ ☐ ಅಪರೂಪವಾಗಿ ☐ ಕೆಲವೊಮ್ಮೆ

☐ ಪದೇ ಪದೇ ☐ ಪ್ರತಿಸಾರಿ

೪೭) ನನ್ನ ಇಲಾಖೆಯಲ್ಲಿ ಸ್ವಂತ ಭಾವನೆಯನ್ನು ಹೇಳಲು ನನಗೆ ಸ್ವಾತಂತ್ರ್ಯವಿದೆ.

☐ ಇಲ್ಲವೇ ಇಲ್ಲ ☐ ಅಪರೂಪವಾಗಿ ☐ ಕೆಲವೊಮ್ಮೆ

☐ ಪದೇ ಪದೇ ☐ ಪ್ರತಿಸಾರಿ

೪೮) ನನ್ನ ಜಾತಿ ಹಿನ್ನಲೆ ಕಾರಣದಿಂದ ನನ್ನ ಇಲಾಖೆಯಲ್ಲಿ ಸ್ನೇಹ ಸಂಬಂಧಗಳನ್ನು ಕಳಕೊಳ್ಳುತ್ತೇನೆ.

☐ ಇಲ್ಲವೇ ಇಲ್ಲ ☐ ಅಪರೂಪವಾಗಿ ☐ ಕೆಲವೊಮ್ಮೆ

☐ ಪದೇ ಪದೇ ☐ ಪ್ರತಿಸಾರಿ

೪೯) ನಾನು ಬೇರೆ ಜಾತಿ ಹಿನ್ನೆಲೆಯಿಂದ ಬಂದವನಾದರು ಬೇರೆ ಜಾತಿ ಜನರು ನನ್ನ ಸ್ನೇಹವನ್ನು ಇಷ್ಟಪಡುತ್ತಾರೆ.

☐ ಇಲ್ಲವೇ ಇಲ್ಲ ☐ ಅಪರೂಪವಾಗಿ ☐ ಕೆಲವೊಮ್ಮೆ

☐ ಪದೇ ಪದೇ ☐ ಪ್ರತಿಸಾರಿ

೫೦) ಇಲಾಖೆಯಲ್ಲಿ ನನ್ನ ಸಹೋದ್ಯೋಗಿಗಳೊಡನೆ ತಮಾಷೆ ಮಾಡಲು ಸಂತೋಷಪಡುತ್ತೇನೆ.

☐ ಇಲ್ಲವೇ ಇಲ್ಲ ☐ ಅಪರೂಪವಾಗಿ ☐ ಕೆಲವೊಮ್ಮೆ

☐ ಪದೇ ಪದೇ ☐ ಪ್ರತಿಸಾರಿ

೫೧) ನನ್ನ ಕೆಲಸದ ಸ್ಥಳದಲ್ಲಿ ಇತರೆ ಜಾತಿ ಗುಂಪುಗಳಲ್ಲಿ ಚೆನ್ನಾಗಿ ಹೊಂದಿಕೊಳ್ಳುತ್ತೇನೆ.

☐ ಇಲ್ಲವೇ ಇಲ್ಲ ☐ ಅಪರೂಪವಾಗಿ ☐ ಕೆಲವೊಮ್ಮೆ

☐ ಪದೇ ಪದೇ ☐ ಪ್ರತಿಸಾರಿ

೫೨) ನನ್ನ ಕೆಲಸದ ಸ್ಥಳದಲ್ಲಿ ನನ್ನ ಸಹೋದ್ಯೋಗಿಗಳು ನನಗೆ ಮಾಡುವ ಉಪಕಾರಗಳ ಬಗ್ಗೆ ನಾನು ಸಂದೇಹಪಡುತ್ತೇನೆ.

☐ ಇಲ್ಲವೇ ಇಲ್ಲ ☐ ಅಪರೂಪವಾಗಿ ☐ ಕೆಲವೊಮ್ಮೆ

☐ ಪದೇ ಪದೇ ☐ ಪ್ರತಿಸಾರಿ

೫೩) ಇಂತಹ ಸಂದೇಹ ಸ್ವಭಾವ ಬಾಲ್ಯದೆಸೆಯಿಂದ ನನ್ನಲ್ಲಿದೆ.

☐ ಇಲ್ಲವೇ ಇಲ್ಲ ☐ ಅಪರೂಪವಾಗಿ ☐ ಕೆಲವೊಮ್ಮೆ

☐ ಪದೇ ಪದೇ ☐ ಪ್ರತಿಸಾರಿ

೫೪) ನಾನು ಬೇರೆ ಜಾತಿ ಹಿನ್ನೆಲೆಯಿಂದ ಬಂದವನಾದರೂ ನನ್ನ ಸಹೋದ್ಯೋಗಿಗಳು ನನ್ನನ್ನು ಅವರ ಮನೆಗಳಿಗೆ ಆಹ್ವಾನಿಸುತ್ತಾರೆ.

☐ ಇಲ್ಲವೇ ಇಲ್ಲ ☐ ಅಪರೂಪವಾಗಿ ☐ ಕೆಲವೊಮ್ಮೆ

☐ ಪದೇ ಪದೇ ☐ ಪ್ರತಿಸಾರಿ

೫೫) ನಾನು ಬೇರೆ ಜಾತಿ ಹಿನ್ನೆಲೆಯಿಂದ ಬಂದವನಾದರೂ ನನ್ನ ಸಹೋದ್ಯೋಗಿಗಳು ನನ್ನ ಮನೆಗೆ ಬರುತ್ತಾರೆ.

☐ ಇಲ್ಲವೇ ಇಲ್ಲ ☐ ಅಪರೂಪವಾಗಿ ☐ ಕೆಲವೊಮ್ಮೆ

☐ ಪದೇ ಪದೇ ☐ ಪ್ರತಿಸಾರಿ

೫೬) ನಾನು ಬೇರೆ ಜಾತಿ ಹಿನ್ನೆಲೆಯಿಂದ ಬಂದವನಾದರೂ ನನ್ನ ಕೈಕೆಳಗಿರುವ ಇತರೆ ಜಾತಿಯವರು ನನ್ನ ಆಹ್ವಾನವನ್ನು ಸ್ವೀಕರಿಸಿ ನನ್ನ ಕುಟುಂಬ ಕಾರ್ಯಗಳಲ್ಲಿ ಭಾಗವಹಿಸುತ್ತಾರೆ.

☐ ಇಲ್ಲವೇ ಇಲ್ಲ ☐ ಅಪರೂಪವಾಗಿ ☐ ಕೆಲವೊಮ್ಮೆ

☐ ಪದೇ ಪದೇ ☐ ಪ್ರತಿಸಾರಿ

೫೭) ನಾನು ಬೇರೆ ಜಾತಿ ಹಿನ್ನೆಲೆಯಿಂದ ಬಂದವನಾದರೂ ಇತರೆ ಜಾತಿಗಳಿಗೆ ಸೇರಿದ ನನ್ನ ಮೇಲ್ವಿಚಾರಕರು ಅವರ ಕುಟುಂಬ ಕಾರ್ಯಗಳಲ್ಲಿ ಭಾಗವಹಿಸಲು ನನ್ನನ್ನು ಆಹ್ವಾನಿಸುತ್ತಾರೆ.

☐ ಇಲ್ಲವೇ ಇಲ್ಲ ☐ ಅಪರೂಪವಾಗಿ ☐ ಕೆಲವೊಮ್ಮೆ

☐ ಪದೇ ಪದೇ ☐ ಪ್ರತಿಸಾರಿ

೫೮) ನಾನುಬೇರೆ ಜಾತಿ ಹಿನ್ನೆಲೆಯಿಂದ ಬಂದವನಾದರೂ ಇತರೆ ಜಾತಿಗೆ ಸೇರಿದ ನನ್ನ ಸಹೋದ್ಯೋಗಿಗಳು ಅವರ ಕುಟುಂಬ ಕಾರ್ಯಗಳಲ್ಲಿ ಭಾಗವಹಿಸಲು ನನ್ನನ್ನು ಆಹ್ವಾನಿಸುತ್ತಾರೆ.

☐ ಇಲ್ಲವೇ ಇಲ್ಲ ☐ ಅಪರೂಪವಾಗಿ ☐ ಕೆಲವೊಮ್ಮೆ

☐ ಪದೇ ಪದೇ ☐ ಪ್ರತಿಸಾರಿ

೫೯) ನಾನು ನನ್ನ ಇಲಾಖೆಯಲ್ಲಿ ಉನ್ನತ ಅಧಿಕಾರಿಯಾಗಿದ್ದರೂ ನನ್ನ ಕೈಕೆಳಗೆ ಇರುವವರ ಕುಟುಂಬ ಕಾರ್ಯಗಳಲ್ಲಿ ಭಾಗವಹಿಸಲು ಅರ್ಹನಲ್ಲ ಎಂದು ನನಗೆ ಅನಿಸುತ್ತದೆ.

☐ ಇಲ್ಲವೇ ಇಲ್ಲ ☐ ಅಪರೂಪವಾಗಿ ☐ ಕೆಲವೊಮ್ಮೆ

☐ ಪದೇ ಪದೇ ☐ ಪ್ರತಿಸಾರಿ

೬೦) ನಾನು ಬೇರೆ ಜಾತಿ ಹಿನ್ನೆಲೆಯಿಂದ ಬಂದಿದ್ದರಿಂದ ಇತರೆ ಜಾತಿ ಹಿನ್ನೆಲೆ ಸ್ನೇಹಿತರ ಕುಟುಂಬ ಕಾರ್ಯಗಳಲ್ಲಿ ಭಾಗವಹಿಸಲು ನಾನು ಅರ್ಹನಲ್ಲ ಎಂದು ಭಾವಿಸುತ್ತೇನೆ.

☐ ಇಲ್ಲವೇ ಇಲ್ಲ ☐ ಅಪರೂಪವಾಗಿ ☐ ಕೆಲವೊಮ್ಮೆ

☐ ಪದೇ ಪದೇ ☐ ಪ್ರತಿಸಾರಿ

೬೧) ಕುಟುಂಬಕಾರ್ಯಗಳಿಗೆ ಬರುವಾಗ ಜಾತಿ ಮುಖ್ಯ ಪಾತ್ರ ವಹಿಸುತ್ತದೆ.

☐ ಇಲ್ಲವೇ ಇಲ್ಲ ☐ ಅಪರೂಪವಾಗಿ ☐ ಕೆಲವೊಮ್ಮೆ

☐ ಪದೇ ಪದೇ ☐ ಪ್ರತಿಸಾರಿ

೬೨) ನಾನು ಬೇರೆ ಜಾತಿ ಹಿನ್ನೆಲೆಯಿಂದ ಬಂದವನಾದರೂ ಇತರ ಜಾತಿಗೆ ಸೇರಿದ ನನ್ನ ಸಹೋದ್ಯೋಗಿಗಳು ನನ್ನ ಕುಟುಂಬದವರೊಂದಿಗೆ ತಿನ್ನುತ್ತಾರೆ.

☐ ಇಲ್ಲವೇ ಇಲ್ಲ ☐ ಅಪರೂಪವಾಗಿ ☐ ಕೆಲವೊಮ್ಮೆ

☐ ಪದೇ ಪದೇ ☐ ಪ್ರತಿಸಾರಿ

೬೩) ಇತರೆ ಜಾತಿಗೆ ಸೇರಿದ ನನ್ನ ಸ್ನೇಹಿತರು ಅಥವಾ ಸಹೋದ್ಯೋಗಿಗಳ ಕುಟುಂಬಗಳ ಮನೆಗಳಿಗೆ ನಾನು ಕುಟುಂಬ ಸಮೇತವಾಗಿ ಹೋಗುತ್ತೇನೆ.

☐ ಇಲ್ಲವೇ ಇಲ್ಲ ☐ ಅಪರೂಪವಾಗಿ ☐ ಕೆಲವೊಮ್ಮೆ

☐ ಪದೇ ಪದೇ ☐ ಪ್ರತಿಸಾರಿ

೬೪) ಇತರೆ ಜಾತಿಗಳಿಗೆ ಸೇರಿದ ನನ್ನ ಸ್ನೇಹಿತರು ಅಥವಾ ಸಹೋದ್ಯೋಗಿಗಳ ಮನೆಯನ್ನು ಭೇಟಿ ಮಾಡುವಾಗ ನನ್ನ ಕುಟುಂಬ ಸದಸ್ಯರು ಆರಾಮವಾಗಿರುತ್ತಾರೆ.

☐ ಇಲ್ಲವೇ ಇಲ್ಲ ☐ ಅಪರೂಪವಾಗಿ ☐ ಕೆಲವೊಮ್ಮೆ

☐ ಪದೇ ಪದೇ ☐ ಪ್ರತಿಸಾರಿ

೬೫) ನನ್ನಸಹೋದ್ಯೋಗಿಗಳುಅವರಕುಟುಂಬಸಮೇತರಾಗಿನನ್ನಮನೆಯನ್ನು ಭೇಟಿ ಮಾಡುವಾಗ ನನ್ನ ಕುಟುಂಬ ಸದಸ್ಯರು ಆರಾಮವಾಗಿರುತ್ತಾರೆ.

☐ ಇಲ್ಲವೇ ಇಲ್ಲ ☐ ಅಪರೂಪವಾಗಿ ☐ ಕೆಲವೊಮ್ಮೆ

☐ ಪದೇ ಪದೇ ☐ ಪ್ರತಿಸಾರಿ

೬೬) ಇತರೆ ಜಾತಿಗಳಿಗೆ ಸೇರಿದ ಜನರು ಕ್ಯಾಂಟೀನ್ ನಲ್ಲಿ ಅಥವಾ ಬೇರೆ ತಿನ್ನುವ ಸ್ಥಳಗಳಲ್ಲಿ ನನ್ನೊಟ್ಟಿಗೆ ಕುಳಿತು ತಿನ್ನುತ್ತಾರೆ.

☐ ಇಲ್ಲವೇ ಇಲ್ಲ ☐ ಅಪರೂಪವಾಗಿ ☐ ಕೆಲವೊಮ್ಮೆ

☐ ಪದೇ ಪದೇ ☐ ಪ್ರತಿಸಾರಿ

೬೭) ನನಗೆ ತಿನ್ನುವ ಒಳ್ಳೆಯ ಅಭ್ಯಾಸಗಳು ಇಲ್ಲದ ಕಾರಣದಿಂದ ನಾನು ಇತರರ ಒಟ್ಟಿಗೆ ತಿನ್ನಲು ನೆಮ್ಮದಿಯಾಗಿರಲ್ಲ.

☐ ಇಲ್ಲವೇ ಇಲ್ಲ ☐ ಅಪರೂಪವಾಗಿ ☐ ಕೆಲವೊಮ್ಮೆ

☐ ಪದೇ ಪದೇ ☐ ಪ್ರತಿಸಾರಿ

೬೮) ನಾನು ಕ್ಯಾಂಟೀನ್ ನಲ್ಲಿ ಅಥವಾ ಬೇರೆ ತಿನ್ನುವ ಸ್ಥಳಗಳಲ್ಲಿ ನನ್ನ ಸ್ವಂತ ಜಾತಿ ಜನರ ಜೊತೆಯಲ್ಲಿ ಕುಳಿತು ತಿನ್ನುತ್ತೇನೆ.

☐ ಇಲ್ಲವೇ ಇಲ್ಲ ☐ ಅಪರೂಪವಾಗಿ ☐ ಕೆಲವೊಮ್ಮೆ

☐ ಪದೇ ಪದೇ ☐ ಪ್ರತಿಸಾರಿ

೭೦) ನನ್ನ ಕೆಲಸದ ಸ್ಥಳದಲ್ಲಿ ಇತರೆ ಜಾತಿ ಜನರೊಟ್ಟಿಗೆ ತಿನ್ನಲು ಸೇರುವಾಗ ಅವರು ಅವರ ಸ್ಥಳಗಳನ್ನು ಬದಲಾವಣೆ ಮಾಡುತ್ತಾರೆ.

☐ ಇಲ್ಲವೇ ಇಲ್ಲ ☐ ಅಪರೂಪವಾಗಿ ☐ ಕೆಲವೊಮ್ಮೆ

☐ ಪದೇ ಪದೇ ☐ ಪ್ರತಿಸಾರಿ

೭೧) ಇತರೆ ಜಾತಿ ಜನರು ನನ್ನೊಟ್ಟಿಗೆ ಕುಳಿತು ತಿನ್ನುವಾಗ ನಾನು ನಿಶಬ್ಧವಾಗಿರುತ್ತೇನೆ.

☐ ಇಲ್ಲವೇ ಇಲ್ಲ ☐ ಅಪರೂಪವಾಗಿ ☐ ಕೆಲವೊಮ್ಮೆ

☐ ಪದೇ ಪದೇ ☐ ಪ್ರತಿಸಾರಿ

೭೨)ನಾನು ಕ್ಯಾಂಟೀನ್ ನಲ್ಲಿ ಅಥವಾ ಬೇರೆ ತಿನ್ನುವ ಸ್ಥಳಗಳಲ್ಲಿ ಇತರೆ ಜಾತಿ ಹಿನ್ನೆಲೆ ಹೊಂದಿರುವ ಜನರ ಜೊತೆ ಚೆನ್ನಾಗಿ ಹೊಂದಿಕೊಳ್ಳುತ್ತೇನೆ.

☐ ಇಲ್ಲವೇ ಇಲ್ಲ ☐ ಅಪರೂಪವಾಗಿ ☐ ಕೆಲವೊಮ್ಮೆ

☐ ಪದೇ ಪದೇ ☐ ಪ್ರತಿಸಾರಿ

೭೩) ನಾನು ಬೇರೆ ಜಾತಿ ಹಿನ್ನೆಲೆಯಿಂದ ಬಂದವನಾದರೂ ನಾನು ಮನೆಯಿಂದ ತಂದ ಆಹಾರವನ್ನು ನನ್ನ ಸಹೋದ್ಯೋಗಿಗಳು ಹಂಚಿಕೊಳ್ಳುತ್ತಾರೆ.

☐ ಇಲ್ಲವೇ ಇಲ್ಲ ☐ ಅಪರೂಪವಾಗಿ ☐ ಕೆಲವೊಮ್ಮೆ

☐ ಪದೇ ಪದೇ ☐ ಪ್ರತಿಸಾರಿ

೭೪) ಇಲಾಖೆಯಲ್ಲಿ ನಾನು ಇತರರೊಟ್ಟಿಗೆ ತಿನ್ನುವಾಗ ನನ್ನ ಊಟವನ್ನು ಹಂಚಿಕೊಳ್ಳಲು ಇಷ್ಟಪಡುತ್ತೇನೆ.

☐ ಇಲ್ಲವೇ ಇಲ್ಲ ☐ ಅಪರೂಪವಾಗಿ ☐ ಕೆಲವೊಮ್ಮೆ

☐ ಪದೇ ಪದೇ ☐ ಪ್ರತಿಸಾರಿ

೭೫) ಇತರರು ಅವರ ಮನೆಯಿಂದ ತರುವ ಊಟವನ್ನು ಹಂಚಿಕೊಳ್ಳಲು ನಾನು ಇಷ್ಟಪಡುತ್ತೇನೆ.

☐ ಇಲ್ಲವೇ ಇಲ್ಲ ☐ ಅಪರೂಪವಾಗಿ ☐ ಕೆಲವೊಮ್ಮೆ

☐ ಪದೇ ಪದೇ ☐ ಪ್ರತಿಸಾರಿ

ಭಾಗ ಮೂರು

ರೋಷನ್ ಬರ್ಗ್ ಸೆಲ್ಫ್ ಎಸ್ಟೀಮ್ ಸ್ಕೇಲ್

ಈ ಕೆಳಗಿರುವ ಹೇಳಿಕೆಗಳಲ್ಲಿ ನಿಮ್ಮ ಆಯ್ಕೆ ಅಥವಾ ಉತ್ತರವನ್ನು ಸರಿಯಾದ ಪೆಟ್ಟಿಗೆಯಲ್ಲಿ ಚುಕ್ಕೆ ಗುರುತು ಹಾಕಿ ಸೂಚಿಸಿ.

ಅಂಶ ಒಂದು : ೧

ಅ) ಇತರರಿಗೆ ಸಮಾನವಾಗಿ ಸ್ವಲ್ಪವಾದರೂ ನಾನು ಬೆಲೆಯುಳ್ಳ ವ್ಯಕ್ತಿಯಾಗಿದ್ದೇನೆ ಎಂದು ನನ್ನ ಭಾವನೆ.

☐ ಖಚಿತವಾಗಿ ಒಪ್ಪಿಕೊಳ್ಳುತ್ತೇನೆ ☐ ಒಪ್ಪಿಕೊಳ್ಳುತ್ತೇನೆ

☐ ಒಪ್ಪಿಕೊಳ್ಳುಮದಿಲ್ಲ ☐ ಖಚಿತವಾಗಿ ಒಪ್ಪಿಕೊಳ್ಳುಮದಿಲ್ಲ

ಆ) ನನ್ನಲ್ಲಿ ಹೆಚ್ಚು ಒಳ್ಳೆಯ ಗುಣಗಳಿವೆ ಎಂದು ನನ್ನ ಭಾವನೆ.

☐ ಖಚಿತವಾಗಿ ಒಪ್ಪಿಕೊಳ್ಳುತ್ತೇನೆ ☐ ಒಪ್ಪಿಕೊಳ್ಳುತ್ತೇನೆ

☐ ಒಪ್ಪಿಕೊಳ್ಳುಮದಿಲ್ಲ ☐ ಖಚಿತವಾಗಿ ಒಪ್ಪಿಕೊಳ್ಳುಮದಿಲ್ಲ

ಇ) ಎಲ್ಲದರಲ್ಲಿ ನಾನು ಸೋತಿದ್ದೇನೆ ಎಂಬುವ ಭಾವನೆಗೆ ನನ್ನ ಮನಸ್ಸು ಬಗ್ಗಿದೆ.

☐ ಖಚಿತವಾಗಿ ಒಪ್ಪಿಕೊಳ್ಳುತ್ತೇನೆ ☐ ಒಪ್ಪಿಕೊಳ್ಳುತ್ತೇನೆ

☐ ಒಪ್ಪಿಕೊಳ್ಳುಮದಿಲ್ಲ ☐ ಖಚಿತವಾಗಿ ಒಪ್ಪಿಕೊಳ್ಳುಮದಿಲ್ಲ

ಅಂಶ ೨:

ಅ) ಇತರೆ ಜನರ ಹಾಗೆ ನಾನು ಬಹಳ ಕಾರ್ಯಗಳನ್ನು ಮಾಡಬಲ್ಲೆ.

☐ ಖಚಿತವಾಗಿ ಒಪ್ಪಿಕೊಳ್ಳುತ್ತೇನೆ ☐ ಒಪ್ಪಿಕೊಳ್ಳುತ್ತೇನೆ

☐ ಒಪ್ಪಿಕೊಳ್ಳುಮದಿಲ್ಲ ☐ ಖಚಿತವಾಗಿ ಒಪ್ಪಿಕೊಳ್ಳುಮದಿಲ್ಲ

ಆ) ನನ್ನ ಹತ್ತಿರ ಹೆಮ್ಮೆ ಪಡುವಂತಹುದು ಹೆಚ್ಚಾಗಿಲ್ಲ ಎಂದು ನನ್ನ ಭಾವನೆ.

☐ ಖಚಿತವಾಗಿ ಒಪ್ಪಿಕೊಳ್ಳುತ್ತೇನೆ ☐ ಒಪ್ಪಿಕೊಳ್ಳುತ್ತೇನೆ

☐ ಒಪ್ಪಿಕೊಳ್ಳುಮದಿಲ್ಲ ☐ ಖಚಿತವಾಗಿ ಒಪ್ಪಿಕೊಳ್ಳುಮದಿಲ್ಲ

ಅಂಶ ೩:

ಅ) ನನ್ನೊಂದಿಗೆ ನಾನು ಆತ್ಮವಿಶ್ವಾಸಮುಳ್ಳವನಾಗಿ ವರ್ತಿಸುತ್ತೇನೆ.

☐ ಖಚಿತವಾಗಿ ಒಪ್ಪಿಕೊಳ್ಳುತ್ತೇನೆ ☐ ಒಪ್ಪಿಕೊಳ್ಳುತ್ತೇನೆ

☐ ಒಪ್ಪಿಕೊಳ್ಳುಮದಿಲ್ಲ ☐ ಖಚಿತವಾಗಿ ಒಪ್ಪಿಕೊಳ್ಳುಮದಿಲ್ಲ

ಅಂಶ ೪:

ಅ) ಒಟ್ಟಿನಲ್ಲಿ ನನ್ನಲ್ಲಿ ನಾನು ತೃಪ್ತಿಯಾಗಿದ್ದೇನೆ.

☐ ಖಚಿತವಾಗಿ ಒಪ್ಪಿಕೊಳ್ಳುತ್ತೇನೆ ☐ ಒಪ್ಪಿಕೊಳ್ಳುತ್ತೇನೆ

☐ ಒಪ್ಪಿಕೊಳ್ಳುಮದಿಲ್ಲ ☐ ಖಚಿತವಾಗಿ ಒಪ್ಪಿಕೊಳ್ಳುಮದಿಲ್ಲ

ಅಂಶ ೫:

ಅ) ನನಗೆ ನಾನು ಹೆಚ್ಚಿನ ಗೌರವ ಕೊಡಬೇಕೆಂದು ಆಶಿಸುತ್ತೇನೆ.

☐ ಖಚಿತವಾಗಿ ಒಪ್ಪಿಕೊಳ್ಳುತ್ತೇನೆ ☐ ಒಪ್ಪಿಕೊಳ್ಳುತ್ತೇನೆ

☐ ಒಪ್ಪಿಕೊಳ್ಳುಮದಿಲ್ಲ ☐ ಖಚಿತವಾಗಿ ಒಪ್ಪಿಕೊಳ್ಳುಮದಿಲ್ಲ

ಅಂಶ ೬:

ಅ) ನಾನು ಖಂಡಿತವಾಗಿ ಪ್ರಯೋಜನವಿಲ್ಲದವನು ಎಂದು ಕೆಲಮ ಸಾರಿ ಭಾವಿಸುತ್ತೇನೆ

☐ ಖಚಿತವಾಗಿ ಒಪ್ಪಿಕೊಳ್ಳುತ್ತೇನೆ ☐ ಒಪ್ಪಿಕೊಳ್ಳುತ್ತೇನೆ

☐ ಒಪ್ಪಿಕೊಳ್ಳುಮದಿಲ್ಲ ☐ ಖಚಿತವಾಗಿ ಒಪ್ಪಿಕೊಳ್ಳುಮದಿಲ್ಲ

ಆ) ನಾನು ಒಳ್ಳೆಯವನಲ್ಲ ಎಂದು ಕೆಲವೊಂದು ಸಾರಿ ಯೋಚಿಸುತ್ತೇನೆ.

☐ ಖಚಿತವಾಗಿ ಒಪ್ಪಿಕೊಳ್ಳುತ್ತೇನೆ ☐ ಒಪ್ಪಿಕೊಳ್ಳುತ್ತೇನೆ

☐ ಒಪ್ಪಿಕೊಳ್ಳುಮದಿಲ್ಲ ☐ ಖಚಿತವಾಗಿ ಒಪ್ಪಿಕೊಳ್ಳುಮದಿಲ್ಲ

ಭಾಗ : ನಾಲ್ಕು ಸೆಲ್ಫ್ ಎಸ್ಟೀಮ್-ಇನ್ವೆಂಟರಿ

ಈ ಕೆಳಗೆರುವ ಹೇಳಿಕೆಗಳಲ್ಲಿ ನಿಮ್ಮ ಜೀವನದಲ್ಲಿನ ನಡತೆಗಳು ನಿಜವಾಗಿ ಎಷ್ಟರ ಮಟ್ಟಿಗೆ ಕಾಣಿಸುಮದೋ ಈ ಪೆಟ್ಟಿಗೆಯಲ್ಲಿ ನಿಮ್ಮ ಆಯ್ಕೆ ಅಥವಾ ಉತ್ತರವನ್ನು ಚುಕ್ಕೆ ಗುರುತು ಹಾಕಿ ಸೂಚಿಸಿರಿ.

೧) ನಾನು ಇತರರ ಸಮ್ಮತಿ ಮತ್ತು ಧೃಢ ವಚನ ಹುಡುಕುತ್ತೇನೆ ಮತ್ತು ವಿಮರ್ಶೆಗೆ ಭಯಪಡುತ್ತೇನೆ.

☐ ಇಲ್ಲವೇ ಇಲ್ಲ ☐ ಅಪರೂಪವಾಗಿ ☐ ಕೆಲವೊಮ್ಮೆ

☐ ಪದೇ ಪದೇ ☐ ಪ್ರತಿಸಾರಿ

೧) ನಾನು ಯಾವುದೂ ಸಾಧಾರಣವಾದ ನಡತೆ ಎಂದು ಊಹಿಸಿ ನಾನು ಯಾವಾಗಲೂ ಬೇರೆ ಜನಕ್ಕಿಂತ ವ್ಯತ್ಯಾಸವಾಗಿರುತ್ತೇನೆಂದು ನನ್ನ ಭಾವನೆ.

☐ ಇಲ್ಲವೇ ಇಲ್ಲ ☐ ಅಪರೂಪವಾಗಿ ☐ ಕೆಲವೊಮ್ಮೆ

☐ ಪದೇ ಪದೇ ☐ ಪ್ರತಿಸಾರಿ

೨) ನಾನು ಅಧಿಕಾರದಲ್ಲಿರುವ ಜನರಿಗೆ ಭಯಪಡುವೆನು ಮತ್ತು ಅವರಿಂದ ನನ್ನನ್ನು ನಾನು ದೂರ ಮಾಡಿಕೊಳ್ಳುವೆನು.

☐ ಇಲ್ಲವೇ ಇಲ್ಲ ☐ ಅಪರೂಪವಾಗಿ ☐ ಕೆಲವೊಮ್ಮೆ

☐ ಪದೇ ಪದೇ ☐ ಪ್ರತಿಸಾರಿ

೩) ನಾನು ನನ್ನ ಒಳ್ಳೆಯ ಕಾರ್ಯಗಳನ್ನು ಮತ್ತು ಸಾಧನೆಗಳನ್ನು ಮೆಚ್ಚಿಕೊಳ್ಳುವುದಿಲ್ಲ.

☐ ಇಲ್ಲವೇ ಇಲ್ಲ ☐ ಅಪರೂಪವಾಗಿ ☐ ಕೆಲವೊಮ್ಮೆ

☐ ಪದೇ ಪದೇ ☐ ಪ್ರತಿಸಾರಿ

೪) ಒಂದು ಯೋಜನೆಯನ್ನು ಮೊದಲಿನಿಂದ ಕೊನೆಯ ತನಕ ಹಿಂಬಾಲಿಸಲು ನನಗೆ ಕಷ್ಟವಾಗಿರುತ್ತದೆ.

☐ ಇಲ್ಲವೇ ಇಲ್ಲ ☐ ಅಪರೂಪವಾಗಿ ☐ ಕೆಲವೊಮ್ಮೆ

☐ ಪದೇ ಪದೇ ☐ ಪ್ರತಿಸಾರಿ

೫) ನಾನು ಕೋಪಗೊಂಡಿರುವ ವ್ಯಕ್ತಿಯ ಜೊತೆಯಲ್ಲಿರುವಾಗ ನನಗೆ ಭಯವಾಗುತ್ತದೆ ಅಥವಾ ಒತ್ತಡಕ್ಕೆ ಗುರಿಯಾಗುತ್ತೇನೆ.

☐ ಇಲ್ಲವೇ ಇಲ್ಲ ☐ ಅಪರೂಪವಾಗಿ ☐ ಕೆಲವೊಮ್ಮೆ

☐ ಪದೇ ಪದೇ ☐ ಪ್ರತಿಸಾರಿ

೬) ಒಂದು ಹೋರಾಟವನ್ನು ತಪ್ಪಿಸಲು ನನಗೆ ಸತ್ಯಹೇಳುವುದಕ್ಕಿಂತ ಸುಳ್ಳು ಹೇಳುವುದೇ ಸುಲಭವಾಗಿರುತ್ತದೆ.

☐ ಇಲ್ಲವೇ ಇಲ್ಲ ☐ ಅಪರೂಪವಾಗಿ ☐ ಕೆಲವೊಮ್ಮೆ

☐ ಪದೇ ಪದೇ ☐ ಪ್ರತಿಸಾರಿ

೭) ನನ್ನ ಸ್ವಂತ ನಿರ್ಭಂಧಪಡಿಸುವ ನಡತೆಯಿಂದ ನನಗೆ ಸಮಸ್ಯೆಯಿದೆ. ಉದಾ: ಕುಡಿಯುವುದು, ಔಷಧ ದುರುಪಯೋಗ, ಜೂಜು , ಹೆಚ್ಚಾಗಿ ತಿನ್ನುವುದು , ಧೂಮಪಾನ ,

ಲೈಂಗಿಕ ಉಪಯೋಗ, ವ್ಯಾಪಾರ, ಇತರೆ.......

☐ ಇಲ್ಲವೇ ಇಲ್ಲ ☐ ಅಪರೂಪವಾಗಿ ☐ ಕೆಲವೊಮ್ಮೆ

☐ ಪದೇ ಪದೇ ☐ ಪ್ರತಿಸಾರಿ

೯) ನಾನು ನನ್ನ ಮೇಲೆ ಕರುಣೆ ಇಲ್ಲದೆ ತೀರ್ಪು ಕೊಡುತ್ತೇನೆ. ನಾನೇ ನನ್ನ ನೀಚ ವಿಮರ್ಶಕ ನಾನು ಇತರರಿಗಿಂತ ನನ್ನ ಮೇಲೆ ಕಠಿಣವಾಗಿರುತ್ತೇನೆ.

☐ ಇಲ್ಲವೇ ಇಲ್ಲ ☐ ಅಪರೂಪವಾಗಿ ☐ ಕೆಲವೊಮ್ಮೆ

☐ ಪದೇ ಪದೇ ☐ ಪ್ರತಿಸಾರಿ

೧೦) ಕಷ್ಟಗಳಲ್ಲಿ ನಾನು ಚುರುಕಾಗಿರುತ್ತೇನೆ ಎಂಬುವ ಭಾವನೆ ನನ್ನಲ್ಲಿರುತ್ತೆ, ಮತ್ತು ಜೀವನ ಸುಲಭವಾಗಿ ಹೋಗುವಾಗ ನನಗೆ ಹಾಯಾಗಿರುವುದಿಲ್ಲ ನನಗೆ ಯಾವಾಗಲು ಕಷ್ಟಗಳೇ ಬರುವುದು.

☐ ಇಲ್ಲವೇ ಇಲ್ಲ ☐ ಅಪರೂಪವಾಗಿ ☐ ಕೆಲವೊಮ್ಮೆ

☐ ಪದೇ ಪದೇ ☐ ಪ್ರತಿಸಾರಿ

೧೧) ತಮಾಷೆ ಮಾಡಲು ನನಗೆ ಕಷ್ಟವಾಗಿರುತ್ತದೆ. ತಮಾಷೆ ಆಡಲು ಮತ್ತು ಬಿಡುವಾಗಿರಲು ನನಗೆ ತಿಳಿಯದು.

☐ ಇಲ್ಲವೇ ಇಲ್ಲ ☐ ಅಪರೂಪವಾಗಿ ☐ ಕೆಲವೊಮ್ಮೆ

☐ ಪದೇ ಪದೇ ☐ ಪ್ರತಿಸಾರಿ

೧೨) ಇತರರು ಮೋಸಕ್ಕೆ ಒಳಗಾದಾಗ ನಾನು ಅವರೊಂದಿಗೆ ಆಕರ್ಷಿಸಲ್ಪಟ್ಟು ಹತ್ತಿರ ಸಂಬಂಧ ಬೆಳೆಸುತ್ತೇನೆ. ಈ ರೀತಿಯಾಗಿ ಕರುಣೆಯನ್ನು ಪ್ರೀತಿಯಾಗಿ ಗೊಂದಲ ಹೊಂದಿ ಕರುಣಿಸಿ ತಪ್ಪಿಸುತ್ತೇನೆ.

☐ ಇಲ್ಲವೇ ಇಲ್ಲ ☐ ಅಪರೂಪವಾಗಿ ☐ ಕೆಲವೊಮ್ಮೆ

☐ ಪದೇ ಪದೇ ☐ ಪ್ರತಿಸಾರಿ

೧೩) ನನ್ನ ಜೀವನದಲ್ಲಿ ಕೆಲಸದಲ್ಲಾದಲಿ ಅಥವಾ ಮನೆಯಲ್ಲಾಗಲಿ ಸಂಪೂರ್ಣತೆಯನ್ನು ಕೋರುತ್ತೇನೆ. ಮತ್ತು ನನ್ನ ಜೀವನದಲ್ಲಿ ಇತರರಿಂದ ಸಂಪೂರ್ಣತೆಯನ್ನು ನಿರೀಕ್ಷಿಸುತ್ತೇನೆ.

☐ ಇಲ್ಲವೇ ಇಲ್ಲ ☐ ಅಪರೂಪವಾಗಿ ☐ ಕೆಲವೊಮ್ಮೆ

☐ ಪದೇ ಪದೇ ☐ ಪ್ರತಿಸಾರಿ

೧೪) ನನ್ನ ಜೀವನದಲ್ಲಿ ನವೀನತೆ, ಉತ್ತೇಜನ ಮತ್ತು ಹೊಸತನದ ಅಪೇಕ್ಷೆಯಿಂದ ಎದುರಾಗುವ ಪರಿಣಾಮಕ್ಕೆ ಮುಖ್ಯತ್ವವನ್ನು ಕೊಡದೇ ಅವುಗಳನ್ನು ಹುಡುಕುತ್ತೇನೆ.

☐ ಇಲ್ಲವೇ ಇಲ್ಲ ☐ ಅಪರೂಪವಾಗಿ ☐ ಕೆಲವೊಮ್ಮೆ

☐ ಪದೇ ಪದೇ ☐ ಪ್ರತಿಸಾರಿ

೧೫) ನಾನು ನನ್ನನ್ನು ತುಂಬ ಗಂಭೀರವಾಗಿ ಎಣಿಸುತ್ತೇನೆ ಮತ್ತು ನನ್ನ ಎಲ್ಲಾ ಸಂಬಂಧಗಳನ್ನು ಅದೇ ಗಂಭೀರತೆಯಿಂದ ನೋಡುತ್ತೇನೆ.

☐ ಇಲ್ಲವೇ ಇಲ್ಲ ☐ ಅಪರೂಪವಾಗಿ ☐ ಕೆಲವೊಮ್ಮೆ

☐ ಪದೇ ಪದೇ ☐ ಪ್ರತಿಸಾರಿ

೧೬) ನನಗೆ ಸನ್ನಿಹಿತ ಸಂಬಂಧವನ್ನು ಬೆಳಿಸಲು ಮತ್ತು ನಡೆಸಿಕೊಂಡು ಹೋಗಲು ಸಮಸ್ಯೆಯಿದೆ.

☐ ಇಲ್ಲವೇ ಇಲ್ಲ ☐ ಅಪರೂಪವಾಗಿ ☐ ಕೆಲವೊಮ್ಮೆ

☐ ಪದೇ ಪದೇ ☐ ಪ್ರತಿಸಾರಿ

೧೭) ನಾನು ಇತರರ ಅವಶ್ಯಕತೆಗಳಿಗೆ ಶ್ರದ್ಧೆಯನ್ನು ಕೊಡದೆ ಅಥವಾ ವಹಿಸದೆ ಮೊದಲು ನನಗೆ ಅಥವಾ ನನ್ನ ಅವಶ್ಯಕತೆಗಳಿಗೆ ಶ್ರದ್ಧೆಯನ್ನು ಕೊಟ್ಟು ನನಗೋಸ್ಕರ ನಿಲ್ಲುವಾಗ ನಾನು ಅಪರಾಧಿ ಎಂದು ಭಾವಿಸುತ್ತೇನೆ.

☐ ಇಲ್ಲವೇ ಇಲ್ಲ ☐ ಅಪರೂಪವಾಗಿ ☐ ಕೆಲವೊಮ್ಮೆ

☐ ಪದೇ ಪದೇ ☐ ಪ್ರತಿಸಾರಿ

೧೮) ನಿರ್ಭಂಧಪಡಿಸುವನಡತೆಯಿರುವಜನರೊಟ್ಟಿಗೆಸೇರಲುಇಷ್ಟಪಡುತ್ತೇನೆ. ಉದಾ:ಕುಡಿಯುಮದು, ಔಷಧ ದುರುಪಯೋಗ. ಜೂಜು, ಊಟ , ವ್ಯಾಪಾರ ,ಲೈಂಗಿಕತೆ,

ಧೂಮಪಾನ, ಹೆಚ್ಚು ಕೆಲಸ ಮಾಡುಮದು ಅಥವಾ ಉತ್ತೇಜನ ಕೋರುಮದು.

☐ ಇಲ್ಲವೇ ಇಲ್ಲ ☐ ಅಪರೂಪವಾಗಿ ☐ ಕೆಲವೊಮ್ಮೆ

☐ ಪದೇ ಪದೇ ☐ ಪ್ರತಿಸಾರಿ

೧೯) ನನಗೆ ಇತರರೊಟ್ಟಿಗೆ ಜವಾಬ್ದಾರ ಭಾವನೆಯಿಂದ ಇರುಮದು ಮತ್ತು ನನಗಿಂತ ಇತರರೊಂದಿಗೆ ಆಸಕ್ತಿ ಇಡಲು ಸುಲಭವಾಗಿದೆ.

☐ ಇಲ್ಲವೇ ಇಲ್ಲ ☐ ಅಪರೂಪವಾಗಿ ☐ ಕೆಲವೊಮ್ಮೆ

☐ ಪದೇ ಪದೇ ☐ ಪ್ರತಿಸಾರಿ

೨೦) ನಂಬಿಕೆಗೆ ಅನರ್ಹರು ಎಂದು ರುಜುವಿದ್ದರೂ ನಾನು ಜನರಿಗೆ ಶ್ರದ್ಧೆ ವಹಿಸುಮದರಲ್ಲಿ ನಂಬಿಕೆಯಾಗಿರುತ್ತೇನೆ.

☐ ಇಲ್ಲವೇ ಇಲ್ಲ ☐ ಅಪರೂಪವಾಗಿ ☐ ಕೆಲವೊಮ್ಮೆ

☐ ಪದೇ ಪದೇ ☐ ಪ್ರತಿಸಾರಿ

೨೧) ನಾನು ಏನಾದರೂ ಮಾಡಿ ಸಂಬಂಧವನ್ನು ಉಳಿಸಲು ಪ್ರಯಾಸಪಡುತ್ತೇನೆ. ಯಾಕೆಂದರೆ ನನ್ನನ್ನು ಒಬ್ಬಂಟಿಗನಾಗಿ ಬಿಟ್ಟು ಬಿಡುತ್ತಾರೆಂದು ಭಯ.

☐ ಇಲ್ಲವೇ ಇಲ್ಲ ☐ ಅಪರೂಪವಾಗಿ ☐ ಕೆಲವೊಮ್ಮೆ

☐ ಪದೇ ಪದೇ ☐ ಪ್ರತಿಸಾರಿ

೨೨) ನಾನು ಬೇರೆ ಕಾರ್ಯಗಳನ್ನು ಅಥವಾ ಸಂಭವಿಸಬಹುದಾದ ಪರಿಣಾಮವನ್ನು ಗಮನಿಸದೇ ತಟ್ಟನೇ ನೂಕುತ್ತೇನೆ ಮತ್ತು ಚುರುಕಾಗಿ ಕ್ರಿಯೆ ಮಾಡುತ್ತೇನೆ.

☐ ಇಲ್ಲವೇ ಇಲ್ಲ ☐ ಅಪರೂಪವಾಗಿ ☐ ಕೆಲವೊಮ್ಮೆ

☐ ಪದೇ ಪದೇ ☐ ಪ್ರತಿಸಾರಿ

೧೩) ನಾನು ಭಾವನೆಗಳಿಂದ ಇರುಮದು ಅಥವಾ ಭಾವನೆಗಳನ್ನು ವ್ಯಕ್ತಪಡಿಸಲು ನನಗೆ ಕಷ್ಟವಾಗಿರುತ್ತದೆ. ನನಗೆ ನನ್ನ ಭಾವನೆಗಳ ಜೊತೆ ಸಂಪರ್ಕವಿಲ್ಲ ಎಂದು ಎಣಿಸುತ್ತೇನೆ.

☐ ಇಲ್ಲವೇ ಇಲ್ಲ ☐ ಅಪರೂಪವಾಗಿ ☐ ಕೆಲವೊಮ್ಮೆ

☐ ಪದೇ ಪದೇ ☐ ಪ್ರತಿಸಾರಿ

೧೪) ನನಗೆ ನನ್ನ ಭಾವನೆಗಳ ಮೇಲೆ ಮತ್ತು ಇತರರು ತೋರಿಸುವ ಭಾವನೆಗಳಲ್ಲಿ ನಂಬಿಕೆಯಿಲ್ಲ.

☐ ಇಲ್ಲವೇ ಇಲ್ಲ ☐ ಅಪರೂಪವಾಗಿ ☐ ಕೆಲವೊಮ್ಮೆ

☐ ಪದೇ ಪದೇ ☐ ಪ್ರತಿಸಾರಿ

೧೫) ನಾನು ಸಾಧಾರಣವಾಗಿ ಹೊಸ ಸಮಾಜ ಸನ್ನಿವೇಶದಲ್ಲಿ ಸಂಕೋಚಪಟ್ಟು ಮತ್ತು ಪಕ್ಕಕ್ಕೆ ಹೋಗಿ ಇತರ ಜನರಿಂದ ನನ್ನನ್ನು ದೂರಮಾಡಿಕೊಳ್ಳುತ್ತೇನೆ.

☐ ಇಲ್ಲವೇ ಇಲ್ಲ ☐ ಅಪರೂಪವಾಗಿ ☐ ಕೆಲವೊಮ್ಮೆ

☐ ಪದೇ ಪದೇ ☐ ಪ್ರತಿಸಾರಿ

೧೬) ವೈಯಕ್ತಿಕವಾಗಿ ಮತ್ತು ಸಾಮಾಜಿಕವಾಗಿ ನನ್ನನ್ನು ಸ್ವಪ್ರಯೋಜನಕ್ಕಾಗಿ ಉಪಯೋಗಿಸಿಕೊಳ್ಳುತ್ತಾರೆಂದು ನನ್ನ ಭಾವನೆ, ಸಾಧಾರಣವಾಗಿ ಮೋಸ ಹೋಗಿದ್ದೇನೆ ಎಂಬುವ

ಭಾವನೆ ನನಗಿದೆ.

☐ ಇಲ್ಲವೇ ಇಲ್ಲ ☐ ಅಪರೂಪವಾಗಿ ☐ ಕೆಲವೊಮ್ಮೆ

☐ ಪದೇ ಪದೇ ☐ ಪ್ರತಿಸಾರಿ

೧೭) ನಾನು ಬಹಳ ಸಮಯಗಳಲ್ಲಿ ತುಂಬಾ ಜವಾಬ್ದಾರಿಯುಳ್ಳವನಾಗಿರುತ್ತೇನೆ. ಅದರೆ ಬೇರೆ ಸಮಯಗಳಲ್ಲಿ ತುಂಬಾ ಜವಾಬ್ದಾರಿಯಿಲ್ಲದವನಾಗಿ ಇರುತ್ತೇನೆ.

☐ ಇಲ್ಲವೇ ಇಲ್ಲ ☐ ಅಪರೂಪವಾಗಿ ☐ ಕೆಲವೊಮ್ಮೆ

☐ ಪದೇ ಪದೇ ☐ ಪ್ರತಿಸಾರಿ

೧೮) ನನ್ನ ಮೇಲೆ ಒತ್ತಡ ಹೆಚ್ಚಾದಾಗ , ನನ್ನ ಮೇಲೆ ನನಗೆ ಕೋಪ ಮತ್ತು ಗಾಬರಿಯಾಗಿ ನನ್ನ ಜೀವನದ ಮೇಲೆ ಅಥವಾ ನನ್ನ ಸನ್ನಿವೇಶದ ಮೇಲೆ ಅಧೀನ ತಪ್ಪಿಹೋಗುತ್ತದೆ.

☐ ಇಲ್ಲವೇ ಇಲ್ಲ ☐ ಅಪರೂಪವಾಗಿ ☐ ಕೆಲವೊಮ್ಮೆ

☐ ಪದೇ ಪದೇ ☐ ಪ್ರತಿಸಾರಿ

೧೯) ನಾನು ಸರಿಯಾಗಿ ಆಲೋಚಿಸದೇ ತಟ್ಟನೆ ನೂಕುವ ಕಾರಣದಿಂದ ಆಗುವ ದುರ್ಗುಣಾಭಾವ ಪರಿಣಾಮಗಳನ್ನು ಸರಿ ಮಾಡಲು ಅಥವಾ ಹೊಲಸನ್ನು ಶುಭ್ರಗೊಳಿಸಲು ತುಂಬಾ ಸಮಯವನ್ನು ಮತ್ತು ಶಕ್ತಿಯನ್ನು ನಾನು ಕಲಿಯುತ್ತಿದ್ದೇನೆ.

☐ ಇಲ್ಲವೇ ಇಲ್ಲ ☐ ಅಪರೂಪವಾಗಿ ☐ ಕೆಲವೊಮ್ಮೆ
☐ ಪದೇ ಪದೇ ☐ ಪ್ರತಿಸಾರಿ

೨೦) ನನ್ನ ಪ್ರಸ್ತುತ ಸಮಸ್ಯೆಗಳು ನನ್ನ ಕಳೆದು ಹೋದ ಕಾಲದಿಂದ ಬರುತ್ತದೆ ಎಂದು ನಾನು ಒಪ್ಪಿಕೊಳ್ಳುಮದಿಲ್ಲ ಕಳೆದು ಹೋದ ಕಾಲದಿಂದಿರುವ ಭಾವನೆಗಳು ನನ್ನ ಪ್ರಸ್ತುತ ಜೀವನವನ್ನು ತುಂಬಿದೆಯೆಂದು ನಾನು ಒಪ್ಪಿಕೊಳ್ಳುಮದಿಲ್ಲ.

☐ ಇಲ್ಲವೇ ಇಲ್ಲ ☐ ಅಪರೂಪವಾಗಿ ☐ ಕೆಲವೊಮ್ಮೆ
☐ ಪದೇ ಪದೇ ☐ ಪ್ರತಿಸಾರಿ

ಭಾಗ ಐದು

ಸೋಷಿಯಲ್ ಡಿಸ್ಟನ್ಸ್ ಸ್ಕೇಲ್

ಪ್ರೊ.ಕುಪ್ಪುಸ್ವಾಮಿಯವರು ಮಾರ್ಪಡಿಸಿದ ಬೊಗಾರ್ಡಸ್ ಸೋಷಿಯಲ್ ಡಿಸ್ಟನ್ಸ್ ಸ್ಕೇಲನ್ನು ಎಫ್ರಾಥ ಸಾರಥಿ ಪ್ರಸ್ತುತ ಪರಿಶೋಧನೆಯಲ್ಲಿರುವ ಜನರಿಗೆ ತಕ್ಕಂತೆ ಬದಲಾಯಿಸಿದ್ದಾರೆ. ನಿಮ್ಮ ಆಯ್ಕೆ ಅಥವಾ ಉತ್ತರವನ್ನು ಸರಿಯಾದ ಪೆಟ್ಟಿಗೆಯಲ್ಲಿ ಚುಕ್ಕೆ ಗುರುತು ಹಾಕಿ ಸೂಚಿಸಿ.

೧) ಇತರೆ ಜಾತಿ ಸದಸ್ಯರೊಂದಿಗೆ ಬಂಧುತ್ವ ಸ್ಥಾಪಿಸಲು ನನಗೆ ಸಾಧ್ಯತೆ ಇದೆ.

☐ ಇಲ್ಲವೇ ಇಲ್ಲ ☐ ಅಪರೂಪವಾಗಿ ☐ ಕೆಲವೊಮ್ಮೆ
☐ ಪದೇ ಪದೇ ☐ ಪ್ರತಿಸಾರಿ

೨) ಇತರೆ ಜಾತಿ ಸದಸ್ಯರ ಊಟದ ಕೋಣೆಯಲ್ಲಿ ಊಟ ಮಾಡಲು ನನಗೆ ಸಾಧ್ಯತೆ ಇದೆ.

☐ ಇಲ್ಲವೇ ಇಲ್ಲ ☐ ಅಪರೂಪವಾಗಿ ☐ ಕೆಲವೊಮ್ಮೆ
☐ ಪದೇ ಪದೇ ☐ ಪ್ರತಿಸಾರಿ

೩) ಇತರೆ ಜಾತಿ ಸದಸ್ಯರ ಜೊತೆಯಲ್ಲಿ ಹತ್ತಿರದ ಸ್ನೇಹಕ್ಕೆ ಕೃಷಿ ಮಾಡಲು ನನಗೆ ಸಾಧ್ಯತೆ ಇದೆ.

☐ ಇಲ್ಲವೇ ಇಲ್ಲ ☐ ಅಪರೂಪವಾಗಿ ☐ ಕೆಲವೊಮ್ಮೆ
☐ ಪದೇ ಪದೇ ☐ ಪ್ರತಿಸಾರಿ

೪) ಇತರೆ ಜಾತಿ ಸದಸ್ಯರು ನನ್ನ ಮನೆಗೆ ಅತಿಥಿಗಳಾಗಿ ಬರಲು ಸಾಧ್ಯತೆ ಇದೆ.

☐ ಇಲ್ಲವೇ ಇಲ್ಲ ☐ ಅಪರೂಪವಾಗಿ ☐ ಕೆಲವೊಮ್ಮೆ

☐ ಪದೇ ಪದೇ ☐ ಪ್ರತಿಸಾರಿ

೫) ಇತರೆ ಜಾತಿ ಸದಸ್ಯರು ನನ್ನನ್ನು ಅವರು ನೆರೆ ಹೊರೆಯವರಾಗಿ ಒಪ್ಪಿಕೊಳ್ಳಲು ಸಾಧ್ಯತೆ ಇದೆ.

☐ ಇಲ್ಲವೇ ಇಲ್ಲ ☐ ಅಪರೂಪವಾಗಿ ☐ ಕೆಲವೊಮ್ಮೆ

☐ ಪದೇ ಪದೇ ☐ ಪ್ರತಿಸಾರಿ

೬) ಇತರೆ ಜಾತಿ ಸದಸ್ಯರೊಂದಿಗೆ ಆಕಸ್ಮಿಕ ಪರಿಚಿತ ವ್ಯಕ್ತಿಯಾಗಿರಲು ನನಗೆ ಸಾಧ್ಯತೆ ಇದೆ.

☐ ಇಲ್ಲವೇ ಇಲ್ಲ ☐ ಅಪರೂಪವಾಗಿ ☐ ಕೆಲವೊಮ್ಮೆ

☐ ಪದೇ ಪದೇ ☐ ಪ್ರತಿಸಾರಿ

ನಿಮ್ಮ ಸಮಯವನ್ನು ಕೊಟ್ಟು ಸಹಕರಿಸಿ ಪ್ರಶ್ನೆಗಳಿಗೆ ಉತ್ತರ ನೀಡಿದ್ದಕ್ಕೆ ನಿಮಗೆ ವಂದನೆಗಳು.

ಎಫ್ರಾಥ ಸಾರಥಿ

Select Bibliography

Books:

Adams, Jay E. *The Christian Counselor's Manual.* Michigan: Baker Book House, 1973.

Adler, Alfred. *Understanding Human Nature.* London: Allen & Unwin Ltd, 1927.

Aiyappan, A. *Social Revolution in a Kerala Village: A Study in Cultural Change.* Bombay: Asia Publishing House, 1965.

Ambedkar, B.R. *Annihilation of Caste.* Jalandhar: Beem Patrika Publication, 1970.

Ambedkar, B.R. *Dr. Ambedkar on Poona Pact,* 49. Letter written by Gandhi in objection to the separate electorate from Yeravada Central Prison, on August 18th, 1932.

Ambedkar, B.R. *Mr. Gandhi and the Emancipation of the Untouchables.* Bombay: Thacker & Co., Ltd. 1943.

Ambedkar, B.R. *Dr. Ambedkar on Poona Pact.* Jalandhar: Bheem Patrika Publication, 1973.

Ambedkar, B.R. *The Untouchables.* Vol. 7. Bombay: Govt. of Maharashtra, 1990.

Ambedkar, B.R. *What Congress and Gandhi have done for the Untouchables?.* Bombay: Thacker and Co., n.y.

Azaraiah, M. *Mission in Christ's Way in India Today.* Madras: CLS, 1989.

Basotia, G.R. & K.K. Sharma. *Research Methodology Made Simple.* Jaipur: Mangal Deep Publications, 2002.

Chatterjee, Sarajit Kumar. *The Scheduled Castes in India.* New Delhi: Gyan Publishing House, 2008.

Chaube, S.P. *Developmental Psychology.* New Delhi: Neelkamal Publications, 2003.

Clebsch, W. and C. Jaekle. *Pastoral Care in Historical Perspective.* Englewood Cliffs, NJ: Prentice Hall, Inc., 1964.

Colledge, Ray. *Mastering Counselling Theory.* New York: Palgrave MacMillan, 2002.

Dahiwale, S.M. *Emerging Entrepreneurship among Scheduled Castes of Contemporary India: A Study of Kolhapur City.* New Delhi: Hindustan Publishers, 1989.

Devasahayam, V. "Doing Dalit Theology: Basic Assumption." *Frontiers of Dalit Theology.* Edited by V. Devasahayam. Delhi: ISPCK, 1997.

Feltham, Colin (Edited). *Controversies in Psychotherapy and Counselling.* New Delhi: Sage Publications, 1999.

Freud, S. *New Introductory Lectures on Psychoanalysis.* Vol. 2. Penguin Freud Library, 1933.

Freud, S. *The Ego and the Id.* Vol. 11. Penguin Freud Library, 1923.

Gandhi, M.K. *Caste Must go, the Sin of Untouchability.* Ahmedabad: Navjivan Publishing House, 1964.

Gerkin, Charles. *Prophetic Pastoral Practice.* Nashville, TN: Abingdon Press, 1991.

Ghurye, G.S. *Caste and Race in India.* 5th Edition. Bombay: Popular Prakashan, 1969.

Glasser, William. *Reality Therapy.* New York: Harper & Row, 1965.

Graham, Larry Kent. *Care of Persons, Care of Worlds: A Psychosystemic Approach to Pastoral Care.* Nashville: Abingdon Press, 1992.

Hall, Calvin S. and Gardner Lindzey. *Theories of Personality.* New York: John Wiley & Sons, 1973.

Hasnain, N. (ed)., *Weaker Sections: Psycho-Social Perspective.* New Delhi: Gyan Publishing House, 1998.

Heinrich, C. *The Psychology of a Suppressed People.* London: The Aberdeen University Press, 1937.

Hiltner, Seward. *The Christian Shepherd.* Nashville: Abingdon Press, 1959.

Hutton, J.H. *Caste in India: Its Nature, Function and Origins.* 4th Edition. London: 1963.

Issacs, H.R. *India's Ex-Untouchables.* New York: John Day Company, 1965.

Jangam, R.T. *Political Sociology.* New Delhi: Oxford & IBH Publishing Co., 1980.

Jung, C.G. *Psychological Types.* New York: Harcourt, Brace & World, 1933.

Jung, C.G. *The Archetypes and the Collective Unconscious.* 2nd edition. New Jersey: The Princeton Press, 1968.

Kapila, S. *Methods of Social Research.* Jalandhar: New Academic Publishing Co., 2001.

Ketkar, Shridhar. *The History of Caste in India.* Ithaca: Taylor and Carpenter, 1909.

Krishnan, Asha. *Ambedkar and Gandhi.* Mumbai: Himalaya Publishing House, 1997.

Kroeber, A.L. *Caste, Encyclopedia of the Social Sciences.* New York: McMillan, 1980.

Kshirsagar, R.K. *Dalit Movement in India and Its Leaders.* New Delhi: M.D. Publications, 1994.

Lindzey, Gardner, et.al., *Psychology.* 2nd edition. New York: Worth Publishers, 1978.

Maslow, Abraham. H. *Motivation and Personality.* New York: Harper & Row, 1970.

Maslow, A.H. and Bela Mittelmann. *Principles of Abnormal Psychology.* New York: Harper & Brothers, 1941.

Massey, James. "Down Trodden: The Struggle of India's Dalits for Identity, Solidarity, and Liberation." Geneva: WCC, 1997.

Massey, James. "Ingredients for a Dalit Theology." *Towards a Dalit Theology.* Edited by M.E. Prabhakar. Delhi: ISPCK, 1988.

Mendelsohn, Oliver & Marika. Vicziany. *The Untouchables: Subordination, Poverty, and the State in Modern India.* New Delhi: Foundation Books, 2000.

Nelson-Jones, Richard. *Essential Counselling and Therapy Skills.* New Delhi: Sage Publication, 2002.

Nirmal, A.P. "Towards a Christian Dalit Theology." *A Reader in Dalit Theology.* Edited by A.P. Nirmal. Madras: GLTCRI, 2000.

Nirula, D. *Dalits: A Bruised Dignity.* New Delhi: A.P.H. Publishing House, 2005.

Oden, Thomas. *Classical Pastoral Care.* Vol. 3. Secunderabad: OM Books, 2005.

Peace, Richard. *Learning to Love Ourselves.* Downers Grove: InterVarsity Press, 1970.

Prabhakar, M.E. "Introduction." *Towards a Dalit Theology.* Edited by M.E. Prabhakar. Delhi: ISPCK, 1988.

Progoff, Ira. *Jung's Psychology and Its Social Meaning.* New York: The Julian Press, 1953.

Raj, M.C. *Dalitology.* Tumkur: Ambedkar Resource Centre, 2001.

Rajshekar, V.T. *Caste: A Nation with the Nation.* Bangalore: Books for Change, 2002.

Ram, Nandu. *The Mobile Scheduled Caste: The Rise of New Middle Class.* Delhi: Hindustan Publishing House, 1998.

Rao, Sayaji III, *Maharaja of Baroda. Speeches and Addresses.* London: Macmillan Co., 1912.

Rice, Stainly. *Hindu Customs and their Origin.* London: George Allen Unwin, 1937.

Risley, H.H. *The People of India.* 2nd Edition. London: W Thacker Co., 1915.

Rogers, Carl. "A Theory of Therapy, Personality, and Interpersonal Relationship, as Developed in the Client-Centered Framework." *Psychology: A Study of a Science.* Edited by S. Koch. Vol. 3. New York: McGraw-Hill, 1959: 210.

Rogers, Carl. *A Way of Being.* Boston: Houghton Mifflin, 1980.

Rogers, *Client-Centered Therapy; Its Current Practice, Implications, and Theory.* Boston: Houghton Mifflin, 1951.

Sargent, S. Stansfeld. *Basic Teaching of the Great Psychologists.* New York: Barnes & Noble, Inc. 1944.

Sartre, Jean-Paul. *Being and Nothingness.* New York: Washington Square Press, 1966.

Shaffer, L.F. *The Psychology of Adjustment.* New York: Hougton Mifflin Co., 1936.

Sharma, G.S. *Legislation and Cases on Untouchability and Scheduled Castes in India.* New Delhi: Allied Publishers, 1975.

Showeb, M. *Educated and Mobility among Harijans.* Delhi: Vohra Publishers, 1986.

Srinivas, M.N. *Caste in Modern India and Other Essays.* Bombay: Asia Publishing House, 1962.

Srinivas, M.N. *Social Change in Modern India.* Bombay: Orient Longman Ltd., 1972.

Srinivas, M.N. ed. *Caste: Its Twentieth Century Avatar.* New Delhi: Viking, 1996.

Webster, John C. B. *Religion and Dalit Liberation: An Examination of Perspectives.* New Delhi: Manohar, 1999.

Wilson, K. "An Approach to Christian Dalit Theology." *Towards a Dalit Theology.* Edited by M.E. Prabhakar. New Delhi: ISPCK, 1988.

Wise, Carroll A. *The Meaning of Pastoral Care.* New York: Harper and Row, 1966.

Magazines, Articles and Journals:

Baldwin, M. W. & L. Sinclair. "Self-Esteem and "if then" Contingencies of Interpersonal Acceptance." *Journal of Personality and Social Psychology* 71, 6 (1996): 1130-1141

Baumeister, R.F., D.M. Tice, and D. G. Hutton. "Self-Presentational Motivations and Personality Differences in Self-Esteem." *Journal of Personality* 57, 3 (1989): 547-579.

Brown, J.D. & K.A. Dutton. "The Thrill of Victory, the Complexity of Defeat: Self-Esteem and People's Emotional Reactions to Success and Failure." *Journal of Personality and Psychology* 68, 4 (1995): 712-722.

Brown, J.D. "Evaluations of the Self and Others: Self-Enhancement Biases in Social Judgments." *Social Cognition* 4 (1986): 353-376.

Campbell, J.D. "Self-esteem and Clarity of the Self-Concept." *Journal of Personality and Social Psychology* 59, 2 (1990): 538-549.

Downey, G., A.L. Freitas, B. Michaelis, & H. Khouri. "The Self-Fulfilling Prophecy in Close Relationships: Rejection Sensitivity and Rejection by Romantic Partners." *Journal of Personality and Social Psychology* 75, 2 (1998): 545-560.

Gill-Austern, Brita L. "Rediscovering Hidden Treasures for Pastoral Care." *Pastoral Psychology* 43, 4 (1995): 233-253.

Gomez, Felipe. "Christology and Pastoral Practice from Below." *East Asian Pastoral Review 1* (1982): 4-14.

Graffin, Horace L. "Revisioning Christian Ethical Discourse on Homosexuality: A Challenge for Pastoral Care in the 21st Century." *The Journal of Pastoral Care* 53, 2 (1999): 209-219.

Graham, Steven M. and Margaret S. Clark. "Self-Esteem and Organization of Valenced Information About Others: The "Jekyll and Hyde" – ing of Relationship Partners." *Journal of Personality and Social Psychology* 90, 4 (2006): 652-665.

Gupta, A. Sen and A.K. Singh. "Test of Emotional Stability." *Psychological Studies* 30, 1 (1985): 121-123.

Hasty, Cathy. "Using a Modification of the Classic Drama Triangle to Enhance Pastoral Care." *Journal of Pastoral Care* 55, 2 (2001): 147-157.

Heimpel, Sara A. Joanne V. Wood, Margaret A. Marshall & Jonathon D. Brown. "Do People with Low Self-Esteem Really Want to Feel Better? Self-Esteem Differences in Motivation to Repair Negative Moods." *Journal of Personality and Social Psychology* 82, 1 (2002): 128-147.

James, N. Butcher, et.al., New Subscales for the MMPI-2 Social Introversion (*Si*) Scale. *A Journal of Consulting and Clinical Psychology* 1, 3 (September 1989): 169-174.

Jha, Vikas. and M. Imran Ali. "Atrocities on Dalits in Haryana and Rajasthan – A Comparitive Study: Religion as Oppressive." *Religion and Society* 51, 1 (March 2006): 44-58.

Jha, Vivekananda and Prabhati Mukherjee. "Stages in History of Untouchables." *The Indian Historical Review II* (July 1975): 14-31.

John, Mathai P. et.al., "Evaluation of the Reliability of the Scale for Assessment of Negative Symptoms." *Psychological Studies* 28, 3 (1984): 124-136.

Khan, Abdul Majeed. *Affective Syndrome Crisis in Schedule Caste: A Fresh Look. Psychological Studies* 24, 3 (1981): 358-372.

Kumar, Pramod. "Supervisor's Authoritarianism and Ingratiation among Workers." *Psychological Studies* 31, 2 (1986): 165-168.

Leary, M.R., E.S. Tambor, S.K. Terdal, & D.L. Downs. "Self-Esteem as an Interpersonal Monitor: The Sociometer Hypothesis." *Journal of Personality and Social Psychology* 68, 3 (1995): 518-530.

Long, Brid. "Theological Reflection in the Supervision of Pastoral Care." *Journal of Pastoral Care* 52, 2 (1998): 117-131.

Massey, James. "An Analysis of the Dalit situation with Special Reference to Dalit Christians and Dalit Theology." *Religion and Society* 52, 3-4 (Sep-Dec 2007): 57-86.

Massey, James. "Dalits and Human Rights." *Religion and Society* 49, 2-3 (June – Sep 2004): 1-9.

McFarlin, D.B., R.F. Baumeister, & J. Blascovich. "On Knowing When to Quit: Task Failure, Self-Esteem, Advice, and Nonproductive Persistence." *Journal of Personality* 52, 2 (1984): 139-155.

Mohan, A. "The Growth of Contemporary Buddhism and Its Significance for Church's Mission." *Indian Journal of Theology* 47, 1-2 (2005): 107-117.

Murray, L.S., J.G. Holmes, & D. W. Griffin. "Self-Esteem and the Quest for Felt Security: How Perceived Regard Regulates Attachment Processes." *Journal of Personality and Social Psychology* 78, 2 (2000): 478-498.

Murray, Sandra L. Paul Rose, Gina M. Bellavia, John G. Holmes, & Anna Garrett Kusche. "When Rejection Stings: How Self-Esteem Constrains Relationship-Enhancement Processes." *Journal of Personality and Social Psychology* 83, 3, (2002): 556-573.

Nargolkar, V.S. "Removal of Untouchability, Goals and Attainments." *Indian Journal of Social Work* XXX, 3 (Oct.1969): 189-201.

Neiss, Michelle B. et.al., "Executive Self, Self-Esteem, and Negative Affectivity: Relations at the Phenotypic and Genotypic Level." *Journal of Personality and Social Psychology* 89, 4 (2005): 593-606.

Oomen, George. "The Emerging Dalit Theology: A Historical Appraisal." *Indian Church History Review* XXXIV, 1 (June 2000): 19-37.

Parvathamma, C. "The Weaker Sections of Society-The Scheduled Castes in India." *Sociological Bulletin* 30, 1(March 1981): 50-56.

Patil, Ravindra. "Search for Identity among Dalit Middle Class in Maharastra." *Social Action* 50, 1 (Jan-Mar 2000): 70-79.

Raj, H. Sam Sananda and Immanuel Thomas. "Certain Correlates of Self-Esteem: A Factor Study." *Psychological Studies* 31, 2 (1986): 119-124.

Rath and Sircar. "Intercaste Relation as Reflected in the Study of Attitudes and Opinions of Six Hindu Caste Groups." *The Journal of Social Psychology* 51, 2 (1960): 122-135.

Rogers, Carl. "The Necessary and Sufficient Conditions of Therapeutic Personality Change." *Journal of Consulting Psychology* 21, 1 (1957): 95-103.

Roger, Carl. "What We Know About Psychotherapy."*Pastoral Psychology* 12, (April 1961): 31-33.

Rosenberg, M. C. Schooler, C. Schoenbach, & F. Rosenberg. "Global Self-Esteem and Specific Self-Esteem: Different Concepts, Different Outcomes." *American Sociological Review* 60, (1995): 141-156.

Sahu, D.K. "Ministry from the Margin." *Indian Journal of Theology* 45, 1-2 (2003): 1-9.

Saussy, Carroll. "Faith and Self-Esteem." *Journal of Pastoral Care* XLII, 2 (Summer 1988): 125-137.

Sharp, Jim R. "Solution-Focused Counseling: A Model for Parish Ministry." *The Journal of Pastoral Care* 53, 1 (Summer 1999): 72-79.

Shyam, Radhey & Sudesh Yadav. "A Study of Depression, Self-Esteem and Social Support amongst Institutionalized and Non-Institutionalized Aged." *Journal of Personality and Clinical Studies* 18 (2002): 79-86.

Singh, Manmohan. *Unbroken People* 2, 8 (Jan 2007): 14-16.

Suls, Jerry. Katherine Lemos, and H. Lockett Stewart. "Self-Esteem, Construal, and Comparisons with the Self, Friends, and Peers." *Journal of Personality and Social Psychology* 82, 2 (2002): 252-261.

Velaskar, Padma and G.G. Wankhede. "From Old Stigma to New… Exploring the Changing Identity to Urban Educated Dalits." *The Indian Journal of Social Work* LVII, 1 (Jan 1996): 115-134.

Vignoles, Vivian L. Jen Golledge, Eugenia Scabini, Camillo Regalia and Claudia Manzi. "Beyond Self-Esteem: Influence of Multiple Motives on Identity Construction." *Journal of Personality and Social Psychology* 90, 2 (2006): 308-333.

Vohs, Kathleen D. and Todd F. Heatherton. "Self-Esteem and Threats to Self: Implications for Self-Construals and Interpersonal Perceptions." *Journal of Personality and Social Psychology* 81, 5 (2001): 1103-1118.

Wankhede, G.G. "Social and Educational Problems of Scheduled Castes: Some Critical Insights." *The Indian Journal of Social Work* 60, 3 (July 1999): 397-418.

West, Gordon F. and JoLynne Reynold. The Applicability of Selected Rational –Emotive Therapy Principles for Pastoral Counselling." *The Journal of Pastoral Care* 51, 2 (1997): 187-194.

Wood, Joanne V., Sara A. Heimpel, and Ian R. Newby-Clark. "Snatching Defeat from the Jaws of Victory: Self-Esteem Differences in the Experience and Anticipation of Success." *Journal of Personality and Social Psychology* 89, 5 (2005): 764-780.

Young India, 12 June, (1924).

Young, H. "Practicising RET with Bible-Belt Christians." *British Journal of Cognitive Psychotherapy* 2 (1984): 60-76.

Dictionaries and Encyclopedia:

New Webster's Dictionary, New York: Delair Publishing, 1971, 493.

Ridley, C.R. "Self-Esteem." *Dictionary of Pastoral Care.* Edited by Rodney J. Hunter, 1161.

The Encyclopedia of Psychic Disorders. Vol. III. New Delhi: Viva Books Pvt Ltd, 2004, 64, 106.

The Oxford Thesaurus. Oxford: Clarendon Press, 1993.

Unpublished Papers:

Jogdand, P.G. "Dalit education and Dalit Identity: A Case of Dalits in Maharastra" Paper presented in National Seminar on Dalits and the New Education System, organized by ISI, New Delhi, January, 1998.

Waghmare, B.S. "Dilemma of Dalit Middle Class and Ambedkarism," Paper presented in Seminar Organised by the Department of Sociology, Pune, University of Pune, October, 1991.

Reports:

National Commission for Scheduled Castes and Scheduled Tribes, *Highlights for the Report for the year 1994-95 & 1995-96.* New Delhi: Government of India, 1997.

Newspapers:

Chopra, Deepak. "We are the World, Let's Heal Ourselves." *Times of India.* (Bangalore) 14 Feb 2006.

India Today, (Bangalore) 5 June 2006.

Indian Currents, 4-10 May 2009.

Webliography

http://www1.umn.edu

www.selfesteem2go.com

www.Coping.org

jjmess@tampabay.rr.com

www.postambedkar.htm